PRAISE FOR MICHELE BORBA'S OT

No More Misbehavin'

"Michele Borba offers insightful, realistic, and straightforward advice that is sure to get immediate results."
—Sally Lee, Editor-in-Chief, *Parents Magazine*

"This will be the only discipline book you'll ever need to raise good kids."
—from the Foreword by Jack Canfield, coauthor, *Chicken Soup for the Soul* and *Chicken Soup for the Parent's Soul*

"A sensitive, thoughtful, eminently practical book that will help parents help their children change behaviors that will improve the child's, and the entire family's, well-being and happiness. A wonderful contribution!"
—Alvin Rosenfeld, M.D., child psychiatrist and coauthor, *The Over-Scheduled Child*

"The most complete toolkit for coping with behavior I have ever seen. Destined to be a classic for all parents and teachers, *No More MisBehavin'* is powerful and practical."
—Annie Leedom, founder and president, www.parentingbookmark.com

"Based on the good old-fashioned idea that kids who behave are happier than those who don't, *No More Misbehavin'* shows parents exactly how to turn their love into *action* with a step-by-step plan for permanently removing bad behaviors. Excellent!"
—Elaine Hightower, coauthor with Betsy Riley, *Our Family Meeting Book: Fun and Easy Ways to Manage Time, Build Communication and Share Responsibility Week by Week*

"Michele Borba's new book provides parents with an innovative strategy for dealing with children's challenging behaviors. Her suggestions are practical, doable, and proven. Any parent looking for concrete solutions for troubling kid behaviors need look no further. Simply outstanding!"

—Naomi Drew, author,
Hope and Healing: Peaceful Parenting in an Uncertain World

"This book offers hands-on, practical, and effective solutions to everyday problems that all parents encounter from time to time. These strategies are guaranteed to reduce your parenting headaches and help you enjoy your kids! I'll certainly be recommending this book to the parents with whom I work."

—Dr. Jane Bluestein, author,
Parents, Teens and Boundaries: How to Draw the Line
and *The Parent's Little Book of Lists:*
DOs and DON'Ts of Effective Parenting

"*No More Misbehavin'*s clear, no-nonsense advice will be a blessing to parents paralyzed by stubborn childhood behaviors ranging from biting to bullying to heel-dragging in the face of chores. This step-by-step, here's-how manual is almost like having Michele Borba as your personal parenting trainer."

—Tom Lickona, author,
Educating for Character and *Raising Good Children*

Building Moral Intelligence

"A much-needed antidote to the waves of incivility, intolerance, and insensitivity sweeping through our nation's youth culture. Dr. Michele Borba offers parents a treasure trove of ideas for building the most neglected intelligence around: our kids' moral intelligence. I'd like to see a copy of this book in every home across America!"

—Thomas Armstrong, author,
7 Kinds of Smart, Multiple Intelligences in the Classroom,
and *Awakening Your Child's Natural Genius*

"Michele Borba is an inspiring educator, an experienced parent, and a terrific writer. She has identified the core issues for parenting moral kids and presented them with passion, wit, and enormous practicality. Her new book gives us solid empirical research but also specific day-to-day activities that will really make a difference in our children's lives."
—Michael Gurian, author, *Boys and Girls Learn Differently, The Wonder of Boys, The Good Son,* and *A Fine Young Man*

"While many people in public life decry the lack of character and moral development among our kids, few take this concern further, into the realm of practical steps to address the issue in the lives of real children and youth. Michele Borba has done so in her book *Building Moral Intelligence.* As one whose work takes him into prisons to interview kids who kill, I can testify to the need for adults to cultivate moral intelligence— and the consequences when we don't. This book is a tool for parents to use in the struggle."
—James Garbarino, author, *Lost Boys: Why Our Sons Turn Violent and How We Can Save Them*

"This smart and helpful book integrates much of what we know about raising moral children. I especially like the book's constructive way of pulling together a wide range of theoretical approaches and coming up with a wealth of sensible child-rearing tips."
—William Damon, professor and director, Stanford University Center on Adolescence

"This how-to guide to teaching children moral intelligence fills a deep need. It is practical, filled with excellent activities, and based on solid research."
—Kevin Ryan, director emeritus, Boston University Center for the Advancement of Ethics and Character

"This is perhaps the best written guide for parents and educators concerned with the deep character and moral intelligence of their children or students. It is wise, literate, and valuable."

—Peter Scharf, director, Center for Society,
Law and Justice at the University of New Orleans,
and author, *Growing Up Moral*

"Michele Borba articulates the core traits that build and promote responsible citizenship among the young and old alike. Creating safe schools begins with responsible behavior. Dr. Borba explains in clear, concise, and effective ways how to make that happen. Her book is a 'must read' for parents, educators, and community leaders."

—Ronald D. Stephens, executive director,
National School Safety Center

Parents Do Make a Difference

"Michele Borba's new book is invaluable. Drawing on a lifetime of rich experience, the author understands parents' concerns and speaks to them wisely and compassionately. Best of all, she spells out what parents need to know in easily accessible language and easily learnable stages."

—Nathaniel Branden, author,
The Six Pillars of Self-Esteem and *A Woman's Self-Esteem*

"Packed with helpful suggestions and insights. This book is a wonderful guide to help kids become winners."

—Louise Hart, author, *The Winning Family:
Increasing Self-Esteem in Your Children and Yourself*
and *On the Wings of Self-Esteem*

"Michele Borba has done it again—she's written another must-have, must-read book! Parents of children will ask, 'Why didn't they have this when my kids were younger?' and then buy it for their grown kids so the grandkids will be raised sensibly. I highly recommend this book to anyone who cares about kids."

—Hanoch McCarty, coeditor,
A 4th Course of Chicken Soup for the Soul,
and coauthor, *Acts of Kindness*

"This book is loaded with practical, proven ideas for teachers and parents to use in their efforts to be the best influence they can be. Children of all ages will be helped to develop skills they need to be their personal best in the new millennium."

—Dorothy Rouse, board member and former teacher,
Los Gatos Union School District, Los Gatos, California

"By applying the strategies from *Parents Do Make a Difference* I experienced such stunning success with a severely disturbed foster child that it caused an astonished juvenile court judge to label her transformation 'miraculous.' He even led his courtroom to a round of applause for her success and credited her rehabilitation to Dr. Borba's techniques. One could only imagine how using these techniques could profoundly impact the lives of all children."

—Dawn Hamill, foster child advocate

"I strongly endorse Michele Borba's new book, *Parents Do Make a Difference*. Grounded in solid research, her message has the potential to truly help parents help their children be more successful in school and in life."

—Richard Herzberg, executive director,
Bureau of Education and Research

Don't Give Me That Attitude!

24 Rude, Selfish, Insensitive
Things Kids Do and How to Stop Them

Michele Borba, Ed.D.

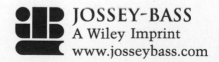

JOSSEY-BASS
A Wiley Imprint
www.josseybass.com

Copyright © 2004 by Michele Borba. All rights reserved.
Published by Jossey-Bass
A Wiley Imprint
989 Market Street, San Francisco, CA 94103-1741   www.josseybass.com

Note to the Reader: All of the letters in this book have been received from parents over the past few years. The names of the parents and children, as well as their location, have been changed to protect their privacy.

Jossey-Bass books and products are available through most bookstores. To contact Jossey-Bass directly call our Customer Care Department within the U.S. at 800-956-7739, outside the U.S. at 317-572-3986, or fax 317-572-4002.

Jossey-Bass also publishes its books in a variety of electronic formats. Some content that appears in print may not be available in electronic books.

Library of Congress Cataloging-in-Publication Data
Borba, Michele.
  Don't give me that attitude! : 24 rude, selfish, insensitive things
kids do and how to stop them / Michele Borba.— 1st ed.
    p. cm.
Includes bibliographical references.
  ISBN 0-7879-7333-5 (alk. paper)
  1. Attitude change in children. 2. Child rearing. I. Title.
  BF723.A76B67 2004
  649'.64—dc22

                                            2003022251

Printed in the United States of America

FIRST EDITION
PB Printing 10 9 8 7 6 5 4 3 2 1

Contents

Acknowledgments

To the folks at Jossey-Bass for your incredible support on all four of the books we've worked together on: it has been an absolute pleasure working with such a professional and dedicated publishing team. Most especially I thank Alan Rinzler, undoubtedly the best editor in the business. You have no idea how lucky an author is to work with such an extraordinary wordsmith. I send him thanks for so many things: for helping me cultivate the idea, formatting ideas, his unceasing dedication to producing only the best, and supporting each and every step along the way. Every author should be so blessed to have such an editor. Thank you, Alan; again, it's has been an honor. Special thanks go to Debra Hunter, Paul Foster, Jennifer Wenzel, Sachie Jones, Karen Warner, Seth Schwartz, Carol Hartland, Beverly Miller, and Paula Goldstein. Heartfelt appreciation to Jennifer Wenzel for endless support, brilliant marketing, and limitless creativity.

To all the folks in the Wiley office in New York, especially to the publicity department and one great dynamo, Ellen Silberman. Thanks not only for your hard work, tenacity, and energy, but also your personalized touches (I finally know how to catch a New York cab). Huge gratitude also goes to the Canadian Wiley group, especially Meghan Brousseau and Jamie Broadhurst. Making the jaunts to Toronto and Vancouver is always something I look forward to. I know that not only will the publicity campaigns be top notch but so enjoyable because I get to spend time with these great dedicated folks.

I extend special gratitude to the staff of *Parents* magazine, especially senior editor Diane Debrovner, for the honor of serving on your advisory board but also the privilege of speaking with many of your writers about several attitudes presented in this book. These women not only were enjoyable, but their pointed queries about kid attitudes helped me enormously in thinking through the steps to stop them. In particular, I thank Vicky Mlyniec (helpfulness, cruelty, and every other parenting topic); Diane Benson Harrington (manipulative, defiant); Leslie Lampert (the 21-day makeover plan and "drama queens"); Pam Kramer (bad-tempered); Winnie Yu (demanding and controlling); Deb Waldman (fresh); and Susan Brody (annoying behaviors). I also thank reporters Katy Kelly ("trophy parenting"), Andrea Atkins (out-of-control behavior), and Jane Clifford (character development) and most especially Charlotte Latlava (discipline 101) and Francesca Donlan ("everything!") for their usual superb suggestions, fabulous interviews, and ongoing encouragement.

Huge appreciation is also sent to a few loyal, dedicated professionals who have always been there for me and have become such personal friends: especially Annie Leedom, president of www.netconnectpublicity.com, for her wonderful steadfast friendship, continual optimism, and most appreciated encouragement: you're loved, Annie. Anybody looking for the absolute best Internet publicity campaigns need search no further than Anne Leedom. I also thank Adrienne Biggs of Biggs Publicity for her continual support and creative ways of acquiring great publicity leads that somehow always turn golden, and Steve Leedom, of www.nowimagine.net, for creating my gorgeous Web site, www.moralintelligence.com, and being so available to talk me through the most annoying computer glitches. Thanks also to Celia Rock and Dottie DeHart of the world's best publicity agency, Rocks-DeHart Public Relations, for fabulous ideas and incredible campaigns. Special, special thanks to Dottie DeHart. Wow, does she know publicity! Thank you for giving so generously of your time, resources, and yourself these past five years. I also extend enormous amounts of gratitude to the best agent in the business, Joelle DelBourgo. Every writer should have this woman in her corner. Joelle, it's a pleasure!

Finally, hugs to my own personal "ya-ya" group—Barbara Keane, Patty Service, Judy Baggott, and Bonnie Englund—for the nonstop laughs and giggles. Special appreciation to Andy Keane and Kathy and Jake Been for ideas on curbing know-it-alls and smart alecks. And most especially I thank the ones who have made the biggest difference in my life and on my own attitudes, my family. Deepest love to my husband, best friend, and continuous supporter, Craig; my extraordinarily amazing parents, Dan and Treva Ungaro; and my wonderful mother-in-law, Lorayne Borba. And to the three greatest, good-looking, funniest, and best-attitude kids around, my sons: Jason, Adam, and Zach. Thanks for the joy and the laughter you bring. It's an absolute honor being your mom.

To Alan Rinzler,
A more skilled, supportive, and knowledgeable editor
I could not imagine.
From a most appreciative author.

PART 1

Confronting the Crisis

Sow a thought and you reap an act;
Sow an act and you reap a habit;
Sow a habit and you reap a character;
Sow a character and you reap a
destiny.
—Charles Reade

Dear Dr. Borba,

As much as I hate to admit it, our twelve-year-old son is becoming a spoiled brat. Frankly, there are times I'm just at my wit's end! I love him to death, but I really don't like what he's turning into: self-centered, inconsiderate, and downright rude! He only thinks of himself and can be quite flippant and fresh. I tell him to stop, I ground him and remove privileges, but his selfish, rude ways are still there. How do I get him to stop giving me this attitude? There has to be a better way!

—Jenny K., a mom from Portland, Oregon

Bad Attitude Act Out

"What do I get if I do it?"

"I want it, and I want it now!"

"Why should I care how she feels?"

"Get real. I'm doing it my way!"

Sound familiar? These outbursts from selfish, rude, fresh, demanding kids are symptoms of a swiftly growing epidemic that is sweeping the country. Now this doesn't mean there aren't any good kids left in the world; of course, there are! In fact, studies suggest that this generation is volunteering more than ever before. But let's stay focused on the crisis at hand. It's there, it's growing, and it won't go away until we decide it's a big enough problem to do something about. Experts differ as to the most appropriate way to label this breed of self-centered, insensitive youth, describing their behavior with such psychological terminology as "overindulged," "grandiose," "narcissistic," and even "egocentric-regressed." Most lay folks agree that the plain, old-fashioned term "spoiled brat" fits just fine. And it's also a term that every parent dreads. "Not my kid! A big brat? Never!" It's embarrassing, it's humiliating, it's the crisis we all dreaded might occur with our own sons and daughters.

Even the word "spoiled" sounds as if it's rotten: there's nothing you can do about it, and you have to throw it away.

But we're not talking about apples and oranges here: these are our precious children, our loved ones, our hope for the future. We can't give up and abandon our most treasured human blessings, the relationships we most cherish. We can't ever stop believing that we *can* make a difference in confronting this crisis, that everything we do now will play a crucial role in turning their lives around and shaping their ultimate destiny. We must have faith that there is a way to help our kids defeat the negative consequences and long-term penalties of the Big Brat Factor.

EXPOSING THE BIG BRAT FACTOR

How are things on your own home front these days? Do you ever wonder if your darling cherub could be the next poster child for "most spoiled"? Have you thought (secretly, of course) how much easier selling your kids on eBay would be than raising them for one more minute? Do you sometimes feel as though you've become your kids' ATM machine? If so, chances are your kid has a big dose of the Big Brat Factor.

Take a deep breath, and know you're not alone: millions of other parents are in the same boat. There is an epidemic in our society, and not only that, it's not just in the good old U.S.A. During the past eighteen months, I've worked with parents and educators in Canada, Hong Kong, Malaysia, Finland, and elsewhere, and I can tell you that children worldwide are now victims of this malady. The good news is that this is not a natural disaster but a human dilemma, and that means we can do something about it. The first step is realizing that brats don't come in just one shape or form. In fact, there's a broad variety of brat types that could be living under your very own roof. Check out the following list to see if it inspires the shock of recognition:

The Little Princess–Mr. Fresh Prince Syndrome. Do your kids feel they are entitled to get everything they want and rule the roost? Do you feel you are running a bed-and-breakfast establishment instead of a home? Are you picking up after your kids and doing their chores because you can't bear dealing with their reaction if you ask them to do it themselves? (And heaven forbid if you asked your precious offspring to do something for you!)

The Con Artist. Does your kid manipulate you morning, noon, and night? Does she excuse, blame, fib, threaten, guilt-trip, and play you off against your partner? Is this the same kid you just said no to and somehow she's charmed you to give in? She's good, isn't she?

The Donald Trump Clone. Do you have a "gimme, gimme, gimme" kid? Is he so greedy and materialistic that to him you're nothing but a walking wallet? Is his vocabulary riddled with brand names? Does his closet overflow with stuff he's never worn or used? Are you looking at the want ads for job number four so you can pay for this kid's lifestyle? And how will he ever balance his budget when he's finally living on his own?

The Drama Queen. Does your little munchkin act as if she just lost the Oscar when she doesn't get her way? Is she such a diva that you can't change the TV channel without asking her permission? Do her theatrics leave you drained and exhausted at the end of the day? Why can't this kid take no for an answer?

"Poor Little Me." Does your child feel so sorry for himself that you find yourself always doing everything for him and expecting very little in return? Does he constantly complain about too much homework, friends who are mean to him, or how unfair you treat him? Do you find yourself rescuing him because it's so much easier than listening to his woes and moans?

Cruella De Vil. Is your kid so mean and nasty that you cringe at some of the things she says or does? Is she so insensitive that she can't see how her words and deeds hurt others? Are you afraid to confront her style of put-downs, sarcasm, and cutting remarks because you can't bear to receive yet another one of her stinging insults? How will she ever form loving relationships?

The Emperor Napoleon. Do you have an arrogant kid who acts as if he's out to conquer the world? Is he a smart aleck, know-it-all, little snob? Does he have a superiority complex? Does he treat you as if you are one of his subjects in his master plan to seize the throne? How can *you* be the parent if this kid is the boss?

Miss Bad Manners. Are you afraid to take your kid out in public because she's so fresh and rude? Does she stick out her tongue, interrupt, burp, and talk on her cell in the middle of the movie? Are raised eyebrows becoming all too common from strangers as well as friends when they see how your kid acts?

Couch Potato. Is your kid lazy, irresponsible, and uncooperative? Is he stuck in the family room with the remote control wired to his fingers? Is his chore chart fading away on your refrigerator door? How can you motivate him to wake up and join the human race?

In Your Face. How can you live with a kid who is defiant, rebellious, noncompliant, and never does what you ask? Are you doing stress-reduction exercises on your doorstep to find the courage to deal with what waits within?

Mr. Bigot. Is your kid narrow-minded, intolerant, and biased toward certain ideas, individuals, and groups of people? Does he tell racist jokes or believe in prejudicial stereotypes, and can't tolerate any ideas except his own? Do you feel you can't break through the stone wall of his mind to show him the wonderful reality of human diversity?

The Terminator. Does your kid behave with ruthless aggression in trying to overcome anything and everything that stands in his way? Does he go ballistic when you say no to him, when his friends won't do what he says, when his coaches put him on the bench? Do you worry when the phone rings that his explosive temper may have gotten him into big trouble?

Of course, no kid will fit exactly into any of these general categories; after all, the Big Brat Factor encompasses a wide spectrum of behaviors and attitudes and ranges from minor to major infractions. But seriously ask yourself if there's anything in these brat types that strikes a nerve or sounds even vaguely familiar. Nobody knows your child better than you do, so check your own instincts and ask yourself whether parenting is bringing you more stress than joy, more pain than happiness, more pangs than rewards. Do you fear that you're becoming the kind of parent you swore you'd never be? More nag than nurturer? More yeller than listener? More scolder than cheerleader? Most important, are you really worried that your kid is on the wrong track and needs an immediate makeover for her rude, insensitive ways? Then go with your instinct: it's time!

I have no doubt that you love your kid deeply. Your dream was to be the perfect parent and give your child your absolute best. You imagined that with such a passionate effort and with so much sacrifice and good intentions on your part, there's no way that your kid would turn out anything but wonderful.

So what went wrong? What's the underlying reason for the emergence of this spoiled kid of yours? How could he possibly have become a casualty of this epidemic? After many years of researching child development, being a special education teacher, working with over 750,000 parents and teachers all over the world, and having three kids of my own, I've come to the conclusion that the basic cause for the kind of behaviors that create a spoiled, selfish, insensitive kid who's a victim of the Big Brat Factor is ATTITUDE. The one thing that all these kids share—whether they're arrogant, bad-mannered, impatient, greedy, narrow-minded, lazy, irresponsible, manipulative, uncooperative is a BAD ATTITUDE.

WHAT'S THE DIFFERENCE BETWEEN ATTITUDE AND BEHAVIOR?

I wrote a book in 2002 called *No More Misbehavin': 38 Difficult Behaviors and How to Stop Them*. In this book, I tried to help parents target and eliminate common problems like whining, biting, fighting, poor sportsmanship, bullying, tattling, teasing, and other annoying things that kids do. The focus was on changing children's conduct and replacing their inappropriate habits with a more acceptable way of acting at home, at school, and in the community. My goal was to provide parents with tools and strategies for disciplining their children, for getting them back on the right path, and for creating an atmosphere that would allow family, friends, and teachers to interact with them in a more favorable manner.

And that's what behavior is: the kind of actions our kids do that we see, hear, feel in our gut, and instantly know whether it's a right or wrong way to be in the world. I'm talking about the meltdown in the mall, the beating up on little sister, the lying about homework, the talking back, meanness, tattling. All of these and many, many more are behavioral symptoms that parents must change. I'm sure you've had your share of these bad behaviors, and you know just what I'm talking about.

So what's the difference between changing your child's bad behavior and the subject of this book, which is changing your kid's attitude? What exactly is an attitude?

Behaviors are on the surface; attitudes run deep. Behaviors are actions; attitudes are a way of looking at life. Behaviors you can see; attitudes are often hidden and hard to figure. Behaviors are more reactive and impulsive; attitudes are longer term. Behaviors are a child's way of coping with the world; attitudes are the foundation of her character. Behaviors are here and now; attitudes will determine her destiny.

The spoiled kid crisis we're facing as parents today goes beyond just bad behavior to the underlying root cause of bad attitudes—for example:

- *Bad attitudes are a bad way of looking at life.* Kids who see the world as a cold and cruel place are often selfish and insensitive. And because they do believe it's acceptable, they treat others with meanness, rudeness, and intolerance.
- *Bad attitudes are usually made up of bad behavior habits.* Kids with bad-tempered attitudes usually start out by displaying their anger in unhealthy ways, such as biting, hitting, tantrums, or fighting. If not corrected, those bad behaviors turn into bad habits, and soon the child develops one big bad attitude that says to the world, "I'll use my anger to get what I want."
- *Bad attitudes are often hidden and hard to figure.* Kids who are insecure, fearful, and anxious may conceal or compensate for their feelings with attitudes of pessimism, jealousy, and cynicism.
- *Bad attitudes run deep and can last a lifetime.* Kids who have moms or dads who always pick up the pieces may face a lifetime addiction, dependency, and manipulation.
- *Bad attitudes are the foundation for bad character.* Kids who have learned how to get away with being irresponsible and uncooperative often end up as adults with a skewed moral compass.
- *Bad attitudes can lead to a lifetime of unhappiness and social isolation.* Kids who are spoiled, self-centered, arrogant, and disrespectful may never form lasting attachments or find personal fulfillment.

WE'VE GOT A BIG PROBLEM

Many parents assume that attitude isn't something that develops until the preadolescent or teen years. But times have changed, and any parent paying attention now realizes that even a four year old can have all the full-blown symptoms of a bad attitude. And boy can they make us miserable: their sass, back talk, and greedy, manipulative, bossy, and even defiant ways let us know in no uncertain terms that these little critters are on the road to poor character and a lack of moral intelligence—not to mention the damage their attitude can do to your family harmony. So don't think for a minute that bad attitude starts only when kids start watching MTV, talking on cell phones, sending instant e-mail messages, and playing video games.

Of course, they don't start out that way: the onset of a bad attitude has usually begun with smaller but definitely annoying actions—a whiny tone, a fresh comment, or a quiet rebuttal of an adult's request. Parents usually assumed their kids' conduct was "just a phase" or a single slip, and let it slide. And there lies our mistake. If not nipped early, this ailment spreads easily. Do beware: bad attitudes are highly contagious. If there are other siblings in the house, chances are they will catch it too.

One thing is clear: there does seem to be an epidemic of overindulged, demanding, rude kids with attitudes, and everyone seems to agree. Lawmakers, doctors, clergy, businesspeople, educators, parents, and the general public alike have voiced their concerns about the growing breed of overindulged youth. Just review some of the troubling facts in the Bad Attitude News Alerts scattered throughout this book.

Kids with bad attitude come in all sizes, both genders, all ages, and all cultures. They can be rich or poor; reside in rural, urban, or suburban areas; attend private or public school; have multiple siblings or be only children; live with a single parent or with both. The diversity of their lives seems to have little bearing on whether they acquire the dreaded ailment,

BAD ATTITUDE NEWS ALERT

- A national survey reveals that more than two-thirds of school police officers say younger children are acting more aggressively.
- Three-quarters of Minnesota kids surveyed by Mind-Works agreed that today's kids are materially spoiled and generally irresponsible.
- A poll of twelve to seventeen year olds conducted by the Center for a New American Dream, a nonprofit organization that promotes responsible consumption, showed that the average kid nags nine times to get a product his parents refuse to purchase; about half the parents finally give in.
- Nearly two out of three parents surveyed by a TIME/CNN poll said their kids measure self-worth more by possessions than their parents did at the same age.
- Eighty-five percent of respondents in a recent AOL Time Warner poll said kids in America are spoiled.
- Nine out of ten Americans felt the breakdown of common courtesy has become a serious problem in this country, a major contributor to the increase in violence, and an important factor in the breakdown of our values in this country.
- Only 12 percent of the two thousand adults polled felt that kids commonly treat others with respect; most described them as "rude," "irresponsible," and "lacking in discipline."
- Eighty percent of people think kids today are more spoiled than kids of ten or fifteen years ago. What's

> more, two-thirds of parents admit that their own kids are spoiled.
> - And it isn't getting any better.

although there is one factor that clearly is the greatest predictor for getting this disease: *kids were allowed to develop the bad attitude without opposition, and because there was no resistance or reaction, these bad attitudes flourished and grew.*

WHERE IS THIS COMING FROM?

Of course, there are other known causes that do contribute to the demise of kids' sensitivity, respect, and appreciation. A few more common reasons bad attitudes are flourishing in today's youth include these classic parenting blunders.

Keeping Up with the Joneses. We want our kids to have the same advantages as the kids next door: schooling, social events, the "in" fashions, gadgets, and technological paraphernalia. So we keep our radar extended to watch what the neighbors are doing, and probably far more often than we'd care to admit, we copy their moves. We may not mean to, but we do compete with those who have similar-aged kids. And—like it or not, we indulge our kids with what we think they must have to "keep up" or "stay ahead."

Experiencing Guilt. Economic hardships or just the desire to have a good life cause many parents to work long, hard hours. And that means more time away from the kids. The result is a good dose of parental guilt. The remedy: giving kids presents, having few rules or requirements, and slacking off on the boundaries between kids and executive authority to make up for the parents' lack of presence. Does it work? No. But it sure is effective in creating overindulged kids.

Feeling Stressed and Exhausted. It's a fast-paced world these days, and many parents freely admit they barely have energy to phone for take-out food. So who has time to deal with a kid's bad attitude? It's far easier to let it slide. And so, more often than not, the bad attitude becomes a habit.

Misunderstanding Self-Esteem. One of the biggest parenting blunders is thinking that saying no to will diminish kids' self-esteem and spirit. Nothing could be further from the truth, so let me set the record straight: authentic self-esteem is about feeling worthy about who you are and competent to cope with life. What kid is going to feel worthy and competent with a bad attitude? His reputation suffers, adults give him those "looks," friends pull away, and he loses invitations. Actually, every arena of his life plummets: social, academic, moral, and emotional. Besides, every solid study on self-esteem finds that kids who are raised in less permissive homes tend to have higher self-esteem. These parents say no, set rules, establish clear behavior expectations, and consistently enforce those standards with fair discipline policies. Enough about self-esteem!

Delaying Childbirth. Many couples are postponing parenthood beyond the traditional childbearing years. Others have had trouble conceiving or adopting a child. So when they finally are blessed with their young ones, they may tend to overindulge, spoil, and have unrealistic expectations of their little miracles.

Succumbing to a Culture of Fear. Yes, we are living in a dangerous and uncertain world, but we can't allow the media focus on kidnappings, terrorism, school shootings, snipers, and other disasters all over the world to influence our need to make us feel that we can keep kids safe and secure. Too many parents are overprotecting their children and spoiling them with material possessions and instant emotional indulgence in hopes of compensating for the bombardment of mean and scary images that surround them.

Misusing Quality Time. A rash of parenting books and child experts rushed to tell parents they must spend a set period of perfect moments with their child each day. So if Johnny shows a bad attitude or starts to act up during this special, blissful set-aside period of family bonding, the last thing a parent wants is to spoil those precious moments with any kind of confrontation.

Keeping 'Em Stimulated. In a well-intentioned effort to make their kids creative geniuses, many parents pile too many mind benders, growth gadgets, and other forms of intellectual stimulation on their little tykes. Sometimes what a kid needs most is alone time in the dirt. If you continue this overbearing, structured, and calculating intervention, your kid will grow passive and dependent, expect to be entertained, and be easily bored.

Buying into a Materialistic, Consumer-Driven World. Admit it: we're all susceptible to being seduced by advertising, and so are our innocent kids. Need proof? Since the 1970s, the average number of commercials a kid sees in a year has doubled from 20,000 to 40,000. And not only are kids spending more—a whopping $36 billion annually—but they're becoming more consumer driven. A study by Penn State concluded that today's kids are not only more materialistic, but are also launching their big-time shopping careers at much younger ages. And one of the biggest reasons: we're giving in to their whims.

Desiring Something Better for Your Kids. Over the years I've talked to hundreds of parents, and by far the noblest reason given for indulging kids is wanting them to have a better childhood or future than theirs. When they describe the economic hardships or dysfunctional family life some of them have endured, I sympathize. But it's still not a reason to indulge. They mean well, but they're misdirected. They place their value on material goods instead of the values of virtue, selflessness, character, and sacrifice. The difference is huge, and it sends a terribly wrong message to kids.

Wanting to Be Our Kids' Best Friend. Someplace along the way, the role of "parent" has been turned into "friend." And the parent's "relationship" with their child takes precedence over being authority, behavior manager, and guide. Reprimanding bad attitudes is not part of this agenda. The risk to the parent's popularity with their kid—and his friends—is far too great.

Now don't get me wrong: more often than not, our parenting intentions are honorable. After all, we don't want our kids to be brats; we want the best for them. We want them to be happy, successful, and fulfilled. We hate to reprimand them. We hate to say no. We want our kids to be popular and have just as much as the next kid. So we give them everything we think they need—or want—along with their bad attitudes. We enroll them in lots of activities and drive them to every known event and gathering. But sometimes our good intentions—and usually quite unintentionally—can become terribly skewed.

Here's the problem. We may be overlooking what really matters most in our kids' lives: that they turn into good and decent human beings. After all, years from now, the soccer game goal, SAT score, and those violin lessons will count little compared to the kind of adult your child has become. And one of the biggest things that will hinder your kid's character and reputation as a human being are those selfish, self-centered, rude, defiant makings of bad attitudes.

THE BAD ATTITUDE INTELLIGENCE TEST

Just how much do you know about bad attitudes and how to change them? Answer the following questions true or false. The results may surprise you.

1. Your child's attitudes are predetermined at birth.

    True_____   False_____

2. Your child's attitudes cannot be changed.

    True_____   False_____

3. Your attitude has a lot with your child's attitude.

    True_____   False_____

4. If your child is smart and gets good grades, he's likely to have a good attitude.

    True_____   False_____

5. Being affluent and having a higher education has little to do with your child's good or bad attitude.

    True_____   False_____

6. A bad attitude is just a phase. Let it go—your kid will outgrow it.

    True_____   False_____

7. Parents have more influence on their kids' attitudes than their peers, the media, and school.

    True_____   False_____

8. Your child's attitude is really at the center of her personality, so if you try to change it, you're destroying who she really is.

    True_____   False_____

9. No matter how much pressure kids face today, it's not okay to ease their stresses by doing some tough stuff for them.

    True_____   False_____

10. After age eleven years old, there's not much you can do about your kid's attitude; it's set.

    True_____   False_____

Here are the answers with some explanation. Check out your bad attitude intelligence score.

10 correct = A+   Excellent!
8 correct = B   Pretty good
6 correct = C   Average; you've got some work to do.
5 or fewer = F   You're in trouble; commit this book
                  to memory.

1. False. Although some attitudes may be influenced by biological factors, most are learned.

2. False. Most attitudes can be changed by using the proven, research-based interventions in this book. Long-term commitment is necessary for meaningful change and permanent attitude change. There's no doubt about it: parenting is hard work.

3. True. That old mantra, "attitudes are better caught then taught," is 100 percent correct. Your kids are watching and copying everything you do, even stuff you're not aware of. So watch out, and be ready for change yourself.

4. False. Don't count on it. There's not much connection between your kid's school smarts and having a positive attitude. You have to nurture your child's learning as well as his character. Each is a separate entity.

5. True. Being affluent and having a good education is no guarantee that your kid won't be spoiled, self-centered, rude, or insensitive. In fact, it might be just the opposite.

6. False. Don't wait a moment before putting a halt to your kid's bad attitude. The longer you wait, the tougher it will be to change.

7. True. You have greater influence over your child's attitude than anything or anyone else. Use your power wisely, and don't blame outside influences.

8. False. It's not my intention to help you change your child's personality or temperament. But it is your job as a parent to stop your kid from being selfish, narrow-minded, and noncompliant, and having other bad attitudes that lead to weak character and poor moral intelligence.

9. True. One of your more important roles as a parent is to help your child become independent, self-reliant, and resourceful. Always rescuing and handling your child's problems creates a dependent kid who has trouble coping with the realities of life.

10. False. It's never too late to change bad attitudes. It may get harder as kids get older and more set in their ways, but that is no excuse. Plenty of older kids make big changes in their attitudes, and yours will be no exception.

PREVENTING THE WORST-CASE SCENARIO: WHY YOU BETTER START CHANGING BAD ATTITUDES TODAY

One thing is clear: it's up to us. We must take immediate action, or there will be disastrous long-term effects on our children's potential for happiness and fulfillment. Here are ten outcomes that could happen if we don't make an emergency intervention and allow our kids to hold on to those bad attitudes.

Undermine Character. Character determines your child's reputation as a human being. Virtues like kindness, empathy, respect, tolerance, perseverance, fairness, and honesty form our children's character, beliefs, and attitudes. Bad attitudes comprise all those vices that counter solid character development: disrespect, insensitivity, rudeness, laziness, meanness, and more. Ridding your kid of his bad attitude makes room for those essential virtues to blossom and increases the likelihood of his developing strong character.

Hinder Social Relationships. Well-liked kids are fun to be around. They are good team players, share, encourage, respect differences, and listen openly. They are also fair, respectful, and enjoyable. Kids with attitudes are just the opposite. More often than not, they are poor sports, disrespectful, gossipy, and unforgiving. As a result, they are also more likely to be picked last for the team, play group, or even as friends.

Destroy Reputations. Think about it: kids don't like to be around peers who are rude and demanding, and neither do adults. Bad attitudes can doom a kid's reputation, and rebuilding it is very tough. It's one more reason that we need to curb their attitudes.

Foster Poor Money Management. Overindulged kids are usually given what they want, and they don't worry about saving or have little time to learn money management skills. Now think of these kids as adults: their economic future is rather bleak unless, of course, their parents continue to provide huge allowances. Is that *your* plan?

Make the Kids Less Happy. The latest research suggests that kids who are indulged and "have it all" are actually *less* likely to be happy. They are also more likely to be bored, less enthusiastic, and less likely to be able to derive pleasure from their activities.

Create Weaker Coping Skills. Spoiled kids have their every desire catered to, and as a result they are less able to cope with stress. So how will they learn to deal with life's inevitable frustrations and setbacks? By always rescuing kids, we actually do them a huge disservice: we rob them of learning how to cope. And in today's uncertain world, it may well be one of the most important traits our kids learn.

Destroy Authentic Self-Esteem. A big mistake is thinking that by catering to our kids' desire, we boost their self-esteem. As we've seen, research tells us the opposite: parents who are less permissive and provide clear guidelines and expectations tend to raise kids with higher self-esteem. Kids with positive self-esteem measure their worth based on who they are and what they are capable of, not what they have and who can do it for them. An interesting note is that a recent survey found that nearly two out of three parents felt their children measure their self-worth more by possessions than they themselves did at the same age.

Make Kids Less Compassionate. When you've grown to think the world revolves around you, it's tough to consider other people's concerns and feelings. And slowly those inconsiderate, insensitive attitudes vaporize our kid's warm-hearted or empathic feelings toward others.

Erode Parent–Kid Relations. How often have you had to deal with your kid's bad attitude lately? Chances are these conflicts have not been very positive. Now add up all those times you've had to reprimand your child for her attitude. Each negative encounter slowly erodes our relationship with our kids. It is one more reason that we need to curb their bad attitudes so we can spend our together time building positive and loving relationships instead.

Ruin Family Harmony. Bad attitudes can be damaging to a family atmosphere. After all, negativity breeds, and the kid's insults, demands, and plain disrespect can slowly erode family harmony as well as sibling relationships.

The ramifications of a bad attitude are dangerous. The biggest reason kids learned those bad attitudes is that we allowed it. Now it's time to let them know the jig is up, and we're going to help them make some huge changes. So get ready: it's time for a serious attitude makeover!

BAD ATTITUDE EMERGENCIES:
IMMEDIATE INTERVENTION NEEDED

Almost all bad attitudes include being selfish, self-centered, and insensitive. But aside from these generalities, it is crucial for us as parents to figure out which of our kids' specific attitudes need our urgent attention. Only then can you change them.

You'll probably find that there may be more than one attitude that needs immediate intervention. Some attitudes may overlap. For instance, the bad-tempered kid can also be defiant. The uncooperative child can also be lazy. The arrogant child may also be judgmental or narrow-minded. Bad attitudes can also spiral into even worse bad attitudes. For example, the bad-mannered kid can become fresh, and the fresh kid can become noncompliant. The impatient kid can become bad-tempered; the poor loser can become manipulative. And identifying your kid's bad attitude may not be as easy as spotting a bad behavior since attitudes run deeper and are often hidden. You can usually see your kid's misbehavior—whining, hitting, tattling, talking back, swearing—but the underlying attitude may be invisible and much more difficult to determine. That means you're really going to have reflect on what you've observed and felt about your kid over a period of time in order to figure out which attitude to focus on.

Begin your emergency attitude intervention by studying the list below. Check off the characteristics that best apply to your child. Then you'll know which bad attitude to start on and where to find it in the book.

	Characteristics	Attitude	Page Number
☐	Know-it-all, smart aleck, saying "I'm the best, brightest, smartest," bragging, unrealistic self-appraisal, showing off,	Arrogant	39

feeling privileged or above others, sense of entitlement _"I'm so cool."_		
☐ Incivility, rude, no common courtesy, crude, impolite, interrupts, bad table manners, swears _"Why shouldn't I belch and fart at Grandma's? She can't hear me anyway!"_	Bad-Mannered	56
☐ Blows up, angry outbursts, loses control, physically aggressive, short-fused, hard time getting over it, poor impulse control, yells, frequently frustrated _"Take that!"_	Bad-Tempered	72
☐ Tells lies about grades and scores, copies other kids' work, denies breaking the rules, calling foul for fair, blames someone else for his wrongs, moves pieces when your back is turned _"Why not? Everybody else does."_	Cheats	86
☐ Mean to animals, enjoys humiliating others, preys on those who are different, teases and bullies, says unkind things, no empathy _"Look at those suckers squirm!"_	Cruel	101

Characteristics	Attitude	Page Number
☐ Wants it right now, rude, insistent, uncompromising, relentless, unreasonable expectations *"I want it NOW!"*	Demanding	116
☐ Bossy, dictatorial, wants to be in charge, pushes people around, doesn't listen, won't negotiate, always sets the agenda, won't share *"It's my way or the highway!"*	Domi-neering	129
☐ Rude, impolite, back talks, whiny, sarcastic, insulting, disrespectful, flippant, glib, sassy, in-your-face *"You don't have a clue, Mom. Don't you know anything?"*	Fresh	143
☐ Hoards, materialistic, con-sumer driven, has the gimmes, selfish, never satisfied, ravenous, wants things for himself, doesn't share, demands bribes *"Gimme, gimme, gimme!"*	Greedy	157
☐ Can't wait, wants things now, needs instant gratification, won't stand in line, short atten-tion span, trouble relaxing, impulsive *"Aren't we there yet?"*	Impatient	171

Characteristics	Attitude	Page Number
Poor empathy, tactless, doesn't think of others' feelings, ego-centric, bad case of the "me-me's," coldhearted, selfish, self-centered *"Hey, lighten up, Dude, I was just kidding!"*	Insensitive	185
Needs constant reminders, avoids tasks, blames others for own failures, conveniently forgets, denies, rationalizes, accuses others, misplaces things, misses appointments *"How was I supposed to know it was due today?"*	Irresponsible	199
Envious, never satisfied with who they are or what they have, wishes they could have the good fortunes, qualities, or possessions of others *"She's so pretty, I just hate her."*	Jealous	214
Hypercritical, sarcastic, nasty, opinionated, puts others down, expresses a great deal of negativity *"You're stupid!"*	Judgmental	233
Takes the easy way out, poor work ethic, won't apply herself, wastes time, expects others to	Lazy	247

	Characteristics	Attitude	Page Number
	do her work for her, may feel efforts will fail, gives up easily *"Can you make my bed, Mom?"*		
☐	Twists your words, blames others, wears you down until he wins, exploits guilt, plays one parent against the other, pretends to be sick, expects bribes, dishonest, scheming, depends on others to do it for him, employs blackmail, uses self-pity, cultivates false affection or charm *"If you give it to me, I'll be your best friend!"*	Manipulative	262
☐	Prejudiced, intolerant of other points of view, biased, won't listen, sees only his side, highly opinionated, hateful, bigoted *"All boys are stupid."*	Narrow-Minded	282
☐	Defiant, disobedient, refuses to do what is asked, rebellious, strips parents of authority, battles for power, seeks total control *"Try and make me!"*	Noncompliant	303
☐	Feels as if nothing matters, why bother, nothing's going to work, gives up easily, dismal sense of	Pessimistic	321

future, assume they won't
succeed, dwells on the negative

"What's the point of trying?"

☐ Makes excuses, blames every- one else, cries or loses temper, cheats or lies to win, displays bad sportsmanship, doesn't value camaraderie or teamwork, thin-skinned, can't accept criticism, changes rules mid- stream, quits, fails to congratulate opponents	Poor Loser	337

"I should have won."

☐ Egocentric, bratty, self above all, doesn't share, doesn't take turns, puts his needs and concerns above others, doesn't consider other people's feelings, no empathy, poor emotional intelligence	Selfish	350

"Me . . . me . . . me."

☐ No sharing; won't take turns; won't work on a team; won't support family or friends; doesn't listen to others; hoards toys, tools, and supplies; argu- mentative; criticizes others; bossy; doesn't pull her own weight on a team	Uncooper- ative	364

"I'll do it my way."

Characteristics	Attitude	Page Number
☐ Unappreciative, always wants more, never quite satisfied, oblivious to the luxury or privilege of their lives, feeling entitled, unwilling to reciprocate with gifts or kind acts to others *"This isn't at all what I wanted."*	Ungrateful	377
☐ Unsupportive, unwilling to pitch in, won't do chores or duties, expects to be compensated *"You do it."*	Unhelpful	390

THE SEVEN WORST MISTAKES
IN TRYING TO CHANGE BAD ATTITUDES

So you've tried your hardest to change your kid's bad attitudes, and nothing has worked. You recognize your kid is spoiled, and you've really made an effort to stop his greedy, self-centered, defiant, or flippant ways. And you're still having little success. You've threatened, scolded, bribed, and begged, but nothing seems to work. Frankly, you're at your wit's end.

Why isn't your response working? Why have none of your methods been successful? How can you be sure that your child changes her ways and stops her bad attitudes for good? The first thing you must do is rethink how you're going about it now.

Here are a few of the most common mistakes you may be making in trying to eliminate the Big Brat Factor in your kids.

Thinking "It's Just a Phase." Spoiled behavior and bad attitudes don't go away by themselves. They almost always need parental intervention. The longer you wait, the more likely the attitude will become a habit. So don't call it a phase: jump in and commit yourself to stopping your kid's bad attitude as soon as it starts.

Being a Poor Model. Our own attitudes have enormous influence on our kids' attitudes. After all, what they see is what they copy. So before you start planning to change your kid's attitude, take a serious look at your own. If you really want to change your kid's bad attitude, change your own attitude first.

Not Targeting the Bad Attitude. It's most effective to work on only one attitude at a time, and the more specific your plan is, the better it will be. Don't make a broad, general statement like, "He's got a bad attitude." Instead, narrow the focus to target the specific attitude you want to eliminate: "He's becoming so arrogant." Or "She's so impatient." Do this, and your first step of your attitude makeover will be far more successful.

No Plan to Stop the Bad Attitude. Once you have identified the bad attitude, you need a solid makeover plan to stop it. The plan must (1) address the kid's bad attitude, (2) state exactly how to correct it, (3) identify the new attitude to replace it, and (4) have a set consequence if the bad attitude continues. Part Two provides specific makeovers for each bad attitude.

Not Cultivating a Replacement Attitude. A bad attitude is caused by the absence of a virtue. For example, if a child is insensitive, he lacks empathy. If she is fresh, she lacks respect. Therefore, no bad attitude will change unless your child learns a new attitude to replace it. Without a replacement attitude, chances are the child will revert to her bad old ways. See the Bad Attitude Antidotes and Replacements Chart on page 28.

Going Alone. Big mistake! Any good plan that you devise needs the cooperation of other family members, grandparents, babysitters, coaches, scout leaders, and any other important people in their lives. It may also be valuable to have the support of a group of parents with similar problems, as I suggest in the "How to Use This Book" section at the end of Part One. The more you work together, the more effective your plan will be.

Not Sticking with the Plan. Learning a new habit generally takes time—usually a minimum of twenty–one days. You mustn't give up easily, but commit yourself to a campaign until it works.

BAD ATTITUDE ANTIDOTES
AND REPLACEMENTS

Every bad attitude has an antidote. In an effective makeover, not only do you have to stop the bad attitude, but you must also boost the missing virtue whose absence has created the problem in the first place. For example, if your kid has been fresh and giving you a lot back talk, you better be sure that a crucial part of eliminating his of bad attitude is replacing it with respect. That will not only make your family more harmonious and you less stressful, but you'll also get an added bonus of a better behaved kid with stronger character. What follows is a list of benefits that will result from the twenty-four bad attitude makeovers in this book.

Bad Attitude	*Attitude Antidote and Replacement*
Arrogant	Humility, Graciousness, Modesty
Bad–Mannered	Courtesy, Politeness, Respect
Bad–Tempered	Self-Control, Calmness, Peacefulness
Cheats	Honesty, Integrity, Accountability
Cruel	Kindness, Gentility, Mercy
Demanding	Tact, Tranquility, Consideration
Domineering	Serenity, Patience, Cooperation

Bad Attitude	Attitude Antidote and Replacement
Fresh	Respect, Caring, Reverence
Greedy	Frugality, Altruism, Generosity
Impatient	Patience, Self-Control, Serenity
Insensitive	Sensitivity, Empathy, Tact
Irresponsible	Responsibility, Trustworthiness, Reliability
Jealous	Thankfulness, Trust, Forgiveness
Judgmental	Tolerance, Fairness, Compassion
Lazy	Industriousness, Perseverance, Productivity
Manipulative	Truthfulness, Integrity, Trustworthiness
Narrow-Minded	Tolerance, Open-Mindedness, Flexibility
Noncompliant	Respect, Obedience, Dependability
Pessimistic	Optimism, Hopefulness, Joyfulness
Poor Loser	Good Sportsmanship, Fairness, Forgiveness
Selfish	Selflessness, Generosity, Consideration
Uncooperative	Cooperation, Friendliness, Caring
Ungrateful	Gratitude, Thankfulness, Courtesy
Unhelpful	Helpfulness, Diligence, Generosity

FACING OUR OWN HIDDEN DEMONS

Being selfish, spoiled, or insensitive, a victim of the Big Brat Factor, a member of the bad attitude generation is not just your kid's problem. This crisis is a big crisis for you and your entire family. To help your child change, you need to step back and look at the big picture, and the place to start is by taking a good, honest look in the mirror.

You are the most enormous influence on your kid's attitude. Before you start planning how to change your kid's attitude, take a serious look at your own. Here are a few reasons you may be allowing your kid's bad attitude to continue. They will be the basis of perhaps the most difficult but important makeover: the one you do on yourself. Check the ones that might apply to you.

- ☐ I just don't seem to have the time or energy to deal with his bad attitude.
- ☐ I never saw her attitude as a problem. I assumed it was just a phase or would just go away.
- ☐ I really doubt I can change my kid's attitude. It's her natural temperament.
- ☐ I want to raise my child differently from how I was raised. I'm compensating for what my parents didn't give me.
- ☐ My child has had some tough breaks, and I'm just trying to make things easier for her.
- ☐ My schedule takes me away from my family a lot. This is my way of making up for not being there for my kids.
- ☐ Everyone else gives their kids luxuries. Why should I be any different?
- ☐ I'm afraid that if I change my kid's attitude, I might crush his spirit.
- ☐ I'm trying to be a friend to my kids. I think that's a big part of raising children.
- ☐ I want my child to be happy and have a happy childhood. Always being on his case for his attitude isn't going to help create that image.
- ☐ I'm afraid to say no to my child. He might not love or approve of me.
- ☐ I'm tired and stressed a lot and take it out on my kids. This is my way of making up for not being the kind of parent I'd hoped to be.
- ☐ I don't believe in punishment.
- ☐ Trying to change her attitude might dampen her self-esteem.
- ☐ Other: _____
  _____
  _____

These types of hidden attitudes may interfere with your effectiveness as a parent and may influence your children in a negative way.

HOW DO PEOPLE SEE YOU?

There's no way you can be completely objective about your own attitudes and how they influence your role as parent. One of the best ways to get a clear view of yourself is to imagine yourself in the shoes of your family and friends and ask yourself how they would characterize your parenting style. Which bad attitude types below would your friends and family say are sometimes typical of you as a parent?

- [ ] *Dictator.* "I expect things to be done this way. So do it."
- [ ] *Compromiser.* "Well, let me hear what you think; then maybe we can work something out."
- [ ] *Low expectations.* "I really don't care. Whatever you do is fine."
- [ ] *Wishy-washy.* "I really wish you wouldn't do this. Oh . . . go ahead."
- [ ] *Protector.* "I'm calling up that kid's parent and telling him to make him stop elbowing you under the net."
- [ ] *Egocentric.* "Not now. I don't have time."
- [ ] *Buck-passer.* "It's your father's [or mother's] rule. Wait until I tell him [her] you wouldn't obey."
- [ ] *Nonenforcer.* "I know it's the rule. I changed my mind."
- [ ] *Blamer.* "You have your father's [mother's] genes."
- [ ] *Guilt-ridden.* "I've been gone so much, no wonder you're so defiant. It's all my fault."
- [ ] *Briber.* "If you do what I ask, I'll give you . . . ."
- [ ] *Stressed.* "Listen, I just got home. Talk me to later or maybe never."
- [ ] *Rescuer.* "I'll pick up the pieces, Honey. I know how hard this is for you."

Expert. "I've read all the parenting books, so listen to me."
☐ *Therapist.* "You look so upset. Tell me how you're feeling."
☐ *Other:*_____

_____

_____

YOUR OWN ATTITUDE MAKEOVER

Our daily actions—our looks, our choices, our words, as well as the way we treat our kids, spouse, friends, colleagues, neighbors—have a major influence on our kid's attitude in more ways than we ever realize. You must start changing your own bad attitudes before you can expect your kid to change. I strongly recommend that you start a Makeover Journal to keep an ongoing record of the specific, goals, and strategies and ongoing progress of your efforts. But all good plans start with a first step, so on the lines that follow, write the most important thing you'd like to change in yourself that would also have a positive influence on your child's attitude:

_____

_____

_____

HOW TO USE THIS BOOK

There are many other books on the market that claim to provide a quick and easy solution to all your parenting problems. Most of them offer a simply stated philosophy and a somewhat vague and generalized plan of action. This book is different.

The last thing I want to do is give you the impression that changing a kid's attitudes is something that can be accomplished by spending a few minutes for a couple of days a week on it. We're talking serious time and energy here. This book provides you with specific research-based strategies, guidelines, steps to take, short- and long-term projects, in-depth advice, questionnaires, self-tests, checklists, and other tools and resources.

All the strategies you need to help you change your kid's attitude are provided in this book. But after working with hundreds of parents with these ideas, I'm convinced there are a few supplies and ideas that will enhance your makeover efforts. In fact, you will find many of these same principles in my book *No More Misbehavin': 38 Difficult Behaviors and How to Stop Them*. Readers responded so positively that I offer them again. I strongly recommend you follow the six key tasks of preparation each time you try a new makeover to achieve long-term attitude change.

Use an Attitude Makeover Journal. Each makeover poses questions to help you think about your kid's attitude. I urge you to write your thoughts and action plan in what I call a Makeover Journal. It could be a nice leather journal or a plain spiral notebook; either is fine. Be sure to write in it consistently every day. You'll be able to reread your notations, see attitude patterns that you otherwise might have missed, as well as track your kid's progress. Even the most reluctant parents have told me that using a Makeover Journal has been invaluable for their efforts.

Talk to Essential Caregivers. Consult those who know your kid well—other family, teacher, day care teachers, coach, scout leader, Sunday school teachers, clergy, babysitters—to find out their perspective on your kid's attitude. For instance, does your kid act the same way with them? What do they think is causing the bad attitude? How do they respond? Does it work? What suggestions do they have? When you develop any makeover plan, share it with them. The more you work together, the quicker you'll be in stopping the bad attitude. Consistency is a critical part of an effective makeover.

Track the Targeted Attitude. An important makeover tool is a monthly calendar. Find one that has space for you to write a few sentences each day about your kid's makeover progress. For instance, note the date the attitude first began. Once the makeover begins, write each day the number of times your kid displays the attitude. If your plan is effective, you'll gradually see a decline in the frequency of bad attitudes, and you'll know your plan is working.

Read the Resources. Following each makeover is a list of further readings. Some are for you, and others are for your child. They provide a more thorough background about the attitude and offer more helpful hints for your makeover. Read a selection or two each time you target an attitude to make over.

Form a Parent Support Group. One of the best ways to use this book is by discussing these issues with other parents. You'll realize that other parents' kids have similar behavior problems as yours—which is always a bit comforting—as well as have the chance to hear their suggestions of what works or doesn't work in ridding bad behaviors. So form or join a group: any size is fine—even one other parent will do. Just make sure you all enjoy one another and will commit to meeting regularly.

Be Committed and Relentless. Finally, do not stop until you see the kind of change you hope for. Yes, it will take time, but remember that your child did not develop this attitude overnight. Change in attitude or behavior usually takes a minimum of three weeks, so do not give up.

FINAL THOUGHTS
BEFORE THE BIG ATTITUDE MAKEOVER

Before starting your first attitude makeover, keep in mind a few points. Remember that attitudes are learned, so they can be unlearned. Helping your child unlearn his own bad attitudes means you'll need a specific makeover plan, and that's exactly what I give you in this book. All you need to do is identify the bad attitude you want to change, find the chapter that addresses it, and then be committed and consistent in following the specific plan of action per attitude.

Here's an exercise to help you figure out where to start and how to maintain your commitment:

- *What is your biggest concern?* Ask yourself what concerns you most about your child's attitude. Now put yourself in your child's shoes: How does he feel? How did it affect your relationship with your child? What about his relationship with family members or friends who were witnesses? What do you wish would change? Write your wishes in your Makeover Journal. Now reread those wishes often. Doing so will fuel your desire to change your child's attitude.
- *Which bad attitude will you work on first?* Which attitudes would you like to tune up most in your child? Flip to the Contents in the front of this book, and review the list. Talk to other important caregivers in your child's life to get their opinions. Mark the attitudes that concern you. Choose one that you would like to change now. Granted, there may be several you are concerned about, but stay realistic and practical. Write the attitude on the line below. Now turn to the chapter with the Attitude Makeover and start. There's no time better than the present. Do keep the perspective. No, it won't be easy. No, your child will not change overnight. But change will happen if you are consistent and committed, and keep caring.

The bad attitude I will work on first: _____

- *What is your legacy?* What would you like your great legacy to be for your child? Fast-forward your child twenty-five years from now. What do you hope are the virtues she possesses? What is it about her moral character that you hope has replaced the bad attitudes she may have had as a child? What will you do to ensure that she attains that legacy? Write a letter to yourself describing your hopes and dreams for your child—the legacy you would like to leave. Reread your letter often.

You're ready! Turn to the first attitude you want to change in your child, read the makeover plan, and start. Then be relentless until you see the change of attitude you're looking for.

most popular

Twenty-Four Attitude Makeovers

Teach your children to choose the right path, and when they are older they will remain upon it.
—Proverbs 22:6

Bad Attitude

1

Arrogant
Antidote: Humility, Graciousness, Modesty

"I'm so cool."

Dear Dr. Borba,
Our twelve year old is pretty bright and always has to let everyone
know it. If anybody is wrong, look out: he can be merciless and
really insulting about letting them know that he's right and they're
wrong. I'm waiting for the day somebody just gets fed up and decks
him. Is there any way to stop his know-it-all attitude? He's really
turning into an arrogant little snob.

—Josh F., a father of two from Little Rock, Arkansas

Bad Attitude Act Out

"I'm so pretty, Mommy, I'm going to be Miss America."

"I knew that when I was five."

"Get real. I'm the one here with the smarts."

EMERGENCY ATTITUDE

Immediately stop reinforcing, putting up with, or encouraging your kid's overinflated notions about himself, or about you, or about your family. If you've been putting your younger kid on center stage to parade her talents and beauty (so that everyone "ooohs and ahhhs" her every breath), then cut it out! If you've become a "praiseaholic" each and every time your kid kicks a goal, says a funny joke, ties his shoelace, and swallows, cease! If you've been tooting your horn about your family's status, fame, and fortune so when people see you they run, call a halt. If you've been listening to your kid boasting and bragging about her every little accomplishment and encouraging her to do so too, end it. Then pass your treatment on to your spouse, siblings, relatives, and friends so they can apply the same treatment as well.

To rein in older kids' arrogance, confront them with specific tasks that challenge their limits, even provide the possibility of down right failure. You could put them in a difficult situation with a tough job to do, and also expose them to the true genius of someone who knows a lot more than they do. Examples are cooking dinner for a soup kitchen; sewing a quilt for the AIDS project; building a low-cost house with Habitat for Humanity or a similar organization; doing a daunting intellectual exercise with a math prodigy; experiencing a rigorous outdoor experience such as Outward Bound; or painting with a gifted artist. Choose an activity designed to help your kid recognize his limits, and create a rare humbling moment when he realizes he isn't the best in everything.

He's such a "Know-It-All." "Might as well call her 'Little Miss Smarty Pants.'" "He's such a Little Snot." "What a Smart Aleck!" "She's turning into such a snob."

Could any of these terms describe your kid? If so, beware: no matter what variety of language, they are all labels for the same bad attitude: Arrogance. Warning: the attitude is spreading, and even the younger set is affected by the Big Brat Factor these days.

Arrogant kids have somehow acquired the notion that they are better than others, and they make sure everyone knows it. Their attitude has one goal: making sure the other guy clearly recognizes the message: "I'm better than you." And that also implies—at least in her mind—that everyone else is inferior, and that includes *you*. After all, if she is the Know-It-All, then you're the Know Nothing. We're talking plain arrogance, and it's anything but becoming. That's why kids with arrogant attitude are also self-centered, rude, competitive, and selfish (not to mention very unpopular with all those poor souls on the receiving end).

When kids are little, we may think it's cute when they volunteer all the answers or have a sarcastic comeback. The mistake is thinking they are clever, funny, or even "beyond their years." But beware: you're really dealing with the early stages of arrogance. If not put in her place, the young smart aleck can turn into an older arrogant know-it-all. The simplest cause is that we've mislabeled their smart-aleck attitude as clever or witty: in reality, there's really nothing cute or witty about it in the least. Their snide remarks and quick retorts are often pointed slams at another person or shameless attempts to get attention through laughs and being "cute."

There's another reason kids turn arrogant, and that's our fault as well. Our parental pride can take a turn when we begin showing them off by parading their talents. "Come on, Jenna, everyone wants to hear you sing." "Have we shown you Harold's latest report card?" Of course we're proud, but there's a hidden danger in flaunting our kids' talents: they assume that the world revolves solely around them and they are better than others. There's also the danger that our kids will begin to think they have to keep performing, keep showing off their talents, and keep being the clown to gain our love or approval.

Now don't get me wrong: I'm not debating your child's intelligence, beauty, talent, or skills or doubting your pride in your offspring. She could well be a budding Einstein, the next Virginia Woolf, a young Wayne Gretsky, a future Jackie Joyner-Kersee, a potential Itzhak Perlman, or even the next Picasso or Frida Kahlo. And she may deserve recognition and acknowledgment for her strengths. But this issue is not about how bright your kid is; how good looking; how extraordinarily adroit her math, science, art talents; how proficient her soccer, violin, computer expertise; or how profound her beauty. Instead, it's all about her preoccupation of making sure everyone knows she's better than the other kids. Arrogant children's methods of letting others in on their superiority are usually quite tactless and *always* insensitive. After all, these children dwell on their *own* capabilities and are usually quite blind to those of others.

Certainly, no infant arrives diapered and arrogant. But somewhere growing up, these kids anointed themselves as the Better Ones. And there are many reasons. Unrealistic self-appraisals may have resulted from overly lavished parental pride (and usually with a blind eye to their kid's faults and behavior mishaps). Excellence in an area—academics, sports, music, the arts, or any other—may be such a prime commodity in these kids' homes that letting others in on those talents is valued. Or competition, one-upmanship, or winning at any cost (including the price of humility) may be the family mantra.

There always are deeper underlying causes to any bad attitude that often are overlooked. For instance, an arrogant child may attempt to make others think his ideas are better because deep down, he doesn't feel superior at all: in reality he feels inferior. But boasting or bragging is his way of trying to

Twenty-Four Attitude Makeovers

convince others of his talents. He might be jealous or resentful of other siblings or friends, so to get back he has to play the "I'm better than you" game. Or he may feel his relationship with you or his other parent is contingent on what he knows or does instead of who he is. So he is forever trying to prove himself to gain your love or approval. It could also be a reaction to a critical or negative parenting style.

Whatever the cause, make no mistake: if this arrogant attitude continues, it can have deadly consequences. No teacher, coach, scout leader, or other child's parent appreciates a kid with an "I'm superior" attitude. Besides that, what peer wants to be around another kid who tries to make him feel inferior? That's why all too many arrogant children have such dismal social lives. What any arrogant kid desperately needs is a strong helping of humble pie, so make sure you give him a big piece soon. Make sure you teach him humility, graciousness, and modesty to replace the arrogance that will prevent good character and ultimate fulfillment.

BAD ATTITUDE ALERT

Before you attempt to stop your kid's arrogant, "superior" ways, you need to consider where, why, and how this attitude evolved.

Diagnosis
These questions will help you better understand why your child is using an arrogant attitude and figure out what's going on.

Why. Why is your kid arrogant? Think carefully about what may have caused him to have such a high opinion of himself—or might he be compensating for something he lacks? Does he really have something to feel superior about? Is he gifted in the area he professes to be so knowledgeable about?

And what makes him feel he is so superior? Are you praising and acknowledging that expertise so much that he sees only his strengths and overlooks his weaknesses? Is an arrogant attitude something that is valued in your home? Or are you being too negative and critical, provoking this defensive reaction, this compensation for your withering attacks? Does he see others bragging unduly about their strengths, and so he is modeling their attitude? Or might it be that he is really trying to compensate for feelings of inadequacy? Another thing to consider: does he hear you bragging about his "brilliance" to others, and so he feels he needs to provide you with more things to brag about? Why did he develop such a know-it-all spirit?

What. Are there particular things he is more arrogant about? Is there a special subject or area of expertise that he tends to be more boastful toward—such as math, science, or vocabulary? If so, what is it? Is there a skill or talent he is more prone to show off: hockey, flute, weight lifting, or horseback riding?

Who. Does he display the same arrogant attitude to everyone: friends, the neighbor kids, teammates, a coach, a teacher, relatives, siblings, you, or your partner? Are there some individuals he does not use his know-it-all ways on? For instance: *all* relatives or some; *all* friends or just some? *All* his teammates or just some? Why are some spared dealing with this attitude?

When. Is there a particular time of day, week, month, or year when he is more arrogant? Is there a reason? For instance, if it is at a particular time, could something—such as a musical recital, spelling bee competition, athletic tournament, school debate, or report cards—be coinciding? Also, about when did you first see signs of this attitude? Was there anything happening at the same time that might have triggered his know-it-all ways: a move, an overly competitive school, a pushy relative, a certain teacher?

Where. Are there certain places he is more likely to be arrogant: at school or day care, on an athletic field, with peers, at a musical concert, at home, at a store, at Grandma's? Why? Or is he arrogant every place and everywhere?

Now take a look at your answers. Are you seeing any predictable patterns? Do you have any better understanding of your kid's arrogant attitude and where it's coming from?

WHAT'S WRONG WITH YOUR CURRENT RESPONSE?

Your kid is right in front of you, and her arrogant, know-it-all ways are flying full colors. How do you typically respond? Do you reinforce her professions of greatness by agreeing with her? Do you encourage her by reminding her of other talents she has overlooked? Are you cheering her know-it-all ways because you feel it is a sign of high self-esteem?

If you don't approve of her arrogant attitude, what do you do (or do you do anything?)? For instance, do you let her know you don't approve by giving her one of your sternest looks? Yell? Lecture? Shrug? Remove a privilege? Raise your eyebrows? Do you ignore her attitude and hope it will go away by itself? Or do you let her know that she really doesn't have anything to be so proud of? Do you criticize? Humiliate? Compare her professed talent to that of someone else, such as a sibling, your partner, her peers, or even yourself?

What is the one response you have found does not work in stopping her arrogant ways? Write what you will never do from this moment forward:

I will not _____

_____

_____

FACING YOUR OWN BAD ATTITUDES

Where is your kid learning this attitude? Could it be from you or your partner? Tune into your attitude and that of those close to your child, and look for clues. It may help you discover what's triggering your kid's arrogance.

First, look at your own attitude, and think about the kind of example you are sending. For instance, do you brag frequently about your accomplishments or talents in front of your kids? Do they hear you boasting about yourself to your partner, relatives, or spouse? What about your spouse or relatives? Do they display this attitude?

What do your kids perceive you value more: personal character or personal achievements? Is your attitude in line with those values? Do you emphasize your family's social, financial, or professional status to your kids? Do you (and they) have the view that your family is somehow "better" than other families? Do you stress personal accomplishments, grades, athletic prowess, and test results so much to your kids that they might perceive they need to prove themselves in order to gain your love? How competitive are you about your kids and family? For instance, how important is it for your kids to be "better" than your friends' kids? Do you openly compare your kids' performance, grades, or capabilities to those of their classmates, cousins, neighbors, or friends?

What are your beliefs about how children acquire self-esteem? For instance, do you feel it is more a matter of nature or your nurture? Is self-esteem contingent on a child's personal accomplishments or a parent's acceptance, or both? Do you feel that arrogance is a sign of high, medium, or low self-esteem? Do you feel criticism lowers your child's self-esteem? Do you criticize your child's poor behavior or attitude? If so, how? If not, why? Might your response have anything to do with your child's arrogant attitude?

Is there anything in your own attitude that might be enhancing your kid's arrogance? If so, what is it? What is the first step you need to take in yourself to be a better example of humility to your child?

I will _____

_____

BAD ATTITUDE NEWS ALERT

A famous study found that nine of ten adults felt that as they were growing up, they had to display a high skill, talent, or special ability in order to gain their parents' love. Might your child be in this category? If so, it could very well be a reason for his know-it-all ways. Researchers also found that the need to demonstrate competencies learned in childhood remains a pattern well into adulthood. This time, though, the adult uses his profession as a means of gaining approval and accolades from loved ones. Once again, instead of feeling a sense of quiet, inner confidence in his talents and strengths, he must toot his horn and demonstrate them to others for approval. If this is the case, he is at high risk for developing anxiety, low self-esteem, and the fear of disappointment. Make sure your child knows that your love is based on just who he is—and not on that gold star, goal, SAT score, or great grade.

THE "DON'T GIVE ME THAT ATTITUDE" MAKEOVER

To eliminate your child's arrogant bad attitude, take the following steps.

Step 1. Uncover the Source

Here are some common reasons that your child may be so arrogant. Check off those that might pertain to your situation:

☐ She may feel the need to show off her talents, skills, or intelligence. Have you set a precedent in which your kids display their talents to friends, relatives, or one another?

☐ She may be jealous or resentful. Do you favor one child, or does she feel that you do? Do you compare her capabilities—academic, social, aesthetic, or athletic—to those of classmates, peers, neighborhood kids, cousins, or your friend's kids?

☐ She may need attention or want to improve her social status. Does she feel the way to make friends is by "impressing" them? Does she lack social skills to find friends who accept her for herself?

☐ She may feel that this is the way to gain your approval. Do you emphasize the concept of "what did you get?" (grades, "gold stars," goals, scores) to your kid? Do you reinforce or reward (such as with money or privileges) your child's performance?

☐ She may feel "privileged" or "above others." Do you stress your family's status—financial, social, educational, professional—as being better than others?

☐ She may be self-centered. Have you made your child feel as though no one is as intelligent, talented, or capable as she is?

☐ She may feel inadequate. Is she trying to prove her capabilities to others because deep down she feels not good enough?

☐ She models what she hears. Does she hear other family members boasting and mimic them?

☐ She may be competitive. Is competition to be the best a priority in your house, and so she feels the need to prove she meets your expectations?

Identifying the specific reasons for your child's arrogant attitude will aid tremendously in changing it.

Step 2. Point Out Others' Reactions

A big part of changing any habit is for the offender to realize why he should change, and that's a problem with kids. They often have used the attitude so long that they're unaware that arrogance is a real turn-off and doesn't win them any points from friends, teammates, or adults. Help your child recognize how others react to his know-it-all superior ways. Here are a few examples of how you might do so with your child:

- *Ask: How would you feel?* "Sam came over to play, but you spent a lot of time walking him around the house and telling him how much bigger our house is than his. How do you think he feels? Do you think he'd like to come and play with you again?"
- *Point out nonverbal reactions.* "Did you see Kevin smirk when you talked about all your trophies?" "Sara rolled her eyes when you told her Dad makes more money than her dad. Did you notice?"
- *Role-play the other side.* "I heard you bet Meredith that you were smarter in math than she is and showed your report cards. Pretend you are Meredith. What do you think she'd like to say to you?"

Step 3. Emphasize Character, Not Performance

The point is to judge others not on what they have done but based on who they are. That means you need to stress character, not performance. Start with your child, but because modeling is such an important way kids learn, do it also with your whole family. That way you will be more likely to really walk your talk. Here are some ways to emphasize to your kid that in the end, it's his character that matters most:

- *Stop rewarding; just expect and accept.* Stop bribing or rewarding your kid's efforts. The best self-esteem is internalized: your child must gain a sense of pride that he accomplished something for the joy of doing it and did it *on his own.* Also, find a level of expectation that is appropriate for each child's specific ability, temperament, and level of development. Some kids just do better than others at certain things during certain times.

- *Halt the "parading."* I know you're proud, but stop putting your kid on center stage to always perform. It's all right on the soccer field or in a musical concert, but lower the curtains in your home.

- *Emphasize effort, not the product.* Put your acknowledgments into the little steps and efforts your child makes, not the final result.

- *Stress unconditional love.* Continually emphasize to your child, "Who you are is what matters most. Not your grades, test scores, appearance, or friends. Win or lose—you are who I love."

Step 4. Acknowledge Others

Arrogant kids often focus on their own strengths and overlook those of others, so a big part of tempering your kid's arrogance is to help him recognize the accomplishments and achievements of others. Here are a few strategies to help your child start looking for the greatness in others and acknowledge it:

- *Greet others.* The most basic form of acknowledgment is a simple "Hello," "Good morning," or "How are you?" Promote their use by your child. Though they seem like such minimal gestures, simple salutations are the first steps toward helping kids become more tuned into others and less tuned into themselves.

- *Encourage encouragement.* Tell your child that one of the secrets of people who are appreciated (as well as liked) by others is that they frequently encourage others. An arrogant kid may not be aware of supportive, encouraging statements that focus on building others up (instead of themselves), so brainstorm a few together: "Nice try!" "Super!" "Great job!" "Good game!" You might even post a list as a reminder. Then say the encouragers frequently so your child will "catch them" and then encourage her to start using them with peers.

- *Enforce the 1 X 7 Rule.* Encourage your child to praise a person's specific strengths, skills, or talent at least once a day, every day for a week. It could be a family member, friend, or stranger just as long as your child practices the art of praising someone other than herself. Be sure to help your kid recognize the kinds of traits that can be praised, so model a few examples: "Great kick!" "You're quite an artist." "You sure know a lot about history!" At the end of the day, ask your child who she praised and how the recipient responded. *Hint:* This is also a great activity to do as a family: because everyone is on board using the same 1 X 7 Rule, there are more examples for your child to learn from.

Step 5. Reinforce Authentic Self-Esteem and Humility

Reinforce your child's humility as soon as it happens, and let her know how pleased it makes you feel. Remember that true self-esteem is a quiet, inner contentment in which the child doesn't feel compelled to let others know of her accomplishments and accolades. Nor does she feel the urge to compare herself to others or put the other guy down. Here are some examples:

"Jessica, I know how proud you must feel about your grades. I'm proud of how hard you worked. I also appreciate that you just told Dad and me and didn't call all your friends this time."

"Jeremy, I heard how you commented on how much more Dr. Hallowell knows than you do about migrating butterflies. I remember when you claimed to be the world's foremost authority."

The First 21 Days

Start a Humility Crusade in your home by encouraging all family members to look more for the good in others and less in themselves. Follow these steps:

1. Pick your favorite skill, hobby, or focus of interest, from Barbies to the Middle East conflict.
2. Find two or three experts who know a whole lot more than you do, and read up on everything they've said on the subject.
3. Have a family discussion on several of these topics that highlights modesty, focusing on other people's thinking, and serious learning.

Another aspect of the crusade could have these steps:

1. Focus on the specific content of an arrogant remark, like a claim to know more, or do better, or be superior in some way.
2. Dig down and find out the real feelings underneath. Does your child really feel that this is true, or is he only pretending?
3. If he thinks it's true, point out the reality of the situation: that he is not the best, doesn't have the most, and so on, and show him that it doesn't matter. You love him anyway.
4. If it isn't true, show empathy for his insecurity and need to compensate. Again, show him that you love him no matter what and find out what you can do to help him overcome the fear and anxiety that actually provokes this arrogance.

ATTITUDE MAKEOVER PLEDGE

How will you use these steps to turn your kid's arrogant attitude around and achieve long-term change? On the lines below, write exactly what you agree to do within the next twenty-four hours to begin changing your child's attitude so he is less of a know-it-all and more considerate of other people's ideas and opinions.

_____

_____

_____

THE NEW ATTITUDE REVIEW

All attitude makeovers take hard work, constant practice, and parental reinforcement. Each step your child takes toward change may be a small one, so be sure to acknowledge and congratulate every one of them along the way. It takes a minimum of twenty-one days to see real results, so don't give up! And if one strategy doesn't work, try another. Write your child's weekly progress on the lines below. Keep track of daily progress in your Attitude Makeover Journal.

WEEK 1

_____

_____

_____

WEEK 2

_____

_____

_____

WEEK 3

_____

_____

_____

ONGOING ATTITUDE TUNE-UP

Where does your child's attitude still need improvement? What
work still needs to be done?

_____

_____

_____

ATTITUDE MAKEOVER RESOURCES

For Parents

Everyday Blessings: The Inner World of Mindful Parenting, by Myla
Kabat-Zinn and Jon Kabat-Zinn (New York: Hyperion, 1997).
Shows parents how to recognize who their children really are and
be grateful for each child's uniqueness.

No More Push Parenting: A Mother's Tale from the Trenches, by Elisabeth
Guthrie and Kathy Matthew (New York: Broadway Books, 2002).
Great solutions for parents caught up by the need to push their kids
to the top and those parents who don't want to push but are afraid
their kids won't measure up.

Raising Confident Girls: 100 Tips for Parents and Teachers, by Elizabeth
Hartley-Brewer (Cambridge, Mass.: Fisher Books, 2001). Excellent
ideas to help your daughter gain authentic self-esteem and feel good
about who she is without having to put on false airs. Also by the
author for parents of boys: *Raising Confident Boys: 100 Tips for Parents and Teachers,* by Elizabeth Hartley-Brewer (Cambridge, Mass.:
Fisher Books, 2003).

Worried All the Time: Overparenting in an Age of Anxiety and How to Stop It, by David Anderegg (New York: Free Press, 2003). Fascinating analysis on why anxiety-driven parenting may be doing kids more harm than good, and down-to-earth advice on how to pull back.

For Kids

The Emperor's New Clothes, by Hans Christian Andersen (New York: North-South Books, 2002). The all-time classic about the emperor who always wanted to put on airs to convince his subjects of his greatness. Ages 4 to 8.

Kissing Coyotes, by Marcia K. Vaughan and Kenneth Spengler (Illustrator) (Flagstaff, Ariz.: Rising Moon, 2002). Jack Rabbit boasts idly without much consideration for how he might actually accomplish the feats that he brags about. One day he goes a little too far in his claims, and his desert friends have had enough. Ages 4 to 8.

The Tower: A Story of Humility, by Richard Evans (New York: Simon & Schuster, 2001). Determining that greatness means having everyone look up to him literally, a proud young man in long-ago China builds a tower and isolates himself from his fellow villagers. Loneliness is a small price to pay, and anyway, "Why would he want to associate with those so much lower than himself?" A wonderful lesson in humanity. Ages 4 to 8.

Pride and Prejudice, by Jane Austen (A & E, 1995). The filmed version of Jane Austen's classic novel about the prejudice that occurred between the nineteenth-century classes and the pride that would keep lovers apart. Look carefully at the "supposed arrogance" of a few of the characters, particularly the uncle. What becomes apparent at the end is that some people put on airs to cover up insecurities or traumatic earlier experiences. A good lesson for us all. Ages 10 up.

2

Bad-Mannered
Antidote: Courtesy, Politeness, Respect

"Why shouldn't I belch and fart at Grandma's? She can't hear me anyway!"

Dear Dr. Borba,
Our friends spent the weekend, and my wife and I are mortified.
Our once-polite ten year old forgot every manner created. His bad
manners bordered at times on just plain vulgar. While all we adults
stood with our mouths open, he seemed to think his attitude was
"cute." We have three months to shape this kid up before our big
family reunion. Is there any hope, or should we move overseas?

—Kevin B., father of three from Kansas City, Missouri

Bad Attitude Act Out
"It's their fault if their feet got under my shoes. Why should I say 'excuse me' to them?"

> "So what if I talked during the sermon? I couldn't
> turn off my cell phone, or I'd have missed that call."
> "Don't worry about it, Dad. Nobody heard me burp."

EMERGENCY ATTITUDE ℞

Kick off an intensive program in mandatory manners training
in your home 24/7. Have your child sign an agreement to
abide by strict ground rules for civility and courtesy. Don't
assume your child knows how to be courteous: check the list
on page 63 of eighty-five important manners kids should learn,
roll up your sleeves, and teach, model, and reinforce them one
at a time until your kid is cured of a bad-mannered attitude.
For example, with a younger child who never says "please" or
"thank you," look for opportunities to use the words yourself
when talking to your child or others, point out when he could
use them, encourage him to use the words at appropriate
moments, and congratulate him whenever he remembers to do
so. With an older kid who answers the phone in a flippant tone
and never takes a message, spell out expectations to her clearly
and unequivocally. Write out a script if necessary containing
the language you would like her to use, the information you
need to receive in any message, and the tone of voice that
would be most appropriate. Then practice with her until she
can show you she knows what to do and how to do it.

Incivility and rude behaviors are clearly on the rise. A
recent survey conducted by *U.S. News and World Report*
found that nine out of ten Americans felt the breakdown of

common courtesy has become a serious problem in this country. And courtesy does count! Scores of studies find that well-mannered children are more popular and do better in school. Notice how often they're invited to others' homes. Listen to their teachers speak about them using such positive accolades.

But it isn't that these kids are just nice to be around. Polite kids have an edge on the foundation of good character. Since they are more considerate of others' thoughts and feelings, they are a more respectful and less selfish breed. The foundation for civility is courtesy. So tune up your social graces and make courtesy, politeness, and respect a priority in your home. And squelch any impolite, discourteous attitude any time, any place your kid tries them.

BAD ATTITUDE ALERT

There's no reason to accept or cave into a bad-mannered attitude. Start your makeover by taking a strong look at how your kid developed this discourtesy and incivility.

Diagnosis

It really helps if you write your answers to the questions below in your Attitude Makeover Journal.

What. What does your kid specifically do that you consider impolite? Interrupt? Belch? Forget to say "thank you"? Use the wrong eating utensils? Or are you talking about a more vulgar behavior? Does he swear at you? Slam the door in your face? Use her cell phone in the middle of your family dinner? Over the next week, take a serious look at your kid's ill-mannered ways. Jot down a few rude behaviors that specifically concern you. (A list of proper etiquette is provided in the next section. You might refer to it as you diagnose your kid's attitude problem.)

Why. Why does your kid have this attitude? Are manners modeled in your home? Is he hanging around peers or adults who are impolite? Is he watching or listening to CDs, movies, or TV shows that flaunt rudeness or even vulgarity? Is he allowed to get away with this attitude? Does he somehow think it's cool to be rude? Is he treated in a discourteous manner? Has he in the past? Where has he learned this attitude?

Who. Does he display the same rude attitude to everyone? Are there some individuals he does not use this attitude on? If so, who? Why not? Could it have anything to do with the way they are responding to him?

When. Is there a particular time of day, week, or month he is more impolite? Is there a reason? For instance, might he be with a particular group of kids? Watching a TV show? Spending time with an adult who models rudeness?

Where. Are there certain places he is more likely to be impolite (at a certain friend's house, in public, at the movies, at school or day care, at the dinner table, at a restaurant, at the store, at Grandma's)? Why?

Now take a look at your answers. Are you seeing any predictable patterns? Is your kid using this attitude only in certain places or only with certain people? Do you have any better understanding of this attitude and where it's coming from? Write down your thoughts.

_____

_____

_____

WHAT'S WRONG
WITH YOUR CURRENT RESPONSE?

Now reflect on how you typically respond to your kid's rudeness. Think of the last time she displayed this attitude to you. Review the episode, and then push the mental rewind button. How did the episode begin? What might have triggered it? What did you do?

What kind of response has not worked in the past in curbing your kid's rudeness? Was it being rude in return? Excusing it? Taking the blame yourself? Ignoring it? Spanking? Punishing him? Criticizing or trying to correct it? Trying to humiliate him publicly? What is the one thing you will never try again? Write it.

I will not _____

_____

FACING YOUR OWN BAD ATTITUDES

There is an old saying that speaks volumes: "Manners are better caught than taught." The best way to learn manners is by emulating others. Think seriously about what kind of a model you are presenting. Could your child be catching this impolite attitude from you? Is your behavior teaching him to be courteous? For instance, do you consistently treat your kids politely? Have you ever corrected your own impoliteness in front of your child? How do you treat your parents? Friends? Strangers? How would you honestly answer this question: "If my kid watched my manners, would they be worth catching?"

Which of your own manners might need tuning up? When your kid is rude, do you remain courteous and respectful, or are you sarcastic, cynical, or disrespectful? What about the nonverbal messages you send? Do you ever roll your eyes? Smirk? Shrug your shoulders? Walk away?

How do you behave in public? Do you ever cut in at the front of a line? Swear at the other driver for taking the parking place you were getting ready to move into? Interrupt your friends? Talk during a movie? Speak loudly on your cell phone in a restaurant?

What is the first step you need to take to tune up discourteous behaviors in yourself as an example to your kids? Write down specific changes you need to make and are willing to take.

I will _____

_____

BAD ATTITUDE NEWS ALERT

A recent survey conducted by *U.S. News and World Report* found that 78 percent of Americans polled said manners and good social graces have significantly eroded over the past ten years and this erosion is a major contributor to the increase in violence as well as the breakdown of our values in the United States.

THE "DON'T GIVE ME THAT ATTITUDE" MAKEOVER

To eliminate your kid's impolite, rude, bad-mannered attitude, take the following five steps.

Step 1. Set a Moratorium on Bad-Mannered Attitudes and Correct Impoliteness Immediately

The first step to changing a rude attitude is simply to refuse to allow it. Keep in mind that your child is using this attitude because it works, so let him know in no uncertain terms that it will no longer be effective. Call any rude behavior each time you see it: "That's rude! I don't listen to rude talk." Then expect your kid to apologize immediately. Do not answer or give in if he is rude. Feel free to turn and walk away until he is polite: "I'm in the kitchen. When you can talk to me politely, come join me."

Sometimes kids may use an impolite comment and not realize they are being rude. This is especially true with younger kids. In this case, immediately correct the rude behavior, so he understands what he did that was impolite. The best corrections have three characteristics:

1.   They are brief.
2.   They are specific enough, so the child knows exactly what he did that was impolite.
3.   They are instructive, so the child knows what to do to correct his impolite behavior.

Here are some examples of how to use the three parts:

"Starting your dinner without waiting first for Grandma to sit down was impolite. Next time please wait for her to sit and be served."

"Interrupting my conversation with Mom was impolite. Next time, please wait until you see I'm done or say, 'Excuse me, may I say something?'"

"That was impolite! Next time, remember to say 'pardon me' when you walk in front of someone."

Step 2. Point Out the Virtue of Courtesy

The next step to boosting courtesy and squelching a rude attitude is to make sure your child clearly recognizes why manners are important. Once kids understand the impact good manners have on others, they're more likely to incorporate courtesy in their own behavior. You might say:

"Using good manners helps you gain the respect of others. People remember how others act and whether they were polite. It's a great way to build a good reputation."

"Being polite is a great way to meet new friends. People like to be around others who are nice to be with."

"Courtesy is one way to make the world a nicer place. Just think how much better the world would be if everyone was polite and kind to one another."

"When people are polite and civil to one another, they are happier and feel more comfortable. You just can't help but react positively to people who are polite and courteous."

Step 3. Replace Impoliteness with New Manners

One way to purge your child of his impolite attitude is by teaching him new manners to replace the bad ones. There's a whole gamut of manners to choose from: how to meet others, how to be a good host or guest, proper eating etiquette, phone etiquette, Internet etiquette, as well as an array of polite words. I've provided a list of eighty-five important manners kids should learn. Choose one or two manners from the list to teach at a time. As you teach each new manner, be sure to explain why the skill is important and when and how to use it. Kids learn any skill best through repetition, so give your child lots of opportunities to practice the new skill. You might get the rest of the family involved so that everybody is practicing the same skill together. Some families target a new skill each week. Just make sure everyone is supportive; no teasing is allowed.

Eighty-Five Important Manners Kids Should Learn

The list of some of the most important manners etiquette experts say we should teach kids is from my book *Building Moral Intelligence: The Seven Essential Virtues That Teach Kids to Do the Right Thing*. Check off any your child already uses. Those that remain are ones you can help you child learn.

Essential Polite Words

____ Please.

____ Thank you.

____ Excuse me.

____ I'm sorry.

____ May I?

____ Pardon me.

____ You're welcome.

Meeting and Greeting Manners

____ Smiles and looks person in the eye.

____ Shakes hands.

____ Says hello.

____ Introduces self.

____ Introduces other person.

Conversation Manners

____ Starts a conversation.

____ Listens without interrupting.

____ Looks at the eyes of the speaker.

____ Uses a pleasant tone of voice.

____ Appears interested in the speaker.

____ Knows how to end a conversation.

____ Knows how to maintain a conversation.

Table Manners

____ Comes to the table on time.

____ Knows how to set the table correctly.

____ Sits up straight.

____ Places napkin on her lap.

____ Takes his hat off.

____ Makes only positive comments about food.

____ Waits for the hostess to sit before serving or eating.

____ Puts modest portions of food on his plate.

____ Eats food only on his own plate.

____ Eats soup without slurping.

____ Knows proper way to cut meat.

____ Asks, "Please pass the . . ."

____ Doesn't grab serving dishes or reach over someone for food.

____ Knows how to use utensils correctly.

____ Keeps his elbows off the table.

____ Chews with her mouth closed.

____ Doesn't talk with food in his mouth.

____ Places knife and fork sideways on plate when finished.

____ Asks to be excused before leaving table.

____ Offers to help the hostess.

____ Thanks the hostess before leaving.

Hospitality Manners

____ Greets guest at the door.

____ Offers guest something to eat or drink.

____ Stays with the guest.

____ Asks guest what he'd like to do.

____ Shares with the guest.

____ Walks guest to the door and says good-bye.

Anywhere and Anytime

____ Covers mouth when she coughs.

____ Refrains from swearing.

____ Refrains from belching.

____ Refrains from gossiping.

____ Holds a door for a woman or elderly person.

Visiting Manners

____ Greets host's parents.

____ Picks up after himself.

____ If spending the night, keeps room in order and makes bed.

____ Offers to help the parent of the host.

____ Thanks his host and her parents.

Manners Toward Older People

____ Stands up when older person comes into the room.

____ Helps older guests with their coats.

____ Opens the door and holds it open when an older person leaves.

____ Offers his seat if no chair is available.

____ Is considerate of older people's physical needs (hearing, vision, and so on).

____ Holds the car door and helps person into the car if necessary.

____ Is considerate and offers any help.

____ Doesn't address the person's shortcomings (wrinkles, hearing loss, cane, and so on).

Sports Manners

____ Plays by the rules.

____ Shares the equipment.

____ Encourages her teammates.

____ Doesn't brag or show off.

____ Doesn't cheer mistakes.

____ Doesn't boo.

____ Doesn't argue with the referee.

____ Congratulates opponents.

____ Doesn't make excuses or complain.

____ Stops when the game is over.

____ Cooperates.

Phone Manners

____ Turns off cell phone or beeper at movies, concerts, or other public places.

____ If she must use a cell phone at a public place, does so quietly so as not to disturb others.

____ First greets the person and says name.

____ Politely asks to speak to the person he is calling.

____ Answers with a clear and pleasant voice.

____ Asks the caller, "Who's calling, please?"

____ Greets the caller by name if she knows him.

____ Politely says, "Please hold on" while she gets the intended speaker.

____ Takes and gives a message.

____ Politely ends a conversation.

Step 4. Praise Courteous Actions

Reinforce your child's courteous behaviors, and let her know how pleased it makes you feel. Describe exactly what your child did right, so your child is more likely to repeat the virtuous behavior—for example:

"I noticed how you remembered to use such polite words as 'Please' and 'Thank you' when we were visiting Mrs. Walker. It makes me happy to know how well mannered you can be."
"Thank you for waiting until everyone was served before you began to eat. That was being polite."

Do also help your kid recognize that courteous, kind acts—even small ones—can make a big impression on other people. Point them out to help your child see the impact his actions made:

"Greg, holding the door open for Grandma was so polite. Did you see how pleased she was?"
"Wow, nice manners! Did you notice the smile on your coach's face when you thanked her for taking the time to help you train?"

Step 5. If the Attitude Continues, Set a Consequence

Your kid needs to know you are serious about eradicating his rude attitude, so be prepared to enforce a consequence if the attitude continues. If the same rude attitude persists, you might try requiring your kid to repeat the correct polite behavior ten times in a row on the spot, or say or even write a sincere apology note to the offended party. For especially offensive discourtesy, increase the stakes by forbidding your child to attend social gatherings for an appropriate period of time.

One mom told me she has a consequence for rude attitudes that she rarely has to use more than once. She enforces an effective discipline called "Overcorrection." When her daughter displays a specific bad-mannered attitude, she requires her to rehearse the correct manner over and over until she gets it right. The child must give up any social plans and remain home where she practices whatever etiquette rules she broke. For example, if her child demonstrates poor table manners, she requires her to set the table and practice the proper use of utensils. She wasn't excused until she could demonstrate how to use each item correctly. The mom said the etiquette session was so successful she hasn't had to offer a repeat lesson.

The First 21 Days

Institute a Good Manners Outreach Program by specifying one manner each day to practice outside your home. Refer to the list of eighty-five Important Manners Kids Should Learn for possibilities, and each time have a different family member select the one you all will perform. Write the manner on an index card, post it on your refrigerator as a reminder, and at the end of each day compare notes. Talk about when and where it was appropriate to apply, what people did in response, and how it made you feel. After twenty-one days of this Good Manners Outreach Program, your child should be practicing new manners and be well on his way to eliminating his previous bad-mannered attitude.

ATTITUDE MAKEOVER PLEDGE

How will you use these steps to help your kid become less rude and achieve long-term change? On the lines below, write exactly what you agree to do within the next twenty-four hours to begin changing your kid's attitude so he is more polite and courteous.

_____

_____

_____

THE NEW ATTITUDE REVIEW

All attitude makeovers take hard work, constant practice, and parental reinforcement. Each step your child takes toward change may be a small one, so be sure to acknowledge and congratulate every one of them along the way. It takes a minimum of twenty-one days to see real results, so don't give up! And if one strategy doesn't work, try another. Write your child's weekly progress on the lines below. Keep track of daily progress in your Attitude Makeover Journal.

WEEK 1

_____

_____

_____

WEEK 2

_____

_____

_____

WEEK 3

_____

_____

_____

ONGOING ATTITUDE TUNE-UP

Where does your child's attitude still need improvement? What work still needs to be done?

_____

_____

_____

_____

ATTITUDE MAKEOVER RESOURCES

For Parents

More Than Manners! Raising Today's Kids to Have Kind Manners and Good Hearts, by Letitia Baldrige (New York: Rawson Associates, 1997). A road map for guiding kids to succeed in life by enhancing decency, kind hearts, and great manners.

The Gift of Good Manners: A Parent's Guide for Raising Respectful, Kind, Considerate Children, by Peggy Post and Cindy Post Senning (New York: HarperResource, 2002). A wealth of wonderful advice is offered in this comprehensive guide by a renowned manners expert and her sister-in-law.

For Kids

The Berenstain Bears Forget their Manners, by Stan and Jan Berenstain (New York: Random House, 1985). Mama Bear comes up with a plan to correct the Bear family's rude behavior. Ages 3 to 8.

Perfect Pigs: An Introduction to Manners, by Marc Brown and Stephen Brensky (New York: Little, Brown, 1983). A simple introduction to good manners to use with family, friends, at school, during meals, with pets, on the phone, during games, at parties, and in public places. Ages 5 to 9.

Manners, by Aliki (New York: Greenwillow Books, 1990). An assortment of different manners are cleverly illustrated. Ages 3 to 7.

Little Women (MCA/CA Home Video, 1933). A film based on the classic by Louisa May Alcott; four devoted sisters face obstacles with love and courage. The story is rich with lessons in courtesy and morals. Rated PG.

Table Manners for Kids (Public Media Video, 1993). A detailed narration of everything kids need to know about proper table manners.

3

Bad-Tempered
Antidote: Self-Control, Calmness, Peacefulness

"Take that!"

Dear Dr. Borba,
My husband and I are very concerned about our seven year old.
Don't get me wrong: he's a good kid and does well in school, but he
has such a quick temper! The littlest things seem to set him off. He
gets himself so worked up and usually ends up lashing out at his
brothers and friends. We're afraid he's going to hurt someone and get
into serious trouble or lose his friends. Is there anything we can do
to help him?

—Carol R., mom of three from Oklahoma City

Bad Attitude Act Out
"I can't lower my voice, Daddy. I'm mad!"
"Yeah I hit him. He deserved it!"
"Why aren't you pissed, Mom? He cut us off!"

EMERGENCY ATTITUDE R_X

Take a hard look at how you handle *your* temper. Kids do copy our attitudes and behaviors, so keep a lid on, stop yelling, stifle your road rage and other outbursts, and make sure your kid has a good model.

Yelling. Fighting. Hitting. Name-calling. Tantrums. Biting. Sound familiar? They are typical behaviors bad-tempered kids use to make their needs known and to get their way. Yes, they are signs of poor self-control, but they are also signs of selfish and rude attitudes. Need proof? Just be in the company of a screaming, tirading toddler or explosive teenager, and in seconds you know this child sure isn't thinking about others. He is concerned only about getting his agenda met, and the antics he uses to achieve that aim are anything but civil. In fact, he's a leading candidate for membership in the Big Brat Factor All-Stars.

Teaching kids a new way to cope with their intense feelings is not easy, especially if they have been in the habit of using quick tempers to deal out their frustrations. Calming a hot temper is not only teachable but also essential for growing up in a sometimes violent, unpredictable world. Besides, eliminating this behavior will do absolute wonders in creating not only a calmer kid who is far more enjoyable to be with, but also a more peaceful family. So don't wait! Begin your child on the path of self-control, calmness, and peacefulness by starting this attitude tune-up right now.

BAD ATTITUDE ALERT

Nip that bad-tempered attitude in the bud by quickly focusing on how it started.

Bad-Tempered   **73**

Diagnosis

Sure, some kids are born with quicker fuses, but anger can be managed, and tempers can be controlled. And more often than not, quick tempers are learned. The statements that follow describe behaviors usually displayed by kids who flaunt quick tempers and have poor self-control. How many of these behaviors are indicative of your kid?

☐ Frequently interrupts or blurts out answers or questions
☐ Has troubling waiting her turn
☐ Becomes physically agitated, red-faced, starts hyper-ventilating, or can't think straight
☐ Has difficulty managing her own impulses and urges; sometimes needs adult help
☐ Has trouble calming down when excited, frustrated, or angry
☐ Blows up, has angry outbursts, or loses control quickly
☐ Resorts to using physical aggression, such as hitting, kicking, fighting, or pushing
☐ Behaves recklessly
☐ Needs reminders, coaxing, or reprimands to control temper
☐ Has difficulty bouncing back from an upsetting or frustrating situation

How does your kid typically display his quick temper?

Why. Why does your kid have this attitude? Why has he learned that flaunting his temper is effective in getting his needs met? Could he be copying someone's behavior? Does he know how to calm down? Is there a change in your family that might be causing undue stress? Is anything going on at school that might be creating extra pressures on him? Is there any trouble with relationships, romantic and otherwise? If your child is older, have you ever smelled alcohol on his breath? Is he frustrated, picked on, overwhelmed, overscheduled, needing attention, or physically tired? Does he feel he isn't being listened to? Might he be feeling powerless or depressed? Might a bad-tempered attitude be a way to vent his frustrations?

What. Are there particular issues or things he usually gets more upset about? Are they about a conflict with a sibling, homework, chores, a tight schedule? Watch your kid's outbursts closely over the next week. Consider tracking the frequency of incidents on a chart, on a calendar, or in a journal. It may help you tune into what may be provoking the outbursts.

Who. Does he display the same quick temper to everyone? Are there some individuals he does not flare his temper toward? If so, who? Why not? Who does he yell at? Is there someone he does not get so irritated at? For instance, does he yell at his friends, siblings, teacher, you, your partner?

When. Is there a particular time of day, week, or month your kid has a quicker temper? Is there a reason? Also ask yourself when this attitude started. Has your kid always had a quick temper, or are you noticing that she is more upset lately? Why the change? Could it be a sign of trouble in school? With friends? A problem at home?

Where. Are there certain places she is more likely to be more quick-tempered (at school or day care, home, the store, a sporting event, scouting, Grandpa's, with the kid next door)? Why do you think this is so?

Now take a look at your answers. Are you seeing any predictable patterns? Do you have any better understanding of this attitude and where it's coming from?

WHAT'S WRONG
WITH YOUR CURRENT RESPONSE?

What's your current response to your kid's bad-tempered attitude? Do you explode and yell back at him? Do you put your hands over your ears and grimace? Does your blood pressure rise and render you speechless? Do you try to change the subject or offer a bribe to be quiet? Do you spank him? Start by thinking of the last time your kid displayed a short fuse.

Why haven't these responses worked? Most important, what was her reaction to your response? Did it really quiet her down or enrage her even more? Get into her shoes and think about why she responded as she did.

What is one response you will never try again? Write it.

I will not _____

_____

FACING YOUR OWN BAD ATTITUDES

Your attitude is a living textbook to your child, so the first place to start a bad attitude makeover is by reflecting on your temper and how you deal with frustrations. These questions might help: How did your parents handle anger? Did you hear them do much yelling? Did you ever see them throw things or get into a shoving match? How about among your siblings? Who, if anybody, in your family or close friends had a quick temper? How do people respond to them? What responses were effective in calming them down? In escalating their temper?

How do you typically deal with anger now? Does it work or not work for you? How well are you controlling your temper at work? With your partner? With friends? When you're driving? How do you act in front of your kids after a hard, stressful day? How do you try to control your stress? In the middle of an argument, are you able to stop and say: "Let's get calm"? How well do your restrain your temper when other drivers are irrational? What lessons might your kid be learning from these actions?

What is the first step you need to take in yourself to be a better example to your sons or daughters of dealing with their quick tempers? Write down changes you need to make.

I will _____

_____

BAD ATTITUDE NEWS ALERT

A 1998 national survey conducted by the Josephson Institute of Ethics found that almost one in every four middle school and high school males said they had hit a person in the past twelve months "because they were angry."

THE "DON'T GIVE ME THAT ATTITUDE" MAKEOVER

To reduce your child's quick temper, take the following steps.

Step 1. Convey Your Attitude Expectations

Begin by firmly conveying that flaunting quick tempers will no longer be tolerated. Tell your child that while it's normal to be angry from time to time, he may not use a yelling voice, hurtful words, a tantrum, or fists to express his feelings. Then convey your "calmer policy" expectations to all family members. Consider asking them to take a "no yelling" vow. The pledge is written on a piece of paper, signed by all members, and posted as a concrete reminder.

Once everyone is clear on your attitude expectations, absolutely refuse to engage with a quick-tempered kid who yells, hits, or has a tirade. Firmly (and calmly) explain: "That's yelling. I only listen when you use a calm voice." Or "I understand you're upset, but you need to control your temper before I will listen." Then walk away and go about your business until your kid acts correctly. If you have to lock yourself in the bathroom, do so. He needs to know you mean business, so be consistent.

Step 2. Identify Temper Warning Signs

Explain to your child that we all have our own little signs that warn us our tempers are ready to blow and that we should listen to them because they can help us stay out of trouble.

Next, help your child recognize her specific warning signs that she's starting to get upset—for example, talking louder, flushed cheeks, clenched fists, pounding heart, drier mouth, or faster breathing. Once she is aware of her signs, point them out to her when she *first* starts to get frustrated and *before she loses her temper:* "Looks like you're starting to get out of control." "Your hands are in a fist now. Do you feel yourself starting to get upset?"

The more we help our kids recognize those early warning signs when their temper is triggered—usually when they first show signs of tension and stress—the better able they will be to calm themselves and learn to regulate their tempers.

Step 3. Teach Ways to Calm Quick Tempers

Once your kid is aware of his unique signs that warn him his temper is ready to blow, he needs to know how to handle his frustrations or temper. Explain that anger is normal: how we choose to deal with it can be healthy or unhealthy, as well as get us in trouble or keep us out of trouble. There are a number of anger management strategies to cool tempers. The goal is to find the one that works best for your child and then help him rehearse it again and again until it becomes a habit. Here are a few possibilities:

- **Deal with the anger.** Pound clay, hit a pillow, shoot baskets, punch a punching bag. Help your child find the most effective way to calm his temper, and then encourage him to use the technique.
- **Go to a calm spot.** Ask your kid to help you set up a place where he can go to gain control. Put out a few soothing things such as books, music, pens, and paper, and then encourage him to use the spot to cool down.
- **Leave the scene.** Sometimes the best strategy is to leave the scene. Do emphasize that to your kid. Whenever he feels he can't control his temper, feels the urge to fight, or doesn't feel safe, he can walk away. It's always safer.
- **Use self-talk.** Help your child learn to say a simple, positive message to himself to control his temper—for example, "Stop and calm down," "Stay in control," "Chill out," "I can handle this." Have your kid choose a phrase she feels most comfortable saying, and then help her rehearse it a few times each day until she can use it on her own.
- **Teach "Stop and breathe."** Tell your child as soon as he feels he's losing his temper to say to himself: "Stop! Calm down." He then immediately takes a deep, slow breath (or two or three if necessary) from his tummy. Getting oxygen into the brain is one of the fastest ways to relax.
- **Imagine a calm place.** Ask your kid to think of a place he has been where he feels calm and peaceful—for instance, the beach, his bed, Grandpa's backyard, a tree house. Right before his temper starts to flare and he feels those body warning signs kick in, tell him to close his eyes and imagine the spot while breathing slowly. Some kids say it helps them to pretend they are pulling a "stop sign" in front of their eyes. The sign warns them to control their temper.

Step 4. Teach How to Express Frustrations Appropriately

Many kids are quick-tempered because they have never learned ways to stay in control and to express their frustrations in a healthy manner. Find one that works best for *your* kid, and then help him practice it again and again until he learns it and can use it without your guidance. Here are three possibilities:

- *Say how you feel.* Younger kids or those with limited language skills can say how they feel to their offender. You must teach your kid an emotion vocabulary so she can express how she feels (such as *angry, upset, mad, frustrated, furious, stressed, tense, nervous, anxious, irritated, furious, ticked off*). A complete list is provided on page 191. Then encourage her to use her feeling words whenever her temper starts to flare: "I'm mad" or "I'm really, really angry."
- *Use an "I message."* Once your child knows emotion words, he can use them to tell the other person how he feels or what he wants the other to do. The statement must be delivered calmly and focus on the problem. No name-calling or put-downs are allowed because they just fuel the other person's temper: "I'm angry that you took my CD without asking. Next time ask my permission." Or "I am really feeling stressed about this test coming up, so I need some space."
- *Talk to someone about it.* Sometimes it may be counterproductive or even destructive to confront someone with your anger, especially on the spot, just after something has happened to provoke it. So talk to your kids about when to stuff it and vent elsewhere, a useful technique especially for preteens and teens.

Step 5. Reinforce Peaceful Behavior

One of the simplest ways to change kids' behavior is to catch them being good. It's also the technique most parents do the least. Any time you notice your kid handling a difficult situation calmly, expressing his frustrations without yelling, hitting, biting, or having a tantrum, or keeping his temper in control, acknowledge his behavior and let him know you appreciate his efforts: "I noticed you were really mad, but you walked away to control your temper. That's really a good sign." "You used your words this time to tell your brother how upset you were. Good for you!" Remember that attitudes that are reinforced are the ones that kids will continue to use. Reinforce your kid for any efforts he takes to control his temper.

Step 6. Monitor Media Consumption

Kids learn attitudes about temper not only from directly watching parents, teachers, and their peers but also from observing characters in books, movies, and television. And what they are watching is troubling. The typical preschooler who watches about two hours of cartoons daily will be exposed to 10,000 violent incidents per year. By the end of elementary school, the average child will have witnessed 8,000 murders and by age eighteen, 200,000 other vivid acts of violence on the TV screen.

And all those violent images do affect our kids. The American Academy of Pediatrics and five other prominent medical groups conclude that "viewing entertainment violence can lead to increases in aggressive attitudes, values and behavior, particularly in children." The American Psychological Association estimates that televised violence *by itself* contributes up to as much as 15 percent of all of kids' aggressive behaviors. Monitor what your kid watches and listen to what she consumes.

Step 7. Use a Consequence When Inappropriate Temper Displays Persists

What do you do if your kid continues displaying a quick, inappropriate temper? First, stay cool yourself; then it's time for consequences. Make sure you explain the consequence at a relaxed time—not during a screaming match. It must be enforced each time your kid displays his bad-tempered attitude.

Tell a younger kid that each time he displays that quick temper inappropriately (such as yelling, hitting, biting, or a tantrum), he will be sent to time-out (or the "calm-down chair") for a few minutes to help him remember how to control his temper. Just remember that time starts *after* your child gets himself in control.

An appropriate consequence for older kids might be losing a desired privilege such as the telephone or television for a set length (an hour or the evening, depending on the circumstances). Once you set the consequence, then use the same consequence every time. Your kid needs to know you are serious about helping him alter his quick-tempered attitude.

The First 21 Days

Immediately institute a Bad–Temper Cure Policy by setting one rule: "We talk only when we're calm." Write it up as a contract, and have everyone sign it. Then establish a family guideline: "When anyone feels their temper is ready to flare, they take a time-out." The bad-tempered member then walks away and doesn't return until he's completely calm and under control. Everyone in the family should honor that guideline. The best place to practice controlling tempers is in our homes, and intentionally doing so as a family is the most effective way to ensure that your kid can control his temper in the real world. It will most likely take twenty-one days until the rule becomes a habit that all members use consistently no matter where they are. From then on, the habit should become automatic without thinking about it.

ATTITUDE MAKEOVER PLEDGE

How will you use these steps to help your kid control his quick temper and achieve long-term change? On the lines below, write exactly what you agree to do within the next twenty-four hours to begin changing your kid's attitude so he is less quick-tempered.

_____

_____

_____

THE NEW ATTITUDE REVIEW

All attitude makeovers take hard work, constant practice, and parental reinforcement. Each step your child takes toward change may be a small one, so be sure to acknowledge and congratulate every one of them along the way. It takes a minimum of twenty-one days to see real results, so don't give up! And if one strategy doesn't work, try another. Write your child's weekly progress on the lines below. Keep track of daily progress in your Attitude Makeover Journal.

WEEK 1

_____

_____

_____

WEEK 2

_____

_____

_____

WEEK 3

_____

_____

_____

ONGOING ATTITUDE TUNE-UP

Where does your child's attitude still need improvement? What work still needs to be done?

_____

_____

_____

ATTITUDE MAKEOVER RESOURCES

For Parents

Angry Kids: Understanding and Managing the Emotions That Control Them, by Richard L. Berry (New York: Fleming H. Revell Co., 2001). Discusses the root causes of anger in kids and explains ways parents can help them learn techniques for expressing and defusing that anger.

Healthy Anger: How to Help Children and Teens Manage Their Anger, by Bernard Golden (New York: Oxford University Press, 2003). Easy steps to help kids guide and control their anger.

The Angry Child: Regaining Control When Your Child Is Out of Control, by Dr. Tim Murphy and Loriann Hoff Oberlin (New York: Clarkson Potter, 2001). Easy-to-follow strategies that help angry kids manage anger and help parents recognize signs of serious problems.

When Anger Hurts Your Kids: A Parent's Guide, by Patrick McKay (New York: Fine Communications, 1996). A superb guide explaining how parents' anger affects kids and offering ways to regain control.

The Mad Family Gets Their Mads Out: Fifty Things Your Family Can Say and Do to Express Anger Constructively, by Lynne Namka (Charleston, Ill.: Talk, Trust & Feel Press, 1995). Useful ways to help kids who are struggling to express anger constructively and help families learn how to deal with anger in nonviolent ways and relate to each member positively.

Tired of Yelling: Teaching Our Children to Resolve Conflict, by Lyndon D. Waugh (Atlanta, Ga.: Longstreet, 1999). A psychiatrist's parenting solutions for defusing family tension and helping toddlers through teens learn skills of peacemaking.

For Kids

Anger Management Workbook for Kids and Teens, by Anita Bohensky (New York: Growth Publications, 2001). Teaches effective coping behaviors to help stop the escalation of anger and resolve conflicts. Ages 12 to 18.

Harriet, You'll Drive Me Wild! by Mem Fox (New York: Harcourt, 2000). Harriet doesn't means to be troublesome. She's always very sorry for her behavior afterward. Her mother doesn't like to yell and usually gently reprimands her. But as her shenanigans escalate, so does her mom's blood pressure. When that edge is finally reached, Harriet's mom yells and yells. Ages 4 to 8.

Hot Stuff to Help Kids Chill Out: The Anger Management Book, by Jerry Wilde (Kansas City, Mo.: Landmark Productions, 1997). A book that speaks directly to kids and adolescents and provides clear guidelines to help them handle hot tempers more constructively. Ages 10 to 15.

When Sophie Gets Angry—Really, Really Angry (New York: Scholastic, 1999). A little girl who has trouble managing her anger learns how to take time to cool off and regain her composure. Ages 3 to 7.

4

Cheats
Antidote: Honesty, Integrity, Accountability

"Why not? Everybody else does."

Dear Dr. Borba,
Last night my twelve-year-old son showed me the A on his math
test. I was really proud of him, figuring he had studied so hard.
Then I noticed that he'd printed the answers on his hand. When I
confronted him, he said that everybody else was doing the same
thing and that it's no big deal so I shouldn't get so worked up about
it. Well, I happen to think it is a big deal—he cheated! What can I
do to turn his attitude around and get this kid to realize cheating is
wrong?

—Daniel B., a dad of five from Oklahoma City, Oklahoma

BAD ATTITUDE ACT OUT
"But you said I had to get an A. So what's the big
deal?"

> "Chill out, would ya? I'm not so stupid that I'm going to get caught."
>
> "It's okay if I rolled the dice again. Kelly wasn't looking."

EMERGENCY ATTITUDE

If you catch your kid cheating, don't let him take the good grade, blame his school, or excuse it as "something everyone else does." Instead, call the teacher and make your kid face up to the consequence. The short-term pain will be worth the long-term benefit to his character.

If you are concerned about your kid's cheating, you are not alone. Data clearly confirm that cheating is on the rise. Since 1969, the percentage of high school students who admitted to cheating on a test increased from 34 percent to 68 percent. The Ethics of American Youth 2002 survey discovered that three of four high school students admitted to cheating on at least one test during the previous year, and 37 percent admitted they would lie to prospective employers in order to get a good job. Plagiarism among college students has become so rampant that many professors have to rely on a specially designed Web site to scan their students' papers to validate originality. But it isn't just the big kids: the news is filled these days with stories of CEOs and political leaders guilty of fraud, insider trading, excess severance pay, and perjury. Is it any wonder that teachers say that cheating is prevalent even in the early grades?

Make no mistake: cheating *is* a selfish attitude as well as being deceitful, dishonest, and devious. The act goes against the basic grains of integrity and solid character. After all, cheaters aren't concerned about whether their conduct was fair or how it affected others. Usually their biggest fret is worrying about whether they will get caught. This attitude is all about cutting corners and taking the easy way out. The good news is that parents *do* play a significant role in nurturing the virtues of honesty, integrity, and accountability in their kids. Let's just make sure we use that role wisely so our kids do turn out right and this epidemic of cheating is stopped.

BAD ATTITUDE ALERT

Before you start changing your kid's cheating and dishonest attitude, you need to pay close attention and figure out where it is coming from and how it plays out for your child and your family.

Diagnosis

These next questions will help you better understand why your kid is resorting to this attitude.

Why. Reflect seriously on why your kid might be cheating and thinks he should be allowed to get away with it. Usually when attitudes such as cheating or lying suddenly emerge, they are set off by feelings of rejection, jealousy, frustration, hurt, or anger toward an adult. Perhaps you are putting incredible pressure on your kid to be academically successful and get into a prestigious college. It could also be a fear of punishment or of letting a parent down. Other possibilities are overperfectionism, fear of failing, being unprepared or never prepared. Perhaps no one holds him accountable, or cheating is encouraged by his peers, or honesty has never been emphasized. What is your best guess as to why your kid cheats?

What. What type of issues or things does your kid usually cheat about: school, homework, games, sports, chores, household rules, or expectations? Talk to other adults who know your kid well. Are they seeing the same pattern? What do they think is the underlying cause?

Who. Does he cheat with everyone or just with his friends? Siblings? Teacher? Coach? You? Are there some individuals he does not cheat around? If so, who? Why doesn't he cheat with them? Does your kid cheat as a means of aggravating, irritating, or teasing someone such as a sibling and enjoy watching her brother get upset? If so, then you need to address the issue of sibling jealousy and insensitivity. Or does he cheat only when he is on the playing field with a particular friend who always tries to put him down? There is no excuse for cheating, but why your kid is resorting to the attitude can bring up other issues to deal with as well.

When. Is there a particular time of day, week, or month he cheats more? Is there a reason? For instance, might it be test time, a competitive event, or homework that is due? When did the cheating start? Could there have been something that triggered this? Write down your thoughts.

Where. Are there certain places he is more likely to cheat (at school or day care, home, a sporting event)? Why?

Now take a look at your answers. Are you seeing any predictable patterns? Do you have any better understanding of this attitude and where it's coming from?

WHAT'S WRONG
WITH YOUR CURRENT RESPONSE?

Reflect on how you typically respond to your child's cheating. Think of the last time he cheated. What was the incident about? How did you find out he cheated? Did he know you knew, or did you discover his dishonesty another way? Did you confront him with his cheating? Did anyone else get involved? If so, how? Did you ask why he cheated? What did he say? Did you believe him? How did you respond? What was his response back to you? Did he seem remorseful or guilty? Did you share your views as to why cheating is wrong? Why or why not? Did your kid buy into your views? Was your kid held accountable for his cheating? Were any consequences set, and if so, were they enforced? A key question is whether your response helped alter his attitude. In hindsight, would you have done anything differently in your response? If so, what? Why would you have made the change?

Next, get behind the reason your kid may be cheating. Could it be that he is afraid of your response? For example, some kids cheat because they do not want to let their parents down and disappoint them with a poor grade or score. Worse yet, some kids fear *they* will be a disappointment to their mom or dad. Could your response be stoking your kid to cheat? If so, how will you alter your attitude so your kid doesn't feel his score or grade is more important to you than his character?

What is one response that you've tried over and over again and it just hasn't worked? For example, have you threatened your kid with a consequence that was never carried through? Have you said, "Just one more time and I'll . . ."? Have you given a lecture or demanded writing "I will not cheat" one hundred times? Write out the one response you will never make again.

I will not _____

_____

FACING YOUR OWN BAD ATTITUDES

Parents who raise honest kids expect their kids to be honest— and even demand that they are honest. How important is it for your kids to be honest? Is it a trait that you have clearly explained, expected, and reinforced in your kids? If so, when was the last time you expressed how much you value honesty? If you sat your kid down right now and asked him to explain why honesty is important and cheating is wrong, what do you think he would say? What about being fair?

Keep in mind that the best way to encourage honesty in your kid is to be a truthful person yourself. So reflect on how well you model honesty for your family. Here are a few questions to consider: Do you always play games fairly with your kids, or do you sometimes peek at other players' cards? Say your ball was in when it was really on the line? Move your chess piece when the other player is not looking? Brag about cheating on your tax return? Write a note excusing your kid's tardiness by claiming she was ill if she missed school because she overslept? Put something in your pocket at the supermarket? Any time you stretch the truth and cheat, you're actually giving your kid permission to do it also.

If you notice your example of truthfulness needs tuning up, what will you do to be a better model? What is the first step you need to take in yourself to be a better model of honesty to your kids? Write down any changes you need to make in yourself.

I will _____

_____

BAD ATTITUDE NEWS ALERT

A survey conducted by *Who's Who Among American High School Students* found that 80 percent of high-achieving high school students admitted to having cheated at least once, and half said they did not believe cheating was wrong. A recent *U.S. News & World Report* poll found that 84 percent of college students believe they need to cheat to get ahead in the world today. One out of four said they would lie on a job application.

THE "DON'T GIVE ME THAT ATTITUDE" MAKEOVER

To eliminate your child's cheating, take the following steps.

Step 1. Talk About Why Cheating Is Wrong

Don't assume your kid understands why cheating is immoral. Young kids especially won't fully grasp why they shouldn't take something that doesn't belong to them or not tell the truth. First, you must be clear about your own moral beliefs. Do you believe that dishonesty is inherently wrong because it hurts you most of all by diminishing your character and spirit? Do you feel that no matter what the short-term loss might be, being honest and trustworthy is its own reward even when no one is looking? Think through your values. Here are a few ways you might convey them to your child:

- Tell your kid a recent moral choice you've made, like declaring nondocumented income on your tax return or giving back the wrong change even though it's in your favor. Your kids need to know that everyone is tempted to cheat, but honesty and hard work are always the better policy. One of the simplest ways is by modeling how you fight those urges to your kids. Intentionally look for day-to-day opportunities to do so, especially if you are in the middle of any kind of competition (without their knowing you are doing so, of course!).

- Provide your child with good heroes and heroines from history and current events such as George Washington and the cherry tree ("I cannot tell a lie"), Joan of Arc, Honest Abe Lincoln, Rosa Parks, and the women who were the whistleblowers at Enron and the FBI.
- Read stories from the Bible and Aesop's Fables that address honesty and strong moral character.
- Look for examples in your community of people who stood up for an honest cause even when it wasn't popular or convenient.

Spend time listening to your kid as well. You will want to hear your kid's views and where he stands on the issue. Posing questions that include "what," "how," and "why" often help in gauging values, so use them: "Why do you think kids cheat?" "How do you feel about it?" "What do you learn from cheating?"

Don't make the mistake of thinking that a one-time talk on such a serious subject will convince your kid that honesty really is the best policy. State your views over and over, and look for teachable day-to-day moments to review why cheating is wrong. And most important, repeatedly spell out your expectations for honesty: "Everyone in our family is always expected to be honest with one another."

Step 2. Emphasize the Long-Term Consequences of Cheating

Talk to your kid about cheating and the negative results of cheating and dishonesty. Here are a few important points to cover:

- Cheating can get you in serious trouble: probation, expulsion, suspension, or even criminal penalties like fines, tickets, and incarceration.
- People won't trust you, and you get a bad reputation. No one will want to be your friend or do business with you.

- It can become a habit, and you can reach the point where you feel you can't do anything without cheating both among your friends and in school.
- It hurts other people and isn't fair to other students or people who play fair and stick to the rules.
- If you get away with cheating, you find yourself in a situation where you are completely unqualified and unable to handle. You're not only over your head, but you'll also know in your heart you're a fraud.

Step 3. Call Cheating on the Spot

Most kids will cheat at something; whether they continue to do so often depends on how we respond. In fact, if your goal is to raise your kid to be honest and fair, *then you must respond.* Here is what you should do when confronting your kid's cheating:

- ***Don't overreact.*** Stay calm, and do not overreact. Yes it is hard, but it's the best way to respond.
- ***Tell what you saw or heard.*** "I just saw you move your game piece. That's cheating." Be brief. State your observation, and stick to facts.
- ***Be private.*** It's best to cite your observations quietly to your child. Public accusations of cheating usually only aggravate the situation, and your kid will most likely deny the accusation.
- ***Focus on the attitude.*** Do not label your kid "a cheater" or "a liar." It is counterproductive. Focus on the child's action, not his character: "Moving the ball is cheating." "Copying your friend's answers is cheating."
- ***Convey your expectation.*** Tell your kid that you expect him to play fairly by the rules if you are going to continue to play. Be brief but also clear with your expectations for honesty. Here are a few examples: "Let's play fair." "We agreed to stick to the rules." "Let's shake that we'll play fairly."

Step 4. Teach Ways to Buck the Pressure to Cheat

Research reveals that when it comes to cheating, kids are pressured big time by peers. Cheating in school has reached sophisticated new levels. Gone are the days when students tucked meticulously written crib notes inside their pants legs and coughed specially designed codes to peers. Pagers and cell phone text mail messages instantly transmit test answers without the hassle of note passing (and getting caught!). A growing crop of Web sites such as schoolsucks.com provide term papers on any subject for a few bucks. Find out how pressured your kid feels by asking straight out: "Have you been in a situation when other kids want you to cheat or give them answers? What did you do?" Also, try to determine just how prevalent cheating is among your kid's peers: "Do kids cheat in your class? How? What does the teacher do? What happens if they get caught?"

Your child will need more than just a talk to say no. The best way to help her stand up to peer pressure is by teaching her a few assertive strategies such as the ones that follow. Just make sure you help her rehearse them over and over until she can confidently use them on his own.

Peer pressures facing today's kids are enormous. Of course, we always hope that our kids will be able to say no to such negative influences. Doing so is often difficult because such choices are not always popular with their peers. The truth is that it takes real moral strength not to be influenced by others. We must help our children develop the inner strength of character needed to buffer negative pressures and then teach them specific skills of assertiveness. Only then will they be able to stand up to their peers.

- *Assert yourself with confidence.* Teach your kid to stand up for his beliefs and not back down. Show him how to use confident posture: stand tall with feet slightly apart, hold his head high, and look the person straight in the eye. Emphasize that the posture he uses to deliver his lines is usually more important than the words he says.

- *Say no firmly.* Stress that he must say no to the person using a friendly but firm and determined voice. *Then he must not give in.* Remind your child that his job is not to try changing the other person's mind, but to keep himself out of trouble and follow his beliefs.
- *Repeat your decision.* Tell your child it's sometimes helpful to repeat his decision several times like a broken record: "No, it's not right. No, it's not right." It makes him sound assertive and helps him not back down from his stand.
- *Tell reasons why.* Thinking about the possible consequences of the choice helps strengthen kids' convictions not to proceed with what they're asked to do. So tell your kid to give the person the reason he's saying no: "It's not right." " I'll be grounded." "I worked too hard to give you my paper."

Step 5. Set a Consequence for Repeat Cheating

How to handle cheating is heavily debated among parents, especially when it comes to letting kids suffer the consequences. If you're wavering, ask yourself: What really matters more: my kid's grade or his moral development? Remember that excusing, dismissing, or ignoring your kid's cheating is the same as giving it your approval. Besides, isn't it far more important for your kid to learn the essential message: honesty really is the best policy? So, if despite all your efforts, your kid's cheating continues, it's time to set a consequence. And if cheating still continues, spend some serious uninterrupted time with your kid coming to an agreement on how further cheating will be prevented. Here are a few consequences for cheating:

- For younger kids caught cheating in a game, simply stop playing: "That was cheating again. It's not fun to play when you don't play fair. I'm going to stop playing now, and we'll try again later."
- Write an essay or paragraph discussing at least five reasons cheating is bad; younger tykes could draw two reasons.

Older kids who cheat on tests or plagiarize reports should be required to redo the assignment.

Step 6. Acknowledge Honesty

Certainly we should tell our children that it is important to be fair and honest. We also should let them know how much we appreciate their truthfulness whenever they are. So do acknowledge your kid's honest efforts: "I really appreciate your honesty. I can count on you to say the truth." Do be sure to recognize him especially any time he refuses to give in to peer pressure: "I know it was hard to say no to your friend. I admire how you stood up to him and told him he couldn't copy your paper."

The First 21 Days

Make an official Family Cheating Exposé Project to help kids understand the real consequences of cheating, so they understand that no one gets away with it—not even the rich and famous. Pick a few notorious cases from history like the Teapot Dome Scandal, Watergate, and the recent Enron corporation scandal. Read the newspaper to your kid whenever there's a case of corporate, sport, or governmental cheating. Discuss the criminality, the ruined lives, the long-term impact on policies and public trust. Watch a movie like *Catch Me If You Can* or *All the President's Men,* and use it as an opportunity to show how cheating hurts both the victims and the perpetrators. Kids need to know that even sports stars, movie stars, U.S. presidents, CEOs, and archbishops have to pay the penalty for cheating.

ATTITUDE MAKEOVER PLEDGE

How will you use these steps to curb your kid's cheating and achieve long-term change? On the lines below, write exactly what you agree to do within the next twenty-four hours to begin changing your kid's attitude so he is more honest.

_____

_____

_____

THE NEW ATTITUDE REVIEW

All attitude makeovers take hard work, constant practice, and parental reinforcement. Each step your child takes toward change may be a small one, so be sure to acknowledge and congratulate every one of them along the way. It takes a minimum of twenty-one days to see real results, so don't give up! And if one strategy doesn't work, try another. Write your child's weekly progress on the lines below. Keep track of daily progress in your Attitude Makeover Journal.

WEEK 1

_____

_____

_____

WEEK 2

_____

_____

_____

WEEK 3

_____

_____

_____

ONGOING ATTITUDE TUNE-UP

Where does your child's attitude still need improvement? What
work still needs to be done?

_____

_____

_____

ATTITUDE MAKEOVER RESOURCES

For Parents

Golden Rules, by Wayne Dosick (San Francisco: HarperSanFrancisco,
1995). A readable parent guide featuring ten key values parents
should teach their kids.

_My Kid's an Honor Student, Your Kid's a Loser: The Pushy Parents Guide
to Raising the Perfect Child,_ by Ralph Schoenstein (Cambridge, Mass.:
Perseus Books, 2002). Provides excellent points about the consequences of pushing our kids and the impact on their character.

Teaching Your Children Values, by Linda and Richard Eyre (New York:
Simon & Schuster, 1993). A highly usable guide of practical ways to
help children develop values such as honesty, trustworthiness, and
self-discipline.

Why Johnny Can't Tell Right from Wrong, by William Kilpatrick (New
York: Simon & Schuster, 1993). Shows how to correct weak conscience development by providing youngsters with the stories, models, and inspiration they need in order to lead good lives.

For Kids

A Big Fat Enormous Lie, by Marjorie Sharmat Weinman (New York: Dutton, 1978). A little boy learns that lies turns into monsters and telling the truth is the only way to make them disappear. Ages 3 to 8.

Junie B., First Grader: Cheater Pants, by Barbara Park (New York: Random House, 2003). When her father will not let her stay up late to do her homework, Junie B. copies a classmate's paper. "It's not a test, so it's not cheating!" says Junie. Is it or isn't it? Great discussion possibilities. Ages 6 to 10.

Liar Liar Pants on Fire! by Miriam Cohen (New York: Greenwillow, 1985). Great book about a first grader new to the school who lies to impress his classmates. Ages 4 to 7.

Don't Tell a Whopper on Fridays! The Children's Truth-Control Book, by Adolph Moser (Kansas City, Mo.: Landmark Editions, 1999). A kid-friendly book that discusses the problems of lying and the importance of telling the truth. Ages 9 to 12.

Catch Me If You Can (DreamWorks, 2002). An FBI agent (Tom Hanks) tries to catch a resourceful con artist (Leonardo DiCaprio) who's traveling around the country forging checks and various identities for himself. Although the con artist seems to have the "perfect life," there are great moral lessons to be learned. PG-13.

All the President's Men (Warner Brothers, 1976). The true account of two *Washington Post* reporters who followed their conscience and would not give up on covering the Watergate break-in.

5

Cruel

Antidote: Kindness, Gentility, Mercy

"Look at those suckers squirm!"

Dear Dr. Borba,
My wife and I are really concerned about our thirteen-year-old daughter. I don't know another way to describe her other than cruel. She is so mean to her brothers and other kids—even us—and it goes far beyond teasing. She says things that are just unmerciful! We can't understand why she doesn't realize how upset it makes people feel. Meanwhile, we're feeling like hostages. What now?

—Sam L., a dad of three from Toronto

BAD ATTITUDE ACT OUT
"Take cover, Fat Kevin's here. Don't let him sit on you, or he'll break your legs."
"I didn't know that dogs could feel pain like that."

> "Don't even think of being on our team. Your dad's out of work and couldn't afford to buy the equipment."

EMERGENCY ATTITUDE ℞

Set an absolute zero tolerance for any type of verbal or physical abuse by your kid or any other member of your family. Make a 100 percent commitment to turning this attitude around, or you can be sure that things are going to get a lot worse. For example, if you have a younger child who is calling his sister "Fatty," first demand that he apologize sincerely and never use that word again. Give her the opportunity to tell him how she feels when he says that, and be sure that he has really heard her. And if he repeats the behavior, institute a serious ethical consequence like doing her kitchen chores so he'll truly understand the importance of kindness. With an older child who uses her cell phone to send vicious text messages about an ostracized classmate to all of her friends, first role-play with her, switching chairs so she can express how she might feel if she were the victim of this malicious attack; next insist that she apologize in person; and then remove her phone privileges for an appropriate period of time. Kids need to learn in no uncertain terms that cruelty hurts and is never permissible.

Cruel kids can be unmerciful and vicious. In fact, their attitude is self-centeredness and aggression run amok. Mean kids never consider the feelings or needs of others; they are only concerned about *their* needs and getting *their* way. They flaunt their meanness to wear you down and cause you pain, and when they see it working, they have a sense of victory. In fact, they relish others' distress, prey on those who are different, and enjoy watching others' humiliation, discomfort, or sadness. Even more troubling, data show that mean-flaunting kids are on the rise. A national study found that the amount of childhood teasing and being mean to others has significantly increased since the mid-1970s. The National School Safety Center recently warned educators that peer cruelty and bullying is the most underrated problem in schools.

Although kids are hard-wired at birth for the capacity for kindness, achieving it is far from guaranteed, especially in a world that's deluging them with pessimistic, unkind messages. The virtues of kindness, gentility, and mercy must be inspired, nurtured, and taught, and the sooner we do so, the better. When children understand that kindness can make a difference and actually get them what they want and need better than meanness and cruelty can, they will be more likely to incorporate that attitude in their own lives. The sooner you start this makeover, the better.

BAD ATTITUDE ALERT

If you want your kid to stop being cruel, you need to pay close attention, and figure out where this attitude is coming from.

Diagnosis

Think about the last few times your kid was cruel. If possible, talk to other adults who witnessed his meanness. Try to replay the scene in your mind. Here are a few more questions to help you recall the scene and recognize if there is any pattern.

What. What does his mean behavior look like? What cruel things does he do or say that concern you? Here are a few possibilities to check off:

- [ ] Says unkind, mean comments that put down others
- [ ] Is rarely concerned when someone is treated unfairly or unkindly
- [ ] Seems to enjoy seeing others being picked on or alienated (could be in books, movies, or TV shows, hearing about it, or actual personal encounters)
- [ ] Treats animals cruelly
- [ ] Is kind or comforts others only if he expects something in return
- [ ] Insults, intimidates, or ridicules others
- [ ] Looks for the weaknesses in others
- [ ] Rarely pays attention to the concerns of others or helps someone who needs help or is sad

Why. The next big question is to try and figure out why your kid is resorting to using this attitude. There are a few common reasons that kids are cruel. Do any of them apply to your kid?

- [ ] Lack of empathy. He may not fully grasp the emotional impact of his unkindness.
- [ ] Lack of self-esteem. She feels unworthy, so she brings the other person down.
- [ ] Need to retaliate. He has been picked on and teased, and wants to "get back."
- [ ] Desire to be included. As a way of fitting into the group, she puts outsiders down.
- [ ] Lack of problem-solving skills. Not knowing how to solve conflicts, he resorts to insults or name-calling.
- [ ] Jealousy. She envies the other child, so she brings him down to feel better about herself.
- [ ] How he's treated. He is treated unkindly, so he mimics the same unkind behaviors.
- [ ] Desire for power over someone else. Teasing makes her feel superior.
- [ ] Witnesses unkindness. He sees others treated unkindly

and copies the behavior. He could personally be witnessing unkindness or viewing or hearing it second-hand (through behavior around him at home, at school, in the community or on TV, in the movies or news, or CD lyrics).

☐ No expectations requiring kindness. No one is telling him that unkindness is not allowed.

☐ Poor social skills. She doesn't know the skills for getting along, cooperating, negotiating, compromising, encouraging, or listening, so she resorts to bringing the other child down.

Who. Think! Who is your kid most prone to display this attitude toward? A younger brother, certain friends, the neighborhood crew, people with handicaps, kids of a different race, culture, or gender, older folks, animals? Is there any commonality to those your kid targets with his cruel ways? Are there some individuals he does not pick on? Why do they escape his cruelty?

Where. Is there a location where he is most likely to display this attitude—for instance, at home, at school, on the playing field, in the neighborhood, at a relative's home, with a play group, on the school bus, or on the playground? Is there any pattern and if so, why?

When. Is there any time of the day, week, or month that your child seems to exhibit his mean attitude? If so, what might be the reason?

Now take a look at your answers. Are you seeing any predictable patterns? Have you discovered any clues to his attitude? Do you have any better understanding of this attitude and where it's coming from? Write down your ideas in your Attitude Makeover Journal. Compare your thoughts with at least one other caregiver who knows your kid well.

WHAT'S WRONG
WITH YOUR CURRENT RESPONSE?

Next, reflect as to how you typically respond to your child's meanness. It will help you pinpoint what works and does not work in dealing with this attitude. Try to recall the last time your kid was cruel. What did you do or say? Think about the little things you did that are easy to overlook. What tone of voice did you use? Was it critical, sarcastic, judgmental, neutral, or yelling? What did your body language look like? Your facial expressions? What did you say? How did the episode begin, and how did it end? Now put yourself in your kid's shoes. How would she say you responded? For instance, what would she say helped stop her attitude or aggravated the episode?

Does your kid use this attitude with other adults? Do they respond any differently than you do? Does their response work any better than yours in stopping it? Is there one thing you've noticed that you or anyone else does that works to curb your kid's mean attitude? What response does not stop it or is almost guaranteed to make your kid's mean streak flare up? For example, did you try spanking? Yelling? Were you cruel to her in return? Write the one thing you will not do the next time your kid uses this attitude.

I will not _____

_____

FACING YOUR OWN BAD ATTITUDES

So where is your kid getting this mean streak? No one is born mean. In fact, kids are hard-wired for empathy and compassion. But unless we nurture those traits, they will lie dormant, and mean, insensitive behaviors can emerge. Let's take a serious look at the root cause of this attitude. For instance, have you ever been mean to your spouse, family, friends, or kids?

Your child learns a great deal about kindness simply by watching your behavior. How has your example been lately? If you want your child to be kind whenever you are together, *consciously demonstrate kind behavior.* There are many daily opportunities: watching your friend's child, phoning a friend who is down, picking up trash, soothing a child, giving directions, asking someone how she is, baking cookies for your family, always speaking with sensitivity toward others. After performing the kindness, be sure to tell your child how good it made you feel! By seeing kindness through your daily words and deeds and hearing you emphasize how being kind makes you feel good, your child will be much more likely to follow your example. The old saying, "Children learn what they live," has a lot of truth to it.

What is the first step you need to take in yourself to be a better example to your kids for dealing with their mean attitude? Write down changes you need to make.

I will _____

_____

THE "DON'T GIVE ME THAT ATTITUDE" MAKEOVER

To eliminate your child's cruel attitude, take the following five steps.

Step 1. Expect Kindness

Nancy Eisenberg, author of *The Caring Child,* found that parents who express their views about hurtful, unkind behavior and then explain why they feel that way tend to have kids who adopt those views. When you see your child being unkind, take time to name and briefly describe the child's unkind actions. And then make sure he clearly understands what unkind behavior you object to and *why you disapprove.* Then above all, make sure your kid hears this message loud and clear: "Cruelty is wrong, it's hurtful, and it will not be tolerated!" Here are some examples:

"Calling your cousin 'Four Eyes' was cruel. Name-calling is not nice because it puts someone down. That's something I just can't allow."

"Telling your sister fat jokes and calling her 'Fatty' is mean. You're laughing at her, not with her. You may not tease if it hurts the person's feelings."

"Sending your friend that nasty instant message on your laptop was really cruel. And that gossip about Nancy was certainly not true."

Many families create a family covenant that clearly spells out in writing that unkind words and gestures are not permissible in your family. If you'd like to create one for your home, gather everyone around a large piece of paper and emphasize your expectations of saying and doing only caring and supportive behaviors. Ask for suggestions for rules to ensure your family adheres to a strict caring policy, and then vote for the best guidelines. The winning policy is written on a separate piece of paper, signed by all family members, and posted as a concrete reminder.

Step 2. Help Your Kid Experience Kindness

The best way to help kids recognize the power of kindness is not by talking or reading about it but by actually experiencing it. Consider doing community service as a family. Families everywhere are taking time to volunteer their energy and resources to help make our world a better place. By watching their parents' examples, kids are catching their caring spirit and realizing their parents passionately value the trait of caring. There are dozens of ways to get involved, lend a hand, volunteer, or show you care. Food drives, picking up trash in the park, painting battered women's shelters, delivering meals to the homeless or a hospice, and tutoring are just a few ways to help kids feel the joy of kindness.

To find organizations in your area that appreciate volunteers, check the Yellow Pages of your phone book under "Social Service Organizations," and then call to see how you can help make a difference. *Hint:* It's best to try to match your kids' interests and strengths in any service project. For instance, if your kid loves the out-of-doors, then volunteer to plant flowers for a shelter; if she loves to sew, make quilts for a homeless shelter; if he enjoys sports, volunteer to help out at the Special Olympics.

Research by psychologists Elizabeth Midlarsky and James Bryan found that explaining to your child the specific way his act of kindness will benefit someone is effective in nurturing kindness. So look for kind behaviors that naturally occur during the day, and use them as great opportunities to discuss how they affected the recipients. The strategy that follows helps kids identify what the kind deed was and how the gesture made a positive difference. The acronym TIP helps you remember the three parts:

T— *Tell* who was the kindness recipient and describe his need.
I— *Identify* what kindness was said or done.
P— *Point* out how the kind gesture made a difference for the recipient.

Here are some examples of this TIP in action:

"Megan, you were kind to Bill when you helped him pick up his backpack. He was upset, and you made feel better."
"Kara, you saw how upset your brother was because those boys were teasing him. You stood up for him."

Step 3. Monitor Your Kid's Media Consumption

There is no denying that television, the Internet, radio shows, music, movies, and video games are saturating our kids with violent, cruel images, and many newspaper and magazine stories are capitalizing on the sensational and the horrific. This saturation *does* have an impact on our kids' behavior and attitudes. For instance, research shows that children who have been repeatedly exposed to more violent television programming are less likely to demonstrate kindness by helping younger kids who are in trouble. Madeline Levine, author of *See No Evil,* also points out: "Numerous studies have shown that the more people watch media violence, the less sensitive they become to it." So monitor what your kid watches and listens to. Add parental filters to your computer, and set clear standards for TV, CDs, video games, and movies.

Step 4. Help Your Child Have Empathy for Her Victim's Feelings

The critical part of disciplining a child who is flaunting a mean attitude is to help her understand how her actions affected the other person. Unless she learns to consider the other person's feelings and needs and recognize the discomfort or hurt her unkindness caused the recipient, the attitude is likely to continue. Here are a few questions that help kids reflect on the impact their unkind actions had on their victim's feelings:

"Can you see how upset Juan is? How did your attitude make him feel?"
"See, you embarrassed her. What do you say to her now?"
"What if someone said that to you?"

Step 5. Require Your Kid to Make Amends for Cruelty

Martin Hoffman's research found that parents who call attention to the harm done by the child and encourage her to make reparations can increase their kid's kindness. It's also very important for the child to learn that although once she has been cruel, the action can't be taken back, she can ease the other person's discomfort or hurt she caused by making some kind of amend. Here are a few ways kids can take responsibility for their unkindness:

- *Apologize.* The apology must be thought through, said sincerely, and ideally delivered face-to-face. Younger children must learn to say, "I'm sorry," and mean it. Older kids should learn to apologize without adult prompting.
- *Do a kind deed.* If you kid's attitude has affected another family member, he or she is required to do a chore for the offended party, which relieves that person of a duty or helps this person in some other way. A younger kid could help set the table; an older kid could vacuum the house.
- *Set a rule.* "One unkindness equals one kindness." Whenever a child says an unkind comment, she must turn it around and say something kind and caring to the recipient. A word of caution: the turnaround rule works *only* if kids

know what kind comments are *and only if it is consistently enforced*. For some kids, writing the kind comment is far more comfortable than saying it.

- **Perform a service.** For an older child who did an especially egregious cruel act, doing a service might be an appropriate consequence. Find a local organization that uses kid volunteers such as the Boys and Girls Club, a church group, a homeless shelter, or the hospital, and then clearly spell out to your kid the number of hours he must provide to "work off" his mean deeds.

The First 21 Days

Take a few minutes each night to share a kind moment you experienced during the day and invite your kids to do the same. You might start a Care Sharing Session at your dinner table by asking, "What kind things did you do for someone today?" "Did someone do a kind deed for you today?" "How did you think it made them feel?" "How did you feel?" Emphasizing kindness in your family helps kids recognize not only how much you value the trait, but also how kind actions can make our world a better place.

ATTITUDE MAKEOVER PLEDGE

How will you use these five steps to help your kid become less cruel and achieve long-term change? On the lines below, write exactly what you agree to do within the next twenty-four hours to begin changing your kid's attitude so he is kinder and more sensitive of others.

_____

_____

_____

THE NEW ATTITUDE REVIEW

All attitude makeovers take hard work, constant practice, and parental reinforcement. Each step your child takes toward change may be a small one, so be sure to acknowledge and congratulate every one of them along the way. It takes a minimum of twenty-one days to see real results, so don't give up! And if one strategy doesn't work, try another. Write your child's weekly progress on the lines below. Keep track of daily progress in your Attitude Makeover Journal.

WEEK 1

_____
_____
_____

WEEK 2

_____
_____
_____

WEEK 3

_____
_____
_____

ONGOING ATTITUDE TUNE-UP

Where does your child's attitude still need improvement? What work still needs to be done?

_____
_____
_____

ATTITUDE MAKEOVER RESOURCES

For Parents

And Words Can Hurt Forever: How to Protect Adolescents from Bullying, Harassment, and Emotional Violence, by James Garbarino and Ellen DeLara (New York: Free Press, 2002). A powerful must-read for parents and educators who want to stop cruel, vicious kid attitudes.

Odd Girl Out: The Hidden Culture of Aggression in Girls, by Rachel Simmons (New York: Harcourt, 2002). A wake-up call to the hidden world of cruelty among girls that goes on behind our backs.

Queen Bees and Wannabes: Helping Your Daughter Survive Cliques, Gossip, Boyfriends, and Other Realities of Adolescence, by Rosalind Wiseman (New York: Three Rivers Press, 2002). A useful guide and step-by-step instructions to help your daughter learn how to survive the all-too-common cruelness of growing up.

Raising Compassionate, Courageous Children in a Violent World, by Janice Cohn (Marietta, Ga.: Longstreet Press, 1996). Practical ways to help children learn the qualities of kindness, courage, and decency.

The Bully, the Bullied, and the Bystander, by Barbara Coloroso (New York: HarperCollins, 2002). How parents and teachers can help break the cycle of violence and cruelty in our youth from preschool to high school.

The Caring Child, by Nancy Eisenberg (Cambridge, Mass.: Harvard University Press, 1992). One of the most thorough guides to understanding how caring develops.

For Kids

Wilfrid Gordon McDonald Partridge, by Mem Fox (New York: Kane/Miller, 1985). A young boy learns that his friend from the old people's home is losing her memory. He sets out to help her find it, and in doing so learns the power of caring. Ages 4 to 8.

Lord of the Flies, by William Golding (New York: Perigee, 1959). A group of English schoolboys become stranded on a desert island during a nuclear war. Gradually throughout the ordeal, their character transforms from "civilized" and "proper" into cruel, greedy savages without an ounce of kindness. Ages 12 and older.

Please Stop Laughing at Me! One Woman's Inspirational Story, by Jodie Blanco (Avon, Mass.: Adams Media Corp, 2003). An inspirational memory about how one child was shunned and even physically abused by her classmates from elementary to high school. Impossible not to be moved! For young teens.

No More Victims: An Underdog Who Came Out on Top Challenges You to Put a Stop to Bullying in Your School, by Frank Peretti (Nashville, Tenn.: Nelson Publishers, 2001). A powerful account written for older kids and teens urging them to stop the hurt. Ages 11 to 15.

Bad Attitude 6

Demanding
Antidote: Tact, Tranquility, Consideration

"I want it NOW!"

Dear Dr. Borba,
I can't believe I'm admitting this, but my eight-year-old son is wearing me out. He demands to get his way, until he finally does. He asks for so much, and he gives so little. I know I'm making it worse by giving in, but it's just easier. I really think he believes the world revolves around him. He never considers my feelings or how annoying his attitude is. How do I deal with this kid and still survive?

—Ellen W., a mother of three from New Orleans, Louisiana

BAD ATTITUDE ACT OUT

"Take me now, Daddy! You're just sitting there."

"Get me a new Barbie. I'm not waiting until my birthday. I want it now!"

> "MMMMUUUUMMMMM. I need to use the phone. Hang up!"

EMERGENCY ATTITUDE ℞

Don't give in. Any time your child nags, makes an unreasonable request, or demands you do something, stop the conversation immediately. State in no uncertain terms that you will not tolerate this bad attitude. Demand courtesy, schedule an appointment for a reasonable discussion of the request at a later time, and walk away. Once your kid knows you mean business, you'll have taken a great leap forward in changing this bad attitude.

Demanding kids want things to go their way, and they want it *now*. And can these spoiled little critters wear you out! They make it difficult not only for their parents but also for the healthy growth of their own character. That's because demanding kids consider and act only on their own wants, feelings, and desires and don't learn to understand the other person's perspective or stop to consider the feelings of others.

There may be many reasons that your kid is so demanding. He may feel short-changed because you're not spending enough time and energy with him. He may be jealous of the attention you're spending with your partner, at work, or with a sibling. He may be feeling deprived due to a lack of financial resources or especially needy because of setbacks or problems at school. He also may not know a tactful, diplomatic way of expressing his needs or has to resort to nagging because no one ever listens to him. If you listen carefully, in fact, you may realize that when he's demanding material things, he may really be asking for your love. Or you may have just plain spoiled your kid by constantly giving in to his demands. So why should he change his ways? It works.

Keep in mind that kids with this bad attitude have one objective: to have *their* needs and issues met. Our biggest mistake is giving in. Sure, it's easier, but if we continue this pattern, our kids will turn into overindulged, selfish, demanding adults concerned only about their own needs and feelings. That's why we have to tame their attitude now, so the really essential character traits of tact, tranquility, and consideration will have room to grow.

BAD ATTITUDE ALERT

S.O.S.: Better start changing this demanding attitude. Here's how to begin.

Diagnosis

There are many reasons that kids are demanding, constantly interrupt, and want their way. Answering these next questions will help you pinpoint exactly what troubles you and better understand why he is resorting to this attitude.

Why. What do you think is the root cause in the way your family works or doesn't work that motivates this behavior? Or has he just learned that using the behavior is the best way to get his way? Does he need to control others? If so, why? Might he be legitimately needing your attention? Is he jealous? Are his needs frequently unmet? Are family members listening to him? Is life so hectic that she is being overlooked? Sure, demanding kids are irritating, but they may be using that behavior because their own basic needs of being appreciated and heard are not being met. Of course, he may also be demanding because he is self-centered and considers only his own feelings and needs.

What. Are there particular issues or things he usually demands? Is this about wanting stuff, not being listened to, needing more attention and privileges, or something else? Also, what has your kid learned from being demanding?

Who. Does he display the same demanding behavior to everyone? Only to his siblings or younger kids? Are there some individuals he does not use his demanding ways on? If so, who? Why not?

When. Is there a particular time of day, week, or month he is more demanding? Is there a reason? For instance, might he be tired, hungry, or needing attention? Is she with a group of kids who don't listen to her needs? Is she the oldest kid on the team and can bully her way around?

Where. Are there certain places he is more likely to be demanding (at school or day care, home, the store, Grandma's)? Why?

Now review your answers. Talk to others who know your kid well. Are you seeing any predictable patterns? Do you have any better understanding of this attitude and where it's coming from?

WHAT'S WRONG
WITH YOUR CURRENT RESPONSE?

Think about the last time your kid was demanding and how you responded. What were his demands? Were they reasonable? What was your response? How did you deliver that response? For instance, what was your tone of voice? How about your body language? Was it a battle? If so, who won: you or your kid? Did you give into your kid's demands, or did you make him wait? Did you insist on a reasonable discussion or just dismiss him out of hand? Did you lose your temper or storm out of the room?

What did not work in how you responded to your kid? Write it so you can remember never to use it again when he uses this bad attitude.

I will not _____

_____

FACING YOUR OWN BAD ATTITUDES

Kids are not born demanding and inconsiderate, so where is your kid learning this behavior? From siblings? Friends? Neighbors? Relatives? Could it be from you or your partner? Tune into the behavior of those close to your kid, and watch for clues. It may help you discover the source.

Now take a close look at your own behavior: Could your kid be learning this attitude from you? For instance, do you insist things go your way at home? Do you tell your kids what you want them to do and expect them to agree? How is your relationship with your spouse? Do you listen, negotiate, and compromise, or are you more confrontational and dictatorial? Do you listen to your kids, or just expect them to comply with the way you want things to go? Would your colleagues and friends say you are more easy-going or more demanding? Just what kind of example are you sending your kid?

What is the first step you need to take in changing yourself so you can be a better example to your sons or daughters and deal with their demanding behavior? Write down changes you need to make.

I will _____

_____

BAD ATTITUDE NEWS ALERT

If you think this bad attitude will go away by itself without your having to do anything about it, beware! Don't kid yourself. Demanding, bullying kids are very likely to grow into demanding, aggressive adults. Research finds such attitudes are usually learned when kids are young and become remarkably stable. Bottom line: stop a demanding attitude now or it's going to get a whole lot worse!

THE "DON'T GIVE ME THAT ATTITUDE" MAKEOVER

To eliminate your child's demanding attitude, take the following steps.

Step 1. Get to the Bottom of It

Here are some typical reasons that your child may be so demanding. Check off the ones that might apply to your situation.

- [ ] He may need more attention. Have you been distracted by work or other issues in your life? Have you been avoiding him because he's so difficult?
- [ ] He may be jealous. Do you favor a sibling, or does he feel you do? Are there other relationships that interfere?
- [ ] He may feel certain possessions are absolutely necessary to maintain his status among his peers.
- [ ] He may feel entitled to have everything he wants, including your attention. Have you spoiled him by constantly giving in to past demands?

☐ He may not know how to ask for something necessary in a reasonable way. Have you taught him a courteous and diplomatic way to express his needs?

☐ He may feel that no one ever listens to him and the only way he can get your attention is by nagging and whining for stuff. Could this be the case?

Identifying the specific source of your kid's demanding attitude will help greatly in turning it around.

Step 2. State Your New Attitude Expectation

Tell your kid that his demanding, pushy, self-centered "I want it and I want it now" behavior will no longer be tolerated. Tell the little nag that while it's okay to want or need something, he may not use a demanding, rude voice to express his feelings. If he needs or wants something, he must *ask nicely and respectfully*. Walk away, and go about your business until he asks nicely. As long as he keeps demanding, keep walking.

Warning: Once you set this standard, you must not back down. Your kid needs to know you mean business, or he will never learn a new more considerate attitude.

Step 3. Don't Be Afraid to Say No

The only way your child will realize that the world does not revolve around him and that all his desires will not be met is by setting limits that reduce his expectations. Decide now what your limits are and what is unacceptable; then no matter how demanding, annoying, and obnoxious his behavior is, *do not give in when he crosses your line.* It's the surest way for him to learn that demanding more than he deserves won't work. So don't let him win. Make sure you also spread your message to all other immediate caregivers in your kid's life. The more you are on board together with your new response, the faster this attitude will be squelched.

Your kid must learn that he can't always have his way. It's a tough but basic lesson of life. So do thank him for cooperating, empathize with his disappointment, and stay firm. It is sometimes helpful to teach your kids the difference between "need" (a necessity) and "want" (not essential):

Needs: signing the form for tomorrow's field trip; getting to soccer practice on time

Wants: extra money to purchase a CD; a cookie before dinner; telling Mom to get off the phone *now* to call a friend

Once they know the difference, you answer only demands that are asked in a respectful, polite tone (see Step 4) and only ones that are true needs. Here are some examples of parental responses:

"I appreciate how nicely you asked and know you're disappointed that you can't go to the movies. But we had plans to go to Grandma's. You can go tomorrow."

"I heard how nicely you asked and know you're tired, but we agreed that I would buy groceries, not toys."

Step 4. Demand Courtesy

Many kids have learned to be demanding because they don't know how to state their needs any other way. Their voice tones are usually loud, whining, or irritating. Teach a more acceptable tone to use. Please don't assume your kid knows what a nice tone sounds like: show him. Then have him practice the new tone by repeating it back to you. A courteous, less demanding way to make a request is by using "Please," "Pardon me," and "Excuse me." Teach them to your kid, and then model, practice, and reinforce them over and over until he incorporates them into his daily behavior. Also show your appreciation whenever your kid remembers to use those courteous words, and correct him immediately when he forgets. Point out also that repeated "excuse me's" are another way of being demanding. Here are some examples:

"That voice is demanding and rude. Listen to how a nice voice sounds when I want something. Then you make your voice sound like mine."

"No, before you interrupt anyone you say, 'Excuse me.' Try your request again, please."

"John, we agreed that I do not listen to impolite people. How can you ask in a nicer way?"

Step 5. Boost Empathy and Sensitivity

Demanding kids rarely consider the other person's feelings; they consider only their own agenda. They also can be completely oblivious to how inconsiderate their demands are. What they must learn is to think about the other person's feelings and needs. The best news is that empathy—that miraculous virtue that puts you into other people's shoes so you can think and feel where they are coming from—is teachable. That means you can increase your kid's feeling for others, and that will help curb his demanding ways. Although it is teachable, changing your kid's demanding ways so he is more sensitive to others' feelings will take time and diligent, consistent effort. Look for those teachable moments to boost his empathy when your kid is demanding. Here are three ways:

- *Switch roles.* Demanding kids need to consider the other person's needs, so ask your kid to imagine being the other kid: "Pretend you were your guest. You come to the house wanting to play, but you never get to choose the game or make any decisions. How do you feel? Would you want to go back to her house? What can you do next time to make things more enjoyable for your friend?"
- *Gain a new perspective.* The next time your kid barrels ahead with his demands, make him stop and think about how the recipient is feeling: "You be me right now. How would you feel when you're talked to like that? Would you want to agree to those demands?"

- *Imagine the other person.* "Did you notice Dad was resting? Do you think he appreciated your interrupting him right then? Pretend you are Dad. Tell me about his day. Now imagine you are him and you just came home after a day like that. How would you feel if your son woke you up and demanded help with his homework? Tell me. So when would have been a better time to ask him to help you with your project?"

The First 21 Days

Impose a Family Hiatus on Asking—for anything. Get your partner to agree, and then announce to everyone living in the house that no one—not you, your partner, the offending child, or any sibling—will make a single demand for the next three weeks unless it's a normal household routine, vital necessity, or life-threatening emergency. And you must be consistent: no expression of casual desires, no daydreaming about stuff you want, no requests of any kind. You can call it a kind of "wish fast" or "experiment in self-denial." See what happens as everyone adjusts and gets out of the habit. The results may be remarkable.

ATTITUDE MAKEOVER PLEDGE

How will you use these steps to help your kid become less demanding and achieve long-term change? On the lines that follow, write exactly what you agree to do within the next twenty-four hours to begin changing your kid's attitude so he is less demanding and more considerate.

_____

_____

_____

THE NEW ATTITUDE REVIEW

All attitude makeovers take hard work, constant practice, and parental reinforcement. Each step your child takes toward change may be a small one, so be sure to acknowledge and congratulate every one of them along the way. It takes a minimum of twenty-one days to see real results, so don't give up! And if one strategy doesn't work, try another. Write your child's weekly progress on the lines below. Keep track of daily progress in your Attitude Makeover Journal.

WEEK 1

_____

_____

_____

WEEK 2

_____

_____

_____

WEEK 3

_____

_____

_____

ONGOING ATTITUDE TUNE-UP

Where does your child's attitude still need improvement? What work still needs to be done?

_____

_____

_____

ATTITUDE MAKEOVER RESOURCES

For Parents

How to Stop the Battle with Your Child: A Practical Guide to Solving Everyday Problems, by Don Fleming (New York: First Fireside, 1993). The author gives actual problems presented in parent-child scenarios to help parents deal with everyday frustration situations with their kids.

Kids, Parents, and Power Struggles, by Mary Sheedy Kurchinka (New York: HarperCollins, 2000). Practical ways to cope with parenting challenges of disciplining, while understanding the issues behind the behavior.

Parenting the Strong-Willed Child, by Rex Forehand and Nicholas Long (New York: McGraw-Hill, 1996). A program to help parents of strong-willed kids find positive and manageable solutions to their children's difficult behavior.

The Omnipotent Child, by Thomas Millar (New Westminster, B.C.: Palmer Press, 1989). Gives parents the permission to take the role back and be our child's parents by offering practical hints and teaching kids that there will be consequences to negative behavior. Helpful hints for any parent with a demanding, indulged child.

For Kids

The Biggest Pest on Eighth Avenue, by Laurie Lawlor (New York: Holiday House, 1997). Mary Lou and her friends are working hard on a play performance, but their rehearsals and planning sessions are continually interrupted by Mary Lou's pesty brother, Tommy. Ages 4 to 9.

How Rude! The Teenagers' Guide to Good Manners, Proper Behavior, and Not Grossing People Out, by Alex J. Packer, Pamela Espeland, and Jeff Tolbert (Minneapolis, Minn.: Free Spirit, 1977). Sound advice for teens about the world of manners, conveyed in a humorous way. Ages 12 to 15.

Bad Attitude 7

Domineering
Antidote: Serenity, Patience, Cooperation

"It's my way or the highway!"

Dear Dr. Borba,
We are really concerned about our eight-year-old daughter. She is so bossy around her friends. She dictates what she wants so things always turn out her way and let's them know in no uncertain terms what she wants. We know that someday her bossiness might turn into assertive leadership, but we're afraid if she doesn't tame her ways, she's going to end up very unpopular.

—Sheila, a mother from Denver, Colorado

Bad Attitude Act Out

"It's my house, so we're doing it my way."

"No, I won't see that movie. We're seeing the other one, so let's go."

"Give me your cell phone. We're calling my friends, not yours."

EMERGENCY ATTITUDE ℞

Show your kids how being domineering pushes other kids away. It's the best cure for bossiness. For example, with a younger child, watch her closely on the playground, and when she starts trying to take charge, gently take her aside and point out how all her little buddies have moved to the pool. Ask her, "Do you know why you're all by yourself now?" With an older kid, you might attend a few of his athletic practices and watch his behavior from the sidelines. When his domineering attitude starts to surface—he insists they play only his favorite music and everyone else stops dancing and heads for the soft drinks—ask him if he understands the impact of his bossy ways. These kinds of interventions will help your kid give up trying to control everyone and everything around him and rely instead on compromise and cooperation to get what he wants.

Domineering kids are self-centered, spoiled, insensitive, and rude: they appoint themselves in charge and don't consider others' desires or feelings. These kids want things to go their way, so they see that it does: they decide the rules, activities, game plan, and schedule. They can bulldoze their way into a gathering and within minutes redirect everything so it goes their way. Because they act as if their opinions are always right, they rarely listen to their peers. Do take heed: their negative dictatorial traits can be misinterpreted as positive leadership capabilities. Do not be swayed: these kids aren't leaders; they are dictators who rarely consider the feelings and needs of their peers (or "subjects").

Besides, if their bossy ways are not tamed, it can do major damage to their character growth as well as peer relationships. Though we don't want to stifle the self-confidence and high spirits of charismatic kids, we must replace a domineering bad attitude with the virtues of serenity, patience, and cooperation. So let's get started.

BAD ATTITUDE ALERT

Before you start squelching your kid's domineering attitude, reflect on its origins and how it developed.

Diagnosis

Watch and listen to your kid's domineering behaviors more closely for the next few days and ask yourself these questions.

What. In particular, what bossy things does your child say and do that bother you most? The more specific you are at identifying his domineering behaviors, the better able you will be at altering his attitude. Here are behaviors to consider. Mark those your child is displaying.

- [ ] Doesn't listen to others' ideas
- [ ] Always wants things to go her way
- [ ] Rarely negotiates or alters her desires to accommodate others
- [ ] Tells others what to do and expects them to comply
- [ ] Doesn't take turns
- [ ] Tells others the game plan
- [ ] Makes up the agenda or sets the rules
- [ ] Assumes people will do what she wants
- [ ] Hasn't a clue that other people feel pushed around

Who. Tune into which individuals your kid is bossiest toward. For instance, does he tend to be more domineering with siblings, younger kids, the babysitter, a neighborhood group, classmates, teammates, or even you or your spouse? Does he display the same domineering ways toward everyone or just certain individuals? What might be the reason?

When. Is there a particular time of day, week, or month he is bossier? Is there a reason? For instance, might he be tired, hungry, needing attention, or feeling slighted or not listened to?

Where. Are there certain places he is more likely to be bossy (at school or day care, home, play group, Grandma's)? Why?

Why. Now consider why your child has become so bossy and feels the need to control others. Ask yourself why your kid needs to be so dictatorial. There are many reasons your child is using this behavior. Here are a few to consider:

- ☐ Have you or others been bossing your kid? Do you live in a family culture where there is a pecking order of domination? Might she be mimicking the patterns of behavior of those around her?
- ☐ Is your kid insecure, or does she have low self-esteem?
- ☐ Must she need the sense of control?
- ☐ Does she lack friends?
- ☐ Do peers reject her because she lacks social skills?
- ☐ Does your kid have a need for perfectionism and always having things go her way?
- ☐ Have her ideas, feelings, and needs been frequently ignored?
- ☐ Might she need to structure activities to temper her chance of failing in front of others?
- ☐ Is she frequently dominated or bullied by others and attempting to even out the scales?
- ☐ Does she not know more cooperative ways of behaving?

WHAT'S WRONG
WITH YOUR CURRENT RESPONSE?

How do you typically react to your kid's bossiness? Do you boss him back, yell at him, avoid the whole issue, complain, ground him, or prohibit his friends from coming over? What part of the response is *not* working so your kid continues to flaunt his domineering attitude? Is it your voice tone? Inconsistently dealing with the attitude? Ignoring his bossy ways? Yelling at him? What responses do not curb this bad attitude? Why do you think that your response has not been effective in changing your kid's domineering ways?

Is it possible that you or others might be encouraging his bossiness? For instance, might someone (parent, teacher, sibling, peer, relative, caregiver, coach, or yourself) be intentionally or unintentionally reinforcing the attitude by labeling it assertive, independent, confident, outgoing, or a leadership capability? Tune into your own behavior to make sure you are not reinforcing it in any way.

Also, are you sure your kid is quite clear that you—and other caregivers—do not approve of his attitude and why you do not approve? What have you said to make sure he understands your displeasure? How could you be clearer?

List below the one response you will never try again when your kid has a domineering attitude:

I will not _____

_____

FACING YOUR OWN BAD ATTITUDES

How much of your child's bossy behavior is a result of imitating your behavior? Think back to when you were growing up. How would your parents have described you as a kid:

domineering, spirited, and assertive or more laid back, mellow, and quiet? How did your behaviors affect your relationship with your friends? How about how your parents interacted with you?

Has anybody complained about your being bossy lately? Who complained, and what did that person say? Do you ever tell people what to do without stopping to consider their needs or feelings? Do you use that bossy, domineering behavior toward your own kids? For instance, would they say you are more of a bulldozer, or do you see your behavior as assertive? Have you ever corrected your own domineering missteps in front of your child?

If you are guilty of being domineering, what domineering behaviors could you temper so as to be a better example of how to behave to your child? If not you, who else's domineering traits might your kid be copying? Your spouse or a relative? A coach or teacher? A sibling, cousin, or friend? A neighbor kid?

What is the first step you need to take in yourself to be a better example to your sons or daughters of dealing with their domineering behavior? Write down changes you need to make in yourself.

I will _____

_____

THE "DON'T GIVE ME THAT ATTITUDE" MAKEOVER

To eliminate your kid's domineering ways, take the following steps.

Step 1. Hammer Home Why Bossiness Doesn't Work

The first step to squelching any bad attitude is helping your kid recognize not only why it is inappropriate, but also how

BAD ATTITUDE NEWS ALERT

The National Center for Clinical Infant Programs has said that our kids' emotional and social abilities are better predictors of school success than the amount of facts they know or whether they learn to read early. More important are knowing what kind of attitude is expected, how to control impulsive urges, wait and take turns, ask teachers for help, follow directions, and express needs while getting along with other kids. Does your child need help learning any of these skills?

it doesn't get them what they want but instead puts people off. Do not overlook this step! Take time to point out the negative effect your kid's domineering ways can have on others and on her relationships with them. She needs to understand why her domineering ways are not appreciated and why they turn people off. Here are a few points to help you talk to kids at different ages about domineering attitudes:

"I heard a lot of unhappy voices today when you were playing with your friends. Did you notice they were not enjoying themselves? Why do you think they did not want to play with you today? Yes, always ordering kids to do always what you want isn't fun. It's being bossy."

"I heard you tell your friends which search engine to use and what to look for. How often did you ask them which one they wanted to use? How would you feel if your friends never asked you what you wanted to do?"

"Would you want to be in a study group with a kid who always had to have things his way? Some of your members do not like your bossiness. Let's figure out how you can be a better member so the other students will want you in their group."

Of course, telling your child how to talk so she sounds less domineering will not change her behavior. She will need many reminders, especially if she has been bossing others for some time. So the minute you hear her sounding bossy, point it out. To do so in public, you might develop a quiet signal (pulling on your ear or touching your nose) that only you and she are aware of. Each time she displays the behavior, use the code to signal to her that her behavior is inappropriate and needs to stop.

Step 2. Explain and Reinforce Alternative Attitudes

Research shows that kids who share, take turns, and take into consideration the requests of peers usually do so because their parents clearly emphasized that they expect them to. Take time to spell out your ground rules for sharing and cooperation, and explain them to your child. Then expect your kid to use them. Here are examples of how parents have spelled out their requirements for less bossiness and more cooperation:

- *Explain taking turns.* If you want your younger kid to take turns and share, clarify your expectations. For taking turns, use this wording: "Let's make sure to take turns when we play. You go first, and then it'll be Sally's turn and then mine." Sharing can use this phrasing: "Share your computer game so Ryan has a chance to play. He doesn't want to just watch you, so switch sides every ten minutes."
- *Set one sharing rule.* One dad passed on his rule: "If it belongs to you and it's in sight, then you must share it." There are certain possessions that are very special to your child, so putting those items away before a guest arrives minimizes potential conflicts.

- **Compromise.** Describe what it means to your older kid: "When you compromise, it means you're willing to give up a little of what you want, and the other person is too. It's a less bossy way to solve a problem because each person can have at least part of what he wants." He should understand that each person *always* has the opportunity to present his side, and when he does, he should be listened to. That way, everyone tends to feel more satisfied.
- **Negotiate.** Show your older child how to work out the shared use of the family computer so that everyone's interests and goals are met in a timely manner: "Let's work together to make a schedule that's fair for all of us and everyone gets what they need. That's what it means to negotiate."

Step 3. Teach How to Be a Team Player

Bossy kids are self-centered: they want things to go their way and rarely consider or even acknowledge other kids' opinions or desires. One way to curb your child's self-centered, bossy ways is to teach and then expect him to use more cooperative behaviors to help him learn to consider the other kid's desires. Here are a few strategies to help your kid learn to consider the other kid's desires. Remember to teach one skill at a time, and then practice, model, and reinforce it again and again. Only then will your kid be more likely to incorporate the skill into her daily behavior.

- **Explain the balance of power.** Tell your kid that teamwork means a level playing field where everyone is equal.
- **Teach host etiquette.** One simple rule of cooperation is to enforce that the guest always chooses first. If your child is the host, he must ask his guest to select the first game or activity.
- **Use decision breakers.** Domineering kids want to make the decisions, so teach your kid ways to make things fairer, like playing rock, paper, scissors; drawing straws; or flipping a coin.

These strategies are great when two kids can't decide on rules, who gets to choose what to do, or even who goes first.

- **Teach "Grandma's Rule."** The rule is simple and works like a charm to makes things fairer: "If *you* cut the cake, the other person decides which piece to take." The rule can apply to lots of things. For example: if you chose the game, the other person gets to go first; if you poured the lemonade, the other person chooses his glass first.
- **Set a timer.** Teach younger kids to agree on a set amount of time—usually only a few minutes—for using an item. Oven timers or sand timers are great devices for younger kids to use. Older kids can use the minute hands on their watches. When the time is up, the item is passed on.

Step 4. Reinforce Collaboration

One of the simplest ways to boost any attitude is by "catching" your child acting right, so watch for your kid's efforts to be more agreeable and supportive of his peers, and then be sure to reinforce his actions. Remember to explain what he did right, so he'll be more likely to repeat the attitude:

"I noticed you listened to your friend's idea this time and played baseball. I know you wanted to play video games, but you can't always do what you want."
"I heard you ask Roberto what movie he wanted to watch."

Comments like these will slowly help squelch her domineering attitude, replacing it with more thoughtful behaviors.

If your kid continues to dominate others, it's time to set a consequence. One way is not allowing him to play with the kid he dominates until he can temper his dictatorial ways: "Unless you can be more cooperative and less bossy, you will not be able to have Jimmy come over. Let's work on how you can treat him more nicely so he can come over." It sometimes takes a more serious jolt until your kid understands you mean business.

The First 21 Days

Require your child to launch a How Do You Feel About This? Project, which requires to survey every family member about his or her feelings and opinions before undertaking an agreed-on domestic venture; examples are what TV show to watch, which DVD to rent, which restaurant to eat out at, which board or video game to play. The point is to help your child learn democracy in action, the importance of consensus, and how much more effective this is than being domineering. The home is always the best training ground for learning new attitudes and tempering bad habits. So stick to this plan until your child abandons his domineering bad attitude and his tendency to push others around.

ATTITUDE MAKEOVER PLEDGE

How will you use these steps to help your kid become less domineering and achieve long-term change? On the lines below, write exactly what you agree to do within the next twenty-four hours to begin changing your kid's attitude so he is less bossy and more considerate.

_____
_____
_____
_____
_____
_____

THE NEW ATTITUDE REVIEW

All attitude makeovers take hard work, constant practice, and parental reinforcement. Each step your child takes toward change may be a small one, so be sure to acknowledge and congratulate every one of them along the way. It takes a minimum of twenty-one days to see real results, so don't give up! And if one strategy doesn't work, try another. Write your child's weekly progress on the lines below. Keep track of daily progress in your Attitude Makeover Journal.

WEEK 1

_____

_____

_____

WEEK 2

_____

_____

_____

WEEK 3

_____

_____

_____

ONGOING ATTITUDE TUNE-UP

Where does your child's attitude still need improvement? What work still needs to be done?

_____

_____

_____

ATTITUDE MAKEOVER RESOURCES

For Parents

Parenting the Strong-Willed Child, by Rex Foreland and Nicholas Long (New York: McGraw-Hill, 1996). A program to help parents of strong-willed, domineering kids find positive and manageable solutions to their kids' difficult behavior.

Raising Your Spirited Child: A Guide for Parents Whose Child Is More Intense, Sensitive, Perceptive, Persistent, and Energetic, by Mary Sheedy Kurcinka (New York: HarperCollins, 1992). Redefining the "difficult" kid as "spirited," Kurcinka provides tools to understand your own temperament as well as your child's and then gives readers specific tools to help work with their kids. Also helpful by the same author is *Raising Your Spirited Child Workbook.*

The Challenging Child: Understanding, Raising, and Enjoying the Five "Difficult" Types of Children, by Stanley I. Greenspan and Jacqueline Salmon (New York: Perseus Press, 1996). Calm and reassuring advice that helps parents deal with all types of difficult kids.

When Your Kids Push Your Buttons and What You Can Do About It, by Bonnie Harris (New York: Warner Books 2003). How to defuse parenting "road rage" and end the action and reaction cycle between you and your child.

For Kids

Bartholomew the Bossy, by Marjorie Weinman Sharmat and Norman Chartier (New York: Atheneum, 1984). A much-loved author writes the perfect book to help young kids realize that their bossiness isn't always appreciated. Ages 3 to 7.

Bossy Anna (Silver Blades Figure Eights, No 4), by Effin Older (New York: Skylark, 1996). Becoming sick of Anna's persistent bossiness, the Figure Eights tell her to mind her own business but realize when Anna stops coming to the lessons that her efforts had been helping them. Ages 4 to 8.

Franklin Is Bossy, by Paulette Bourgeois (Toronto: Kids Can Press, 1994). Franklin the turtle learns that no one likes a bossy friend. Perfect for ages 3 to 7.

Little Miss Bossy, by Roger Hargreaves (New York: Price Stern Sloan Publications, 1998). Simple text helps youngsters realize the need to treat friends nicer. Ages 3 to 7.

8

Fresh
Antidote: Respect, Caring, Reverence

"You don't have a clue, Mom. Don't you know anything?"

Dear Dr. Borba,

I hate to admit this, but my once-charming twelve year old has become a nightmare. He's an incredible student who gets wonderful grades, but is flunking respect and courtesy. If somebody ever heard the way he talks to me, I'd die. I know he can be nice, because he is usually polite to other adults. I, on the other hand, would like to palm him off to the neighbors. How do I get my old kid back?

—Jenna W., a mom from Vancouver, British Columbia

BAD ATTITUDE ACT OUT
"Grandma, you're too old to know what I'm talking about!"

> "Yeah right, as if I'd take advice from you!"
>
> "Get real! You're so out of it, I can't believe you ever had a boyfriend."

EMERGENCY ATTITUDE

From this moment on, any time your child uses disrespectful words, tones, or gestures toward you, immediately get up, and calmly walk out of her presence. Not just the first time, but each and every time your child does something fresh, your reaction must be consistent and persistent. I don't care if she wants to tell you something important or desperately needs your help, you must make your kid realize that a fresh attitude is intolerable and will no longer be indulged. This goes for little kids and big kids.

Fresh-talking, flippant, sassy kids are on the rise, and can they ever push our buttons! And why not? Offspring with fresh attitudes are sarcastic, rude, and poster kids for the Big Brat Factor. They undermine your authority, challenge almost anything you say, and let you know in no uncertain terms that you don't have a clue. And their antics are also highly selfish and self-centered. Don't kid yourself for one minute that these guys are concerned about how you feel when they zap you with their sarcastic tones and curt jabs.

So where's all this coming from? Most parents would agree that kids have come to think it's cool to be fresh. Reality TV, raunchy song lyrics, and incendiary role models all contribute to the new rude and crude youth culture. It's something you can see and hear in kids' everyday conversations with their peers at home, at school, and on their instant e-mails and cell phone text messages. And of course a primary recipient of this bad attitude is usually going to be you.

Maybe your kid is just trying to be "in" with the "in crowd," but if fresh attitudes are allowed to continue, they can have very negative social consequences. No teacher, coach, scout leader, other child's parent, or almost any other adult, for that matter, appreciates a fresh kid. The good news is that disrespectful attitudes such as giving lip and sassiness can be curbed—that is, as long as you are consistent with your makeover plan and let your kid know in no certain terms that you are serious about teaching her the virtues of respect, caring, and reverence.

BAD ATTITUDE ALERT

Before you can curb your kid's fresh attitude, figure out where, why, what, who, and when your kid is resorting to this horrific conduct.

Diagnosis
Answer these questions.

Why. The first most important question is to figure out why your kid has this fresh attitude. Have you been disrespectful to him? Has he seen you being disrespectful to your partner or other members of your family or friends? Here are some other things to consider: Has he been hanging out with a new crowd? Is he watching or listening to crude entertainment? Has he changed his appearance in trying to find a new image? What has your kid learned from being so fresh? Has it actually been effective? Is there a problem at home? A rift in your relationship? Does he resent you for some reason? Is there something about you or anything else going on right now that might be making him really mad? Does he hang around with friends who are disrespectful to their parents? What is your best guess as to why your kid is using this attitude?

What. Are there particular issues or things he is more sassy about? Are they about needing more privileges, wanting control or independence, needing attention, seeking revenge, or something else?

Who. Does she display the same fresh attitude to everyone? Does she talk differently when her friends are around? Are there some individuals she does not use her sassy tone and fresh ways on? If so, who? Why do you think this is the case? Is there anything different about their relationship with your kid? What about their response to her sassiness?

When. Is there a particular time of day, week, or month when he is fresher? Is there a reason? For instance, might he be needing control, or is he more stressed or overwhelmed than in the past? Did he just go to a concert, dance, or other influential event? Has he been sitting at home all day watching Jerry Springer? Also, when did you notice he first started being fresh and sassy? Can you think back as to what was going on in his world (family, school, friends) that might have triggered this attitude? Did he start hanging around with a new group of friends? Has he changed schools recently?

Where. Are there certain places he is more likely to be fresh (at school or day care, home, during dinner hour, in the car, with a particular kid or group of kids)? Does he use the attitude everywhere or mostly in certain places? If so, why?

WHAT'S WRONG
WITH YOUR CURRENT RESPONSE?

Next, reflect on how you typically respond to your kid's fresh, flippant attitude. For example, are you attentive, preoccupied, concerned, respectful, flip, hurried, interested, or indifferent? Think back to the last time your kid was fresh. What was the incident over? How did it start? What were you doing at the time? How were you acting toward your kid? Is this how you typically react toward her? Get into her shoes: Would she agree with how you described your attitude? Did you make any nonverbal gestures such as rolling eyes, shrugged shoulders, smirking? Was there anything in your attitude that might have set her off? What did she say that you considered to be fresh, and how did you respond? Did you tolerate her fresh attitude? Or did you scold her or blame yourself? Did your response stop the attitude or escalate it? What is the one response you know never works in stopping this fresh attitude? Jot it down.

I will not _____

_____

FACING YOUR OWN BAD ATTITUDES

Your kid isn't born fresh, sassy, and rude, so where is your kid learning this attitude? Could it be from siblings? Friends? Neighborhood kids? Cousins or relatives? What about from you or your spouse? How do you treat one another? Do you ever talk sarcastically and flippantly to each other? Do you use four-letter words? If so, how often? How about the way you treat your friends? Has anybody ever accused you of being fresh or insulting? What was the situation?

Now think about how you typically talk to your kid. Do you talk in a civil, respectful tone toward him? Do you take time to attentively listen to him? Are you ever sarcastic, belittling, cutting, or insulting? Do you ever curse at your kids? What about being overly critical or judgmental? Do you put down your kid in front of others? Compare your child to his siblings? Is your discipline fair or overly punitive? Would your kid agree with your self-evaluation?

Next, seriously reflect on your relationship with your kid. Is it really based on mutual respect? Could the state of your relationship have anything to do with his sassy, disrespectful tone? How would he describe your relationship? For example, would he say it is honest, open, trusting, loving, or relaxed? Or would he say it's strained, closed, or stressful? Why? If your relationship is strained, what can you do to rebuild and reconnect with your kid? And what are you really willing to commit to doing to remedy any rift if it exists between the two of you?

What is the first step you need to take in yourself to be a better example to your sons or daughters when dealing with their fresh attitude? Write down changes you need to make in yourself.

I will _____

_____

_____

BAD ATTITUDE NEWS ALERT

Only 12 percent of the two thousand adults polled in a recent survey felt that kids commonly treat others with respect; most described them as "rude," "irresponsible," and "lacking in discipline."

THE "DON'T GIVE ME THAT ATTITUDE" MAKEOVER

To eliminate your child's fresh attitude, take the following steps.

Step 1. Clearly Identify Your Kid's Fresh Behaviors

The first step in eliminating a fresh attitude is to determine which behaviors you consider inappropriate. Only then can you eliminate them from your kid's repertoire. Where do you draw the line between normal teasing and family banter and a downright rude, disrespectful, fresh attitude? What is your family's rule about four-letter words? Your kid won't know the boundaries unless you do. All kids slip every once in a while, but what is your kid doing or saying that is really fresh? The best test is that a fresh attitude is rude, embarrassing, or hurtful and *always* disrespectful. Keep in mind that freshness can be delivered in three ways: with words, a fresh voice tone, or with body gestures:

- *Fresh words:* "You're a very bad Mommy!" "Get real!" "Don't you know anything?" "Yeah, right!" "That is so stupid!" "Whatever." "That sucks." "F——you!"
- *Fresh tone:* sarcastic, hostile, arrogant, silent, negative, imitates your tone or words mockingly.
- *Fresh body gestures:* smirking, sighing, rolling eyes, vulgar finger gestures.

Make a list of the fresh words, tone, or body gestures your kid typically uses. Talk with others who witness your kid's fresh attitude, and add their observations. Finally, pass your list on to any adult—spouse, day care, grandparents—involved in the attitude makeover so you're on board together.

Step 2. Announce a "No Freshness Policy" and Then Stick to It

Calmly announce your zero tolerance for fresh behavior and language to your kid. Make sure it is a relaxed, uninterrupted time, and then clarify your new policy in a firm, serious tone. This is no time for discussion, negotiation, or compromise. In fact, the whole discussion should be brief. Just express why his fresh attitude will no longer be tolerated: you might explain your family's code of values and your personal beliefs and how a fresh attitude goes against those values. Also let your child know that if his attitude continues, there will be a consequence. Here are a few ways to explain your new standards:

"Please don't use a whiny baby voice when you want something to eat. In this family, we always ask for things respectfully."

"Four-letter words are forbidden in this family."

"I notice that when I talk to you, you roll your eyes. That's disrespectful, and you must stop right away."

"Telling me to 'get a life' when I am talking to you is rude. You may not talk that way."

Step 3. Refuse to Engage with a Fresh-Mouthed Attitude

Kids are much more likely to stop using fresh, sassy attitudes and bad language if they find they don't work in getting what they want. Whenever your kid lays a fresh attitude on you, flat out refuse to respond until he is respectful. *And do so every time he acts fresh.* The best response to a fresh kid is to turn and walk away calmly. No, you're not abandoning your kid; you're letting him know you expect respect and won't deal with him until he acts respectfully. Usually when kids see that you are serious and will not going to give in, they stop.

Beware: Be careful that you don't send any nonverbal messages to your kid. For instance, don't sigh, roll your eyes, shrug your shoulders, or look exasperated. Doing so is technically "responding." Remember that some kids actually enjoy seeing you ticked off, so don't give your child the pleasure. Here are a few examples of how to respond:

"Stop. That's being fresh. When you have a respectful attitude, you can find me in the kitchen."

"I can't understand that sassy voice. I listen only to nice voices."

"We'll talk when you can listen respectfully without rolling your eyes and smirking."

Step 4. Set a Stern Consequence If Fresh Attitude Continues

If you've been clear with your expectations and the fresh attitude and gestures still continue, it's time to set a consequence. Whenever your kid does display that attitude, call it on the spot by briefly describing what she did that was disrespectful—for example, "I've explained before that you may not talk to me in that tone of voice. Since you can't talk respectfully to your family, you may not use your cell or any other phone for the next twenty-four hours. Put it in the drawer, please."

There should be no discussion: just calmly state the consequence, then enforce it and don't back down. He needs to know that his attitude will not be tolerated. Here are a few other consequences for different ages that address fresh, flippant attitudes:

- *Time-out away from activities.* Younger kids who talk back and sass can be removed from the room until they can talk respectfully: "Lydia, that was sassing. Go to time-out for five minutes." Make sure the area is one where she may not receive attention. The simplest rule for determining the time length is one minute for each year of the child's age (five years equals five minutes, ten years equals ten minutes, and so on). Some parents call the location the thinking chair or cool-down corner.

- *Apologizing.* Comments delivered by fresh kids are rude but also hurtful, so make them accountable for their actions. Although they can't take back their spiteful words, they can at least ease the pain by apologizing. Even a four year old can say, "I'm sorry."
- *"Fresh jar."* Establish a "fresh jar"—any jar with a lid that's set aside just for fresh, flippant attitudes. Clearly define what the bad attitude is, and set a fine. For kids short on money, make and post a list of chores that can be done to work off the fine. Each time the child swears, he is fined and must put the set amount of money in the jar. When the jar is filled, donate the money to a charity of your choice.
- *Removal from family.* Older children who are fresh to you or any other family member could lose the privilege of being in the room where you gather most regularly as a family (usually for a few hours or the rest of the day, depending on the crime). If the bad attitude continues, you could establish a stricter criterion: "If you can't treat your family respectfully, then you may not see your friends."
- *Loss of a privilege.* Any child who uses flippant, fresh language on the telephone, including failing to answer the phone in a courteous manner, loses phone privileges for a set period.

Step 5. Find Ways for Positive Contributions

If not nipped right away, fresh-mouthed youths can dish out countless rude and insulting barbs. Their messages are always disrespectful and often quite hurtful. Each sassy, insolent comment wounds more than just the intended victim: they also damage the sender's capacities for empathy and respect. What they desperately need are quality experiences to counter the harm to their moral growth.

An easy way to develop a good attitude is to acknowledge our kids when we see them using it. Studies show that most of the time we do the opposite: instead of "catching" our kids being respectful, we point out when they are acting incorrectly. Any time you see or hear your child demonstrating good attitudes, acknowledge them and express your pleasure. Here are a few examples:

"Jimmy, you spoke in such a nice, sweet voice just now. Good for you!"
"Jenna, I appreciate how you stopped to think before you spoke to your grandmother. Thank you."
"I appreciate the apology, Levar. You hurt my feelings this morning. I also know that it's hard changing a bad habit, but I see that you are trying."

The First 21 Days

Start a Family Instant-Replay Plan every time your kid says something fresh: stop, call a time-out, and help him find a more appropriate and respectful way of expressing what's on his mind. In the heat of the moment, he may not realize the hurtful impact of his fresh attitude even though what he's trying to say may be an honest attempt to express his feelings, concerns, or problems. For example, when he says, "You're clueless," he may be really trying to tell you that because you're of a different generation, you don't know what it's like to be in his shoes when dealing with the stresses and pressures of teachers and peers—for example:

Mom: You called me "clueless," and that really hurts. Can you say that again politely?
Kid: Well, um, you don't know what you're talking about.
Mom: Try that again. What exactly happened to you that I don't know?

> *Kid:* Lauren sent an instant message to her class
> buddy list that I'm a wimp. These days stuff like
> that can get around so quickly.
> *Mom:* Okay, now I understand why you're so upset.
> So can you replay that part about me being clue-
> less?
> *Kid:* Mom, you wouldn't understand unless you
> learned to use the computer.

ATTITUDE MAKEOVER PLEDGE

How will you use these steps and ideas to achieve long-term
change? On the lines below, write exactly what you agree to
do within the next twenty-four hours to begin changing your
kid's attitude so he is less sassy and fresh and more respectful
and considerate.

_____

_____

_____

_____

THE NEW ATTITUDE REVIEW

All attitude makeovers take hard work, constant practice,
and parental reinforcement. Each step your child takes
toward change may be a small one, so be sure to acknowledge and congratulate every one of them along the way. It
takes a minimum of twenty-one days to see real results, so
don't give up! And if one strategy doesn't work, try
another. Write your child's weekly progress on the lines
below. Keep track of daily progress in your Attitude
Makeover Journal.

WEEK 1

_____

_____

_____

WEEK 2

_____

_____

_____

WEEK 3

_____

_____

_____

ONGOING ATTITUDE TUNE-UP

Where does your child's attitude still need improvement? What
work still needs to be done?

_____

_____

_____

ATTITUDE MAKEOVER RESOURCES

For Parents
Backtalk: Four Steps to Ending Rude Behavior in Your Kids, by Audrey
Ricker and Carolyn Crowder (New York: Fireside, 1998). A com-
monsense guide to stopping disrespectful behaviors.

Discipline Without Shouting or Spanking: Practical Solutions to the Most Common Preschool Behavior Problems, by Jerry Wychoff and Barbara Unell (New York: Simon & Schuster, 1985). Nonviolent options for correcting the most common behavior problems for preschoolers, including tantrums, whining, negativity, back talk, and aggression.

Raising Respectful Kids in a Rude World: Teaching Your Children the Power of Mutual Respect and Consideration, by Gary D. McKay, Joyce McKay, Daniel Eckstein, and Steven A. Maybell (Roseville, Calif.: Prima Publishers, 2001). How to establish positive, respectful attitudes in a rude world.

For Kids

Nasty People: How to Stop Being Hurt by Them Without Stooping to Their Level, by Jay Carter (New York: McGraw-Hill, 2003). Great strategies for staying when dealing with difficult, fresh-talking people (and teens). For adults, but good ideas for teens too.

How Rude! The Teenagers' Guide to Good Manners, Proper Behavior, and Not Grossing People Out, by Alex J. Packer, Pamela Espeland, and Jeff Tolbert (Minneapolis, Minn.: Free Spirit Publishing, 1997). Teens will find this manual humorous, nonthreatening, entertaining, and educational for dealing with many kinds of situations. Ages 12 and up.

Social Smarts: Manners for Today's Kids, by Carol Barkin (New York: Clarion Books, 1996). A wide variety of settings in which consideration of others and appropriate etiquette are presented. Ages 9 to 12.

Bad Attitude 9

Greedy
Antidote: Frugality, Altruism, Generosity

"Gimme, gimme, gimme!"

Dear Dr. Borba,
I'm hoping you can help me with my nine year old: he's become so greedy! I've tried to always make him happy and give him what the other kids have, but I think it's backfired. Instead of being satisfied, he just wants more! And he always wants more than anyone else. Now that I created this greedy, selfish monster, can I change his attitude?

—Karen P., a mom from Orlando, Florida

Bad Attitude Act Out
"But I've got to have a clown *and* a pony to ride on at my birthday. That's what Tiffany had."
"Sure, I have six pairs, but the more shoes the better!"
"Grandma gave me only fifty dollars for Christmas!"

EMERGENCY ATTITUDE Rx

Launch a short-term period of denial and deprivation to show your kid that he can actually do without having more of everything. Agree that you—and other family members—will make no nonessential purchases for an agreed-on time. For example, for younger kids, you might eliminate daily treats like candy or toys. For older kids no CDs, DVDs, cute things to wear, accessories, sport shoes, or makeup. The point is to show that constant material acquisition is an addictive habit, and you can get along perfectly well without all this stuff.

Have you noticed that we seem to have a lot of greedy kids these days? The general public agrees and feels that increased numbers of today's youth are self-centered, spoiled, greedy, and materialistic. Instead of being appreciative of what they have, these critters seem to want more, more, more. Kids' ravenous, never-satisfied manner certainly drains a checkbook, but something even more dangerous happens: greediness vaporizes their hearts and souls.

Think about it: if you incessantly prioritize your own wants and desires and put others' needs and feelings on hold, your life outlook is inevitably affected. More often than not, the message learned is that relationships are far less valuable than self and material possessions acquired. The bottom line is that steady dosages of greediness are shattering to our kids' character.

Raising kids in such a materialistic, greedy world doesn't help matters. It isn't easy resisting advertisers who taunt kids to buy-buy-buy, which perhaps is why data reveal that many kids are becoming more consumer driven and at much younger ages. There's big pressure to buy everything that their friends may have bought, as well keeping up with trends that require that they get the latest styles of shoes, cell phones, DVD players, and other electronic gadgets. We're even told that we must buy more to improve our economy, as if consumerism were a crucial part of patriotism.

One of the biggest causes of greediness is the one we hate admitting most: too often we parents have obliged our kids' every whim. Sure, we want our kids to be happy and have what they desire, but motivating them with bribery is a destructive style of parenting, and giving them more than they need just to keep up with the Joneses is equally toxic. In the end, we must keep true to one real parenting goal: raising kids who are satisfied with themselves and recognize the joy of others. So if your child appears to have a case of the "gimmes," always puts himself first, and isn't appreciative of what he has, it's time for a serious makeover. Start today by beginning a long-term commitment to inspire frugality, altruism, and generosity.

BAD ATTITUDE ALERT

Quick! Nip that greediness in the bud by starting right now to figure out how it got started.

Diagnosis
First ask yourself these questions:

Why. Why does your kid have a greedy attitude? There could be a number of causes. For instance, is there an emphasis on materialism in your home? Have his whims and desires been too easily granted? Are you bribing him with stuff every time you want him to do something or behave right? Are you bombarding him with things he doesn't need because you see your friends doing the same thing with their kids? Does she feel that the way to gain peer acceptance is by having the latest fashions or gadgets? Might it be to affirm his relationship with you? For instance, if he is jealous of a sibling or a relationship you have, when you feel guilty and give in to his wants, it "affirms" your love. Has a grandparent or other member of the family overindulged her? Why? By whom? More important, is there one thing you might do to stop it from spiraling further?

What. Are there particular things she is usually more greedy about? Does she want toys, entertainment, clothes, sports paraphernalia, computer gadgets, CDs, or cash?

Who. Does he display the same greedy attitude to everyone? Are there some individuals he does not use his greedy ways on? If so, who? Why not?

When. Is there a particular time he is greedier than others—for instance, on a particular holiday, before school starts, or his birthday? Is there a reason? Do you alleviate your guilt about being away from home, spending too much time on other people or projects, or just plain feeling bad about not being the perfect parent by buying your kid stuff, stuff, and more stuff?

Where. Are there certain places he is more likely to be greedy (at school or day care, home, the store, Grandma's)? Why? For instance, is Grandma an easy target for buying special treats she knows no one else will buy him?

Now review your answers. Are you seeing any predictable patterns? Do you have any better understanding of your kid's greedy attitude and where it's coming from?

WHAT'S WRONG
WITH YOUR CURRENT RESPONSE?

How do you typically respond to your child's greedy demands? Think back to the last time your kid had a greedy streak. What was the issue about? Now focus on *your* behavior. How did you respond? Most important, did you give in to your kid's desires and let him have his way? Did you talk to him about his attitude or ignore it? Did you say, "Go ask your rich Uncle Nat?" "I'll buy you the candy if you sit in the cart and don't say one more word." "Okay, you can have that new outfit if you just start doing your homework." Did you set a consequence or warn him what would happen if he continued his greediness?

What kinds of responses have you discovered do not work in squelching your kid's greediness? Is there one thing you have learned that is *not* effective in dealing with this attitude? List your worst response below:

I will not _____

_____

FACING YOUR OWN BAD ATTITUDES

Your kid was not born greedy, so where is she learning this behavior? Friends? You? Relatives? You're the best role model for helping your child cope with our complicated material world, so what kind of example are you setting? For instance, is he seeing you behave with restraint and wisdom? Or might he be witnessing someone who wants what she sees and buys on the whim? Seriously reflect about whether your behavior is teaching your kid to be greedier or more charitable. Here are a few questions to help you consider the kind of example you are intentionally or quite unintentionally sending your kid. Check ones that may apply to you:

- [ ] Do I model fiscal prudence?
- [ ] Do I buy things impulsively and then run out of money needed for more basic necessities?
- [ ] Do I bribe the kids to get them to comply with normal school or household rules and responsibilities?
- [ ] Do I find myself talking more about things than relationships?
- [ ] Do I compare what I own to what others have? Am I competitive in always having something better than my best friend or the guy next door?
- [ ] Do I go way overboard with gifts for the kids on holidays and birthdays and celebrations?
- [ ] Do I buy the kids fancy stuff instead of spending time with them?
- [ ] Do I always want my kid to have the newest fashion or electronic tools?
- [ ] Do I cave in to my kids' consumer whims because I think it will make them more popular?
- [ ] Do I go in a store and feel the need to buy something even if I know I don't need it?
- [ ] Do I send the kids to expensive camps or after-school programs just because their friends are going?
- [ ] Would my kid say, "It's not what you own but what you are" is true about me?
- [ ] My kids frequently see me doing charitable acts toward others and would agree that charity is a value I deem important.

What is the first step you need to take in yourself to be a better example to your kids for dealing with their greedy behavior? Write down changes you need to make.

I will _____

_____

_____

THE "DON'T GIVE ME THAT ATTITUDE" MAKEOVER

To eliminate your child's greedy attitude, take the following steps.

Step 1. Encourage Experiences That Nurture Strong Values, Skills, and Relationships

The first step to turning off kids' greed is by helping them recognize that having "stuff" does not provide emotional fulfillment. It must be replaced by a central life message: "Who you are is more important than what you have." Of course, merely reciting such lines won't change attitudes. Only through personal example and ongoing experiences that emphasize people over things and values over possessions will kids grasp the concept, and that comes only through your slow, consistent, committed effort. Begin intentionally looking for kinds of experiences that nurture strong values, skills, and relationships. Then encourage your child to try them, followed each time by helping him to see the value of the experience—for example:

"You looked as if you really enjoyed spending the day with Grandpa. He certainly loved being with you. Those are the kind of times you'll remember forever."

"Mom really appreciated your hand-made card. It's so much more meaningful than something you buy. Did you see her expression?"

Step 2. Tame the Gimmes; Then Don't Back Down

The next step to squelching your kid's greedy ways is simply not to tolerate the attitude. Always giving in to your kid's greedy desires doesn't do her any favors. Say *no* more often to your kid's whims and consumer demands, and do so without feeling guilty. Of course, if your kid is used to always getting what she wants, your new response will more than likely not be popular with her. So explain your concerns and the reason for your new policy, and then stick to it. Here are some other methods for taming the gimmes:

- For a younger child, set a reasonable budget for major expenses like a back-to-school wardrobe, birthday parties and presents, and holiday gifts. Stick to it and don't cave in. For an older child, give him your dollar cap, and let him be responsible for deciding how to spend it.
- Whenever possible, encourage family members to make gifts and presents instead of buying a lot of expensive stuff. Many times grandparents, other family members, teachers, and friends really appreciate something you've actually created yourself much more than a store-bought item.
- Pass your "no frills" policy onto other immediate caregivers, particularly grandparents, relatives, and your partner.
- Enlist the aid of friends and grandparents—who often delight in "spoiling" your child—by suggesting they buy only one gift at birthdays or holidays or give money for your child's education fund. The more you stick together, the more effective you will be in curbing your kid's greedy streak.

- Never bribe or reward your child with material gifts just for doing something he should have done anyway.

Step 3. Monitor Media Consumption That Drives Greediness

Television probably wields the greatest influence on fueling kids' greedy attitudes, and commercials are relentless in trying to get kids to want, want, want, and buy, buy, buy. Limit your child's exposure to TV commercials by minimizing his TV viewing. (*Hint:* Children's public television, while not strictly commercial free, offers quality programs with much less advertising.) And when you are watching those commercials with your kid, point out that their purpose is not altruistic. They want his money. When kids are more tuned into the advertisers' motives, they are less likely to want every little thing they see.

Step 4. Praise Charitable Deeds, and Encourage Kids to Value What They Have

Praise is one of the oldest parenting strategies, but research finds that only certain kinds really enhance behavior and changes attitudes. Psychologist Joan Grusec found that kids who were frequently praised by their mothers whenever they displayed generous behavior actually tended to be less generous on a day-to-day basis than other children. Why? More than likely, the children weren't personally committed to the trait—in this case, generosity—that their moms were praising them for. Without their moms' encouraging words, there was really no reason for them to continue doing generous actions on their own, because their good behavior was guided by social approval and not their own internal convictions. Encourage your kids' charitable actions, but be conscious of how you praise and what you say so they understand the value of the deed.

- ***Praise the deed, not the child.*** "That was so kind when you shared your toys with Mariettza."

- **The praise is specific.** "You were a good host in making sure everyone got the same-size piece of cake. I think everyone enjoyed the play group much more this time."
- **The praise is deserved.** "Grandpa loved your painting. You took such time, and he really appreciated it."
- **The praise is genuine.** The best reinforcement is always sincere and lets the child know exactly what she did that was right: "I know it took effort not to buy the toy, but you used good judgment when you said that you really didn't need it."

Step 5. Encourage Savings and Financial Planning

Studies find that a large percentage of kids today are wasteful when it comes to money: most want to spend rather than save. We need to help kids fight their spending urges and teach them money management skills when they are young. Here are eight ways:

- For a young child, buy a piggy bank to save coins. Make a rule that it must be filled before the money is spent.
- Give a weekly or monthly allowance (depending on age) so that she can learn to budget money.
- Make her write down her intended purchase and post it for a few days before she buys it. A younger kid can draw it on her "wish list."
- Older kids should be required to spend their own money on entertainment and nonessential items. Don't give out loans.
- Help a younger child open up a savings account and an older child a checking account so that they can monitor their money and spending.
- Require that a portion of her allowance go to a charity of her choice.
- Require a set portion of her allowance always to be saved.
- Say no to frivolous, rash buying *and don't give in.*

Step 6. Require Giving to Others

One of the best ways to curb kids' greedy attitudes is by requiring that they give to others. Begin by having your family choose a family cause. For example, give part of a weekly allowance to needy kids, adopt an orphan through Save the Children, deliver used toys (in good condition) to the fire department, or bake cookies for the lonely neighbor next door. Once your family decides on a cause, commit to carrying it out. Or give your kids their allowance and require that a portion go to a charity of their choice. That kind of hands-on giving activity can foster an attitude of giving that will help counter greediness more powerfully than almost anything else.

The First 21 Days

Embark on a Family Generosity Project, which represents the opposite of greed and reinforces more positive values that emphasize alternative ways to achieve true happiness. For example, make it a goal to give away 5 percent, 10 percent, or as much as you can of everything in your house: clothing, books, toys, tools, DVDs, CDs, and other expendable objects. Have your kids pack everything up in boxes and help you deliver them to the Salvation Army, Goodwill, Catholic Charities, or another favorite local charity. Their participation will be a big part of learning that it really is better to give than to receive.

ATTITUDE MAKEOVER PLEDGE

How will you use these six steps to help your kid become less greedy and achieve long-term change? On the lines below, write exactly what you agree to do within the next twenty-four hours to begin changing your kid's attitude so he is less greedy and more generous.

_____

_____

_____

THE NEW ATTITUDE REVIEW

All attitude makeovers take hard work, constant practice, and parental reinforcement. Each step your child takes toward change may be a small one, so be sure to acknowledge and congratulate every one of them along the way. It takes a minimum of twenty-one days to see real results, so don't give up! And if one strategy doesn't work, try another. Write your child's weekly progress on the lines below. Keep track of daily progress in your Attitude Makeover Journal.

WEEK 1

_____

_____

_____

WEEK 2

_____

_____

_____

WEEK 3

_____

_____

_____

ONGOING ATTITUDE TUNE-UP

Where does your child's attitude still need improvement? What work still needs to be done?

_____

_____

_____

ATTITUDE MAKEOVER RESOURCES

For Parents

Money Doesn't Grow on Trees, by Neale Godfrey and Carolina Edwards (New York: Simon & Schuster, 1994). A parenting resource to help kids learn financial planning and bust their spendthrift urges.

The Brighter Side of Human Nature, by Alfie Kohn (New York: Basic Books, 1990). Drawing from hundreds of studies, Kohn makes a powerful case that generosity is just as natural as selfishness.

For Kids

Fly Away Home, by Eve Bunting (New York: Clarion Books, 1991). The plight of a homeless boy and his father is told in this poignant tale. The only home that Andrew and his dad have is an airport, and as Andrew's dad says, "It's warm. It's safe. And the price is right." Ages 4 to 8.

Tight Times, by Barbara Shook Hazen (New York: Puffin, 1983). A poignant tale about a boy who more than anything else wants a dog but is not allowed to get one because of "tight times." The book portrays the deep love the family feels for one another even though times are tough and Dad loses his job. Ages 4 to 9.

The Giver, by Lois Lowry (New York: Houghton Mifflin, 1994). In a world without poverty or inequity, Jonas has an experience that questions every value we take for granted. This is wonderful! Ages 9 to 15.

The Marzipan Pig (Family Home Video, 1991). Adapted from the wonderful book by Russell Hoban, here are thirty moving minutes that sensitize kids to feelings (especially loneliness and kindness). A wonderful video for the family to savor.

Places in the Heart (CBS/Fox Video, 1984). This film features Sally Field in an Oscar-winning role as a young widow determined to survive as a cotton farmer during the Depression. Virtues include compassion, self-reliance, perseverance, and self-control.

10

Impatient
Antidote: Patience,
Self-Control, Serenity

"Aren't we there yet?"

Dear Dr. Borba,
Our middle son is so impatient that it's driving everyone in our
family crazy! He can't wait—or maybe it's more accurate to say he
won't wait for anything or anybody. He wants everything ASAP
and can't understand why he can't instantly get his way. I'm finally
realizing just how selfish his attitude is. He's really thinking only
about his needs and never considering anyone else's feelings. His
brothers are starting to resent him, and frankly so am I.

—Kara L., a mom from Long Beach, California

BAD ATTITUDE ACT OUT

"I can't wait! We have to do this NOW!

"MOOOOMMMM! Get off your computer. I need to use
it right away."

"I'm tired of waiting, Dad. Let's go somewhere else."

EMERGENCY ATTITUDE R҉

The next time you yourself behave with impatience, stop, own it, and use it as an opportunity to show your kids a big attitude change in action. For example, you're waiting in line in a restaurant, you're stuck in traffic, you want to use the phone at home, or your computer is taking forever to download; instead of getting all hot and puffy, yelling at the machine, or pacing up and down, use your Assault of the Deadly Impatient Bug as a teachable moment. First, acknowledge to your kid that you nearly succumbed but are still able to regain your patience. Talk out what's going on in your head and share with them your efforts: "I'm really impatient, I need to take a deep breath. I'll go sort the laundry until this darn computer is done downloading. How am I doing? Do I deserve a gold star, or do you think I need more work on being patient?" The more your kid sees you admit your impatient attitude and model healthy ways to beat it, the more likely she is to try it herself. Your child needs to recognize that not only is patience a virtue but it is also a more practical, healthier way to get things done. So repeat this emergency attitude Rx as many times as necessary.

Impatient kids want things *now.* They hate to wait, want everything done instantly (and done in their favor), and really aren't concerned about somebody else's feelings and needs. After all, it's *their* inner clocks that are ticking, and as far as they are concerned, everyone else's watches should be set to comply with *their* time demands.

Standing in line with these kids can be absolute torture. They can't understand why they have to wait: it's an inconvenience to *their* schedule. Heaven help you if the waiter is late, the movie won't start, the airplane is stuck on the runway, the computer is slow downloading, or the game is postponed. Everyone pays the price and must endure the kid's tirades, despite the fact that everyone else is probably inconvenienced as well.

Make no mistake: impatient kids have an attitude, plain and simple, and there are two prime causes. We've become a sprint-paced, instant-message, microwave society that wants things immediately. We have also made the mistake of giving in straight away to our kids and trying to satisfy their whims, wishes, and wants instantly.

Patience is a very important virtue that puts us in harmony with other people and the natural rhythm of events. Patience teaches us to be sensitive to others and more aware of what's going on around us. It boosts character, improves our relationships, is better for them in the long run, and ultimately makes us happier. Let's just make sure our kids recognize this. The first step is to curb their impatient attitudes and replace them with the virtues of patience, self-discipline, and serenity.

BAD ATTITUDE ALERT

As a former special education teacher, I've had lots of experience with impatient kids, and I know that the first step to changing this bad attitude is to understand the underlying causes.

Diagnosis
I always ask myself the following questions.

Why. Why does your kid have this attitude? What is fueling his impatience? Are you an above-average impatient person? Is he used to getting his way instantly? Does he see others get what they need immediately so he wants it as well? Here's another possibility: Is your kid impatient because he's frustrated, fears failure, is anxious or stressed? Get in your kid's shoes in the specific situation where he is most likely to show impatience. Pretend you're him. Why is he impatient? Don't overlook that impatience can also be a sign of frustration, fear of failure, or inability to focus on one thing for any length of time. What about stress? Might your kid's schedule be so overloaded that he literally doesn't have time to relax, be patient, and decompress?

What. Are there particular issues or things he usually is more impatient about? Are they about wanting stuff or needing more attention and privileges? Or is it about not doing a particular subject, chore, or assignment?

Who. Does he display the same impatient behavior to everyone? Are there some individuals he does not use his impatient ways on? If so, who? Why are they spared? Does he respond any differently to those who are more patient and relaxed toward him? If so, who?

When. Is there a particular hour in the day, day of the week, or even month when he is more impatient? Is there a reason? For instance, is he concerned about getting into trouble, wanting to meet his friends, missing a TV show? Does she tend to be more impatient when she is tired, hungry, or stressed? Does he always seem to need the same routine and schedule?

Where. Are there certain places he is more likely to be impatient (at school, at the dinner table, in the car pool, at violin practice)? Why?

Review your answers. Talk to others who know your child well. Do you have any better understanding of her impatient attitude and where it's coming from?

WHAT'S WRONG
WITH YOUR CURRENT RESPONSE?

Yes, some kids have more sensitive temperaments and quicker attention spans, but patience can be taught, attention spans can be stretched, and children can learn to stop and consider the needs of others. Where is your kid learning this behavior? From siblings? Friends? Neighbors? Relatives? Or might you be reinforcing it by always immediately giving in to his requests?

Reflect on how you typically respond to your child's impatience. Do you roll your eyes and tap your feet? Freak out and yell at him? Bribe him to wait a bit longer? Give in to his whims? Try to take a radical step to speed everything up so he gets what he wants more quickly? Think of the last time your kid displayed this bad attitude, and write below what you will never try again.

I will not _____

_____

FACING YOUR OWN BAD ATTITUDES

What kind of example are you setting for your kid? For instance, has anybody complained about your being impatient lately? Who complained, and what did that person say? Do you think the label fit? Think about how well *you* deal with stress, frustrations, or change. Try to think of specific examples and what you did. Here are a few examples: You're stuck in an endlessly long line to get through security at the airport; traffic is stalled, and you're late for an important appointment at work; the bank teller informs you the bank's computer system is down, and you have to wait a few minutes for your transaction to go through; your kid is struggling with his homework and he doesn't get what you're explaining; you arrive at the restaurant on time for your reservation and are told that your table won't be ready for at least forty-five minutes. How mature were you in handling the delay? Even more important, how patient would your kid say you were?

What about everyday life moments? Do you find time to relax, really listen patiently to your kids, and take moments just to think and contemplate your day and life? What about your schedule? Is it so packed that you find yourself stressed and impatient with your family and friends? Do you find yourself impatient about doing things like helping your kid learn to tie his shoes, make her bed, ride a bike, drive a car? When your child is struggling, are you able to be patient? What about when one of your kids makes a mistake? Can you make allowances? What can you do to change your schedule so you can be more patient and enjoy little moments with your family that can add up to mean so much?

Consider whether your attitude is teaching your kid to be patient. Could your kid be learning any of his bad attitude from you? If so, what is the first step you need to take in yourself to be a better example to your sons or daughters of dealing with their impatient behavior? Write down changes you need to make.

I will _____

_____

BAD ATTITUDE NEWS ALERT

Surveys based on pediatrician reports found that impulsivity among American kids has risen *more than 700 percent in twenty years.* Translation: our kids are far less patient and more reckless than children two decades ago. Diagnosis of hyperactivity and short attention spans is spiraling as well.

THE "DON'T GIVE ME THAT ATTITUDE" MAKEOVER

To eliminate your kid's impatience, take the following steps.

Step 1. Make Your Kid Wait—and Don't Give In

The first step to changing your kid's impatient attitude is simply to make him wait. Don't give in to his whims, don't stop your conversation to answer his unnecessary questions, and don't feel sorry for him because he didn't get what he wants just when he wanted it. Not only is it a big part of growing up, but researchers find that patient kids have an advantage in life. Scientific studies have actually proven that patience is crucial for all of us to get what we want and need in life. It helps achieve goals, resolve conflicts, and just plain enjoy life, moment by moment.

Research by Walter Mischel, a psychologist at Stanford University, confirmed just how beneficial patience is by challenging a group of four year olds: Did they want a marshmallow immediately, or could they wait a few minutes until a researcher returned, at which point they could have two marshmallows? The researchers then followed up on the kids upon their high school graduation and found that those who had been able to wait for those marshmallows years before at age four now were far more socially competent: they were found to be more personally effective, self-assertive, and better able to deal with the frustrations of life. The one-third who waited longest also had significantly higher SAT scores by an average of two hundred points on the total verbal and math scores combined than the teens who at age four couldn't wait. Make your kids wait a bit and learn to be patient. Ignore their protests and tirades; in the end, you're doing them a favor.

Step 2. Stretch Your Kid's Patience Little by Little

The most important goal for changing this attitude is to stretch your kid's patience so he can wait for longer and longer periods of time. The first part of this is to help her calm down in the moment. Here are some tips:

- **Freeze.** In a very calm voice, say: "Freeze and don't move until you can get yourself in control."
- **Hold your breath.** Tell your kid not to breathe as long as possible and then take a few long, deep breathes together.
- **Count.** Join your child in slowly going from 1 to 100 (or less with a younger tyke).
- **Sing.** For a young child, ask him to pick his favorite tune such as "Frére Jacques" or "Twinkle Twinkle Little Star."
- **Stretch.** For older children, show them how to relax the tension in their neck or upper back by pretending they're a scarecrow or leaf falling slowly to the ground.

Once your impatient kid has learned to temper his nervous energy and desires, help him stretch the amount of time he can wait little by little. Start by timing how long your kid can wait. If he can hold still for only one minute, don't make him stand there for ten. Take that shorter time as his normal patience level, and then gradually increase his waiting time as his patience improves. If he is also impatient in other areas, such as homework time or doing chores, do the same thing. For instance, time how long your kid can generally stay in his seat when he is doing his homework. If he can hold still for only five minutes, don't make him stay there for twenty. Take that time as his normal work session, and plan breaks at necessary intervals so he can finish his work in appropriate segments. Don't expect this to happen overnight; it won't. But your kid's patience will grow if you stick to this goal.

Step 3. Teach the Difference Between "Needs" and "Wants"

When dealing with impatience related to acquiring some object or material thing, instead of instantly gratifying your kid's urges by buying what he wants or letting him spend his cash, insist he wait (an hour, day, week). During the time, he must think whether he really *needs* the product. After all, there is a difference between "need" and "want," and impatient kids often confuse the two. Some parents have their kids write down or draw a picture of the item desired and post it until the date that he can go out and purchase it. Younger kids can use a calendar to check off each day, until the specified time when they can purchase the item. But if he loses interest before the time is up, even he probably will agree that he didn't really "need" the item after all.

Step 4. Take a Stand Against Interrupting

"I never get to finish my conversation—my kid is constantly interrupting." "I'm on the phone talking, and my kid barges in and wants to tell me something." Sound familiar? One of the biggest parenting complaints is about kids who always interrupt. It's just another sign of an impatient attitude.

Take a stand against unnecessary interruptions: helping your kid learn to wait and *not* interrupt is yet another way to increase patience. Here are a few suggestions to guide you through the weaning process:

- *Acknowledge their presence while waiting.* For younger kids, it is helpful to put your hand gently on their back, give a hug, or put up your pointer finger to signify "one more minute" and you'll give them your undivided attention.
- *Teach the meaning of "necessary."* There are instances when kids should interrupt, but those times need to be spelled out so kids are clear what they are. Discuss which situations justify interruptions (such as emergencies, someone is hurt or could get hurt, or an adult says, "Get your mom now").
- *Give a time frame.* Younger kids especially have difficulties waiting because they have such limited concepts of time.

Visual references providing time references often helps them be patient. Here are a few examples:

A watch: "When the big hand goes all the way around one time, I can help."

A sand timer or oven timer: "Wait until the sand runs out [or timer goes off]."

A refrain: "Slowly say your ABCs or count to 20 [or hum "Twinkle Twinkle Little Star"]. When you're done, I can listen."

- **Point out "inappropriate times."** Discuss inappropriate times to interrupt, such as when someone looks very busy, is on the telephone, is in the middle of a conversation with someone, or is sleeping. This conversation helps your kid become more aware of not only unsuitable moments to interrupt, but also learn to be more considerate of others: "Did you notice Mom was resting? Do you think she appreciated your interrupting her right then? When would have been a better time to ask her to help you with your project?" Or: "I was on the phone talking to Grandpa about how he was feeling. Did you see the worry on my face? Was that a good or bad time to ask me a question? When would have been a better time?"

Step 5. Reinforce Patience

Of course, becoming more patient will not happen overnight. Stress the value of patience as a family, talk about why "patience is a virtue," and acknowledge your kid's attempts to be more patient:

"I know it was hard to wait and you wanted to go home. So thank you for being so patient."

"I noticed how patient you were with your brother today. It's not easy having a three year old around when you're trying to get your work done. I appreciate your patience."

The First 21 Days

Start a Patience Extension Plan for your family. Make a commitment to take every opportunity to show your kids the value of patience in your daily family life, whenever you're stuck, or when you've experienced something that's taking a long time. For example:

"It's going to take a while for Mom to finish blow drying her hair, so sit down here and talk to me, Peter, while we wait. We'll be going as soon as she gets out of the bathroom."

"I see there's a long line here; you must be really busy here tonight at this restaurant. Thanks for letting us wait until there's a window table."

"Let's celebrate, kids. I've been working on that account for eighteen months, and they finally signed up with us just today."

"It took me three weeks to read that book, but I felt so inspired by the time I got to the end."

Take a pledge to cultivate patience as a family. You might start by discussing what things are fueling impatience and then find ways to create less stress so you have more time to enjoy each other—for example:

- Reduce one thing on your weekly schedule.
- Take the phone off the hook for an hour each night and let the answering machine do its magic.
- Set a moratorium on unnecessary errands.
- Turn the TV off for a half-hour at a certain time.

- Add ten minutes after dinner as family time or find a time each night when all family members can be together for even a brief time.

  Then during those added minutes, take that uninterrupted, unstressed time to enjoy each other and listen patiently.

ATTITUDE MAKEOVER PLEDGE

How will you use these steps to help your kid become less impatient and achieve long-term change? On the lines below, write exactly what you agree to do within the next twenty-four hours to begin changing your kid's attitude so he is more patient and considerate of others.

THE NEW ATTITUDE REVIEW

All attitude makeovers take hard work, constant practice, and parental reinforcement. Each step your child takes toward change may be a small one, so be sure to acknowledge and congratulate every one of them along the way. It takes a minimum of twenty-one days to see real results, so don't give up! And if one strategy doesn't work, try another. Write your child's weekly progress on the lines that follow. Keep track of daily progress in your Attitude Makeover Journal.

WEEK 1

_____

_____

_____

WEEK 2

_____

_____

_____

WEEK 3

_____

_____

_____

ONGOING ATTITUDE TUNE-UP

Where does your child's attitude still need improvement? What
work still needs to be done?

_____

_____

_____

ATTITUDE MAKEOVER RESOURCES

For Parents

_Peaceful Parents, Peaceful Kids: Practical Ways to Create a Calm and Happy
Home,_ by Naomi Drew (New York: Kensington Publishers, 2000). If
you were going to buy one book on creating a harmonious home,

this should be it. The author is an expert on the subject, and her ideas are practical.

Tired of Yelling: Teaching Our Children to Resolve Conflict, by Lyndon D. Waugh (Atlanta, Ga.: Longstreet, 1999). A fifteen-step model on how to help your child learn to manage anger and handle conflict.

Your Anxious Child: How Parents and Teachers Can Relieve Anxiety in Children, by John Dacey and Lisa B. Fiore (San Francisco: Jossey-Bass, 1999). Provides specific ways to help children handle stress and cope with difficulties more confidently.

For Kids

Feelings, by Aliki (New York: Greenwillow Books). A wonderful handbook of emotions for children, ranging in topics from anger, jealousy, and fear to pride, joy, and love. Ages 5 to 11.

Today I Feel Silly and Other Moods That Make My Day, by Jamie Lee Curtis (New York: HarperCollins, 1998). Uses whimsical illustrations and a delightful rhyme to address the emotions *grumpy, mean, silly, angry, joyful, confused, quiet, excited, cranky, lonely, happy, discouraged,* and *sad.* Included is a cardboard wheel kids can turn to help them identify the basic feelings. Ages 4 to 10.

Yoga for Children (Wayne Harvey Productions, 1997). A fun video program of stretching and relaxation for children featuring a basic yoga workout that helps kids develop calmness. Ages 4 to 10.

Gandhi (Columbia, 1982). Mahatma Gandhi is magnificently portrayed by Ben Kingsley. The movie chronicles the prejudice he encounters as a young attorney in South Africa, his role as spiritual leader to the people of India and his cause of passive resistance, and his eventual assassination. Ages 12 and up.

Kundun (Touchstone, 1997). A stunning movie depicting the life of the fourteenth Dalai Lama. Great for helping kids understand a bit of Chinese history, the pacifist's views of the Dalai Lama, and the increasing difficulties he faces as a nonviolent man in an increasingly violent world. Ages 12 and up.

11

Insensitive
*Antidote: Sensitivity,
Empathy, Tact*

"Hey, lighten up, Dude, I was just kidding!"

*Dear Dr. Borba,
I just saw a side of my kid I never realized. He was playing basketball with his neighbor friend, Jack, when another friend calls him to go roller blading. So he tells this poor kid to go home, then runs off leaving him stranded. I can't believe he was so insensitive! How do I get him to feel about somebody beside himself?*

—Alan, J., a dad of three from Portland, Maine

Bad Attitude Act Out

"Dougy is a dummy. Why should I care how he feels?"

"So what if I made her cry. She's a dork."

"So Mr. Greenberg's mother just died? So what's that got to do with me?"

EMERGENCY ATTITUDE R⃰

The first and single most important thing you can do to cure your kid's insensitive attitude is to ask her, "How would *you* feel?" If you can help your child get inside someone else's shoes and feel things from the other person's perspective, it would be a huge step to boosting her sensitivity. The next time your child says or does anything insensitive, stop, get her attention, and ask her to play the Role Reversal Game. She must change chairs, switch shoes or hats, or whatever else is possible to become the person she is insensitive toward; then you ask her: "How do you feel that someone said that about you?" For example, with a younger child, ask her to pretend she's little Joey whom she's just called "Stupid." Ask an older child to assume the identity of someone about whom he's just sent out a nasty e-mail blast. Take the time to go over this with your kids so they can really feel deep in their hearts and souls what it's like to be on the receiving end of an insensitive attitude.

Beware: Insensitivity could be just the tip of the iceberg and may indicate other treacherous attitudes just below the surface, like cruelty, freshness, defiance, greed, and other elements of the Big Brat Factor. If this one doesn't have a quick meltdown, other bad attitudes can easily emerge.

Showing children how their insensitive attitude affects someone else is a significant and serious part of building character. All of our kids are born egocentric—after all, an infant's job is to get basic needs met. But our job as parents is to slowly wean them from the "me-me's" and teach them the value of feeling for others. The goal is do so without preaching, punishing, or bribing. One of the best ways is to be prepared for the ideal moment—that perfect situation—when you can use something that is happening to jump in and bring home the message.

Our challenge as parents is how to use those unplanned moments when our kids' attitudes are unacceptable to help them become more responsive to the feelings of others. That kind of opportunity is always the best moment for attitude makeovers. As parents, we must help our kids discover for themselves why they should be more sensitive and realize that uncaring, cold-hearted actions cause great pain to others and ultimately to themselves. Replacing these attitudes with sensitivity, empathy, and tact is essential for long-term character building and ultimate happiness.

BAD ATTITUDE ALERT

Before you start defrosting your kid's insensitive, iceberg attitude, you need to go beneath the surface and find out where this is coming from and how it plays out for your kid and your family.

Diagnosis

Consider how your child has become so insensitive. For instance, have people treated him insensitively? Does he understand that his attitude is hurting other people's feelings? Of course, there are other reasons kids might be insensitive, so answer the following Five W's of Attitude Awareness to help you figure out what's going on.

Why. Why does your kid have this attitude? Have people been insensitive to him? Have you or others had an insensitive attitude toward him? Are feelings not acknowledged or expressed in your home? Is "Boys Don't Cry" or "Girls Talk to Their Friends" the motto in your house? Have you been concerned about your child's emotional intelligence, that is, his ability to read other people's feelings and his own? Has he been angry or depressed lately? Is he burned out? What's going on with him at school or in his social life? Is he numb from the stress of world events, or could he be reacting to a crisis in his own world like divorce, death, or illness? Is there any trauma going on in his life? Is there anything he is gaining from this insensitive attitude? This one is critical. He has an attitude because it works for him at this moment. What has your kid gained from being insensitive? Does he need the distance and safety of insensitivity to guard himself from pain? For example, some really sensitive kids are forced to "numb out" as a way of defending themselves from vicious teasing and bullying at home or in school.

What. Are there particular issues or things about which he usually is more insensitive? Does he talk frequently about how people look, their ethnicity, age, gender, perceived intelligence, or ability?

Who. Does he display the same insensitive attitudes to everyone? Are there some individuals he is more sensitive toward? If so, who are they?

When. Is there a particular time of day, week, or month he is more insensitive? Is there a reason? For instance, might he be tired, hungry, or needing attention? Or is it when he doesn't get his way or feels slighted?

Where. Are there certain places he is more likely to be insensitive (at school or day care, home, the store, Grandpa's)? Why?

Now seriously review your answers. Do you have any better awareness of why your kid is insensitive and where this attitude is coming from?

WHAT'S WRONG
WITH YOUR CURRENT RESPONSE?

How are you currently reacting to your kid's insensitive attitude? Are you yelling at him, avoiding the whole issue, complaining to everyone else, searching for effective consequences, blaming his friends or school, or blaming yourself? Might you or someone else be dismissing his feelings or concerns as irrational, silly, or insignificant?

What part of your response is *not* working so your kid continues to flaunt an insensitive attitude? Is it your voice tone? Your inconsistency? Ignoring it? Yelling at him? Ask yourself what response is the most ineffective, write it down here, and resolve not to use it again.

I will not _____

_____

FACING OUR OWN BAD ATTITUDES

Did you feel that your parents were insensitive? Were feelings allowed to be discussed in your home? Looking back, were you ever insensitive as a kid? When? Toward whom? How did your parents respond, and how do you look at it now?

What kind of example are you setting for your kid today? For instance, has anybody complained about your being insensitive lately at home or at work? Who complained, and what did that person say?

Is your own attitude teaching your kid to be insensitive? Have you ever corrected your own insensitive missteps in front of your child?

What is the first step you need to take in yourself to be a better example to your sons or daughters of dealing with their insensitive behavior? Write down changes you need to make.

I will _____

_____

_____

BAD ATTITUDE NEWS ALERT

Involved dads can make a major contribution to raising sensitive, empathic kids. A long-term study begun in the 1950s found that children whose fathers were positively involved in their care when they were age five were found thirty years later to be more empathic, sensitive adults than those whose fathers were absent. Another study involving first-grade boys in intact families revealed that kids whose fathers took more responsibility for their sons' discipline and schoolwork and were more involved in their children's personal problems were significantly more tuned into the feelings and needs of others. This was true regardless of the father's own level of empathy.

THE "DON'T GIVE ME THAT ATTITUDE" MAKEOVER

To eliminate your child's insensitive attitude, take the following five steps.

Step 1. Don't Tolerate an Insensitive Attitude

Whenever your child displays insensitivity, stop her in her tracks, and call her on it. Explain in no uncertain terms why you consider the child's attitude to be unacceptable. This is the moment to make sure she clearly understands what is wrong about the attitude and why you disapprove. Your timely intervention helps your child shift her focus from herself to considering the impact of her actions on other people—for example:

"That was insensitive. I expect you to treat your friends the same way you'd want to be treated."
"I'm very concerned when I see you treating your friends without considering their feelings. You may not treat people unkindly."

Step 2. Teach Your Kid Emotional Intelligence

There are three steps to building emotional intelligence:

1. *Help your child learn an emotional vocabulary.* In order for kids to be sensitive, they need to be able to read the feelings of others. To do so, they must have an adequate emotional vocabulary. To develop your child's emotional intelligence, teach him feeling words such as in the list that follows. Consider using a different feeling word each day or a new word each week.

An ABC Emotional Vocabulary

afraid	bored	curious
agitated	brave	cynical
alarmed		
angry	caring	depressed
antsy	calm	delighted
anxious	cautious	disappointed
apprehensive	cheerful	discouraged
ashamed	comfortable	disgusted
awful	concerned	distressed
awkward	confident	disturbed
	confused	down
bashful	content	
bewildered	critical	eager
bitter	cross	edgy

embarrassed	inferior	queasy
encouraged	insecure	
enthused	intense	rejected
enraged	irate	resentful
exasperated	irked	reluctant
excited	irritated	restless
exhausted		riled
	jealous	ridiculous
fatigued	jittery	rushed
fearful	joyous	
fidgety		sad
frightened	lazy	safe
frustrated	leery	scared
funny	lonely	secure
furious	loved	sensitive
	loving	shaky
glad		shy
gloomy	mad	shocked
greedy	mean	silly
grouchy	mischievous	sorry
guilty	miserable	sleepy
	moody	stressed
happy		sympathetic
hassled	nervous	surprised
hateful	nice	suspicious
helpless	numb	
hesitant		terrified
hopeful	overwhelmed	tired
horrible		troubled
hostile	panicky	
hysterical	patient	unsafe
hurt	pessimistic	unsettled
	pleased	uncomfortable
impatient	proud	upset
indifferent	puzzled	

vicious	warm	yucky
victorious	weary	
	wonderful	zany
	worried	

2. *Focus on how other people react.* Pointing out the facial expressions, voice tone, posture, and mannerisms of people in different emotional states sensitizes your child to other people's feelings. As occasions arise, explain your concern and share what clues helped you make your feeling assessment:

"Did you see Meghan's face when you were playing today? She looked worried about something. Maybe you should ask her if everything is okay."
"Dad was trying to do the bills when you butted in. Did you notice how he slumped in the chair when you told him about the car?"
"Did you notice Grandma's expression when you were talking with her today? I thought she looked puzzled. Maybe she is having trouble hearing. Why not talk a little louder when you speak with her?"

3. *Ask frequently, "How does the other person feel?"* One of the easiest ways to nurture your child's sensitivity and increase her empathy is to ask her frequently to "get in their shoes" and ponder how another person really feels. (See also the Role Reversal Game in the Emergency Attitude Rx box.) As opportunities arise, pose the question often, using situations in books, TV, and movies as well as real life—for example:

"When you broke your friend's skateboard, how do you think he felt?"
"The tornado destroyed most of the town here in Georgia; see it here on the map? How do you think the people feel?"

Such questions force your child to stop and think about other people's concerns and nurture sensitivity to their needs.

Step 3. Praise Sensitive Actions and Highlight Positive Effects

Reinforce your child's sensitive attitude as soon as it happens. Let her know how pleased it makes you feel:

"Karen, I love how you picked up your baby sister when she started to cry. You patted her so softly. It makes me happy to know how sensitive you can be."

Sensitive, kind acts—even small ones—can make a big difference in people's lives, so point them out to help your child see the impact his actions made:

"Derrick, your coach was so pleased when you called to ask her if she was feeling better since her surgery."
"Suraya, did you see the smile on Ryan's face when you sat next to him on the jungle gym?"

Step 4. Make the Link Between Feeling and Needing

Ask your kid questions to help him discover that people's feelings lead to people's needs. Such questions expand children's awareness of what others might be experiencing. As a result, children become more sensitive to how they might be able to help:

Parent: Look at that little girl crying in the sandbox. How do you suppose she feels?
Child: I think she is sad.
Parent: What do you think she needs to make her feel better?
Child: Maybe she could use someone to hug her because she hurt her knee.

Step 5. Stifle the Bad Attitude
If Insensitivity Continues

If your child continues to display insensitivity toward others' feelings, then it's time to set a meaningful consequence that's appropriate to your child's age and temperament. For example, forbid your child from playing with a friend until your child understands he must treat others kindly. Your rule is: "If you can't treat people nicely, you can't play." Another option is to demand that your child apologize sincerely to the recipient. This might be drawing or writing an apology or apologizing in person or with a telephone call.

The First 21 Days

Declare that for the next three weeks, your family will have a daily Emotional Intelligence Report. Every member of your family must say, write, or draw one strong feeling they observed in another member of the family that day. The report should label the emotion and then describe why they think the person is feeling that way. Here are some examples:

- "Dad looked really upset today. Maybe it was because his boss is resigning."
- "Kelly seems upbeat and happy. Maybe it's because she got invited to the prom."
- "Matt looks so sad. Maybe it's because he just found out his best friend is moving."

Next, your family needs to practice a specific thing to say or do that could support or nurture the other person's feelings or needs at the time by playing the Emotional Support Game. This can help your kid confirm or clarify if she was correct in understanding what was going on and give her an opportunity to be empathic. Here's how it might work:

- "Dad, are you worried that your big project may be canceled now? Let's take the dog for a walk so you can tell me more about it."
- "Kelly, you look really happy about something. Did you get invited to the prom? Ready to go shopping so we can help pick out a dress?"
- "Matt, how about going outside and playing catch? Maybe the new kid next door would like to join us."

ATTITUDE MAKEOVER PLEDGE

How will you use these five steps to help your kid become less insensitive and achieve long-term change? On the lines below, write exactly what you agree to do within the next twenty-four hours to begin changing your kid's attitude so he is less insensitive and more considerate.

_____

_____

_____

THE NEW ATTITUDE REVIEW

All attitude makeovers take hard work, constant practice, and parental reinforcement. Each step your child takes toward change may be a small one, so be sure to acknowledge and

congratulate every one of them along the way. It takes a minimum of twenty-one days to see real results, so don't give up! And if one strategy doesn't work, try another. Write your child's weekly progress on the lines below. Keep track of daily progress in your Attitude Makeover Journal.

WEEK 1

_____

_____

_____

WEEK 2

_____

_____

_____

WEEK 3

_____

_____

_____

ONGOING ATTITUDE TUNE-UP

Where does your child's attitude still need improvement? What work still needs to be done?

_____

_____

_____

_____

ATTITUDE MAKEOVER RESOURCES

For Parents

Raising Compassionate, Courageous Children in a Violent World, by Janice Cohn (Marietta, Ga.: Longstreet Press, 1996). Practical ways to help children learn the qualities of kindness, courage, and decency.

The Moral Intelligence of Children, by Robert Coles (New York: Random House, 1997). Thorough and research-based ideas on how to raise a moral, compassionate child.

For Kids

A Special Trade, by Sally Wittman (New York: HarperCollins, 1978). When she was young, the little girl's grandfather pushed her in the stroller. Now she is five, and Grandfather has a stroke: the girl pushes Grandfather as he once pushed her. Plain glorious. Ages 3 to 7.

Wilfrid Gordon McDonald Partridge, by Mem Fox (New York: Kane/Miller, 1985). A young boy learns his friend from the old people's home is losing her memory. He sets out to help her find it, and in doing so learns the power of caring. Wonderful. Ages 4 to 8.

Stone Fox, by John Reynolds Gardiner (New York: HarperCollins, 1980). Ten-year-old Willy enters a dog-sled race, so that his grandfather's farm might be saved. Ages 7 to 11.

Indian in the Cupboard, by Lynne Reid Banks (New York: Avon, 1980). An Indian toy given to a young boy comes to life, and through it he learns the value of caring. Ages 8 to 12.

Number the Stars, by Lois Lowry (New York: Dell, 1989). Based on the true, compassionate story of a young Danish girl who sacrifices her life to save her friend from the Nazis. Ages 8 to 13.

Bad Attitude 12

Irresponsible
Antidote: Responsibility, Trustworthiness, Reliability

"How was I supposed to know it was due today?"

Dear Dr. Borba,
I'm ashamed to admit this, but our eleven year old is so irresponsible. She never takes care of her things and needs constant reminders to do her homework. Most of the time, my husband or I end up finishing it—it's almost easier then listening to her excuses. We want her to get good grades, but now I think we're going about it all wrong. Help!

—Courtney L., a mom of three from Tucson, Arizona

Bad Attitude Act Out

"You do my table job, Daddy. I'm watching TV."

"Why should I care when the DVD is due back at the store?"

> "It's my teacher's fault: she didn't check to make sure I wrote down the assignment."

EMERGENCY ATTITUDE

Stop immediately doing anything that compensates for your child's irresponsibility. Do not write one more cover-up note to your child's teacher. Do not do put out the garbage when your kid conveniently disappears. Do not take your kid's overdue library book and pay the fine. Do not go back and get your kid's forgotten soccer shoes for the umpteenth time. Instead, make your kid take the consequences of his irresponsible attitude. Remember that your role is guider, not doer, and that single tweak will do much to change your child's bad attitude.

Any of these sound familiar? "I forgot." "Take care of this for me." "It wasn't my fault." "I did some of it, but I left it on the bus." "I don't know where I put it." They are statements of irresponsible, spoiled kids and part of the Big Brat Factor. And are they ever good at finding excuses for their carelessness! Denying, excusing, blaming, rationalizing, and accusing are just a few strategies these kids use to justify their conduct.

Kids with an irresponsible attitude rarely stop to consider how their actions affect others, and so their attitude is selfish. The world revolves around them, so someone else will—and should in their minds—do their jobs, wake them up, find their toys, and replace items they "misplaced." If they do err, they usually never admit their mistakes, apologize, or take ownership. After all, "It's someone else's fault." In fact, usually everyone *but* them is responsible for their irresponsibility. If this attitude isn't turned around, it will dramatically affect every area in their present and future lives: academic, moral, professional, and social. The replacement attitudes of responsibility, trustworthiness, and reliability are essential for our kids' moral character and future well-being. So let's get started!

BAD ATTITUDE ALERT

Before reforming your kid's irresponsible ways, you need to analyze the beginnings of her bad attitude.

Diagnosis

What exactly does your kid do or say that is irresponsible? For instance, does he not take care of his things? Not take care of other people's possessions? Not finish assignments? Not start assignments? Misplace or lose items? Fail to wake up without constant reminders? Need coaxing, yelling, or bribing to finish chores or expect someone to do them for him? On a scale of one to ten, if you tell your child to do something, how often can he be counted on to follow through and keep his word? The more specific you are in your diagnosis, the more effective you will be in creating a makeover plan.

Why. Why does your kid have this attitude? What does he gain from it? For instance, does he get out of doing jobs or assignments? Does someone pick up the pieces for him? Does it save him from the possibility of failure or embarrassment? Is it just plain easier? Have you been irresponsible toward him? Has he ever been taught to be responsible? Does everyone in your family pull their own weight? What has your kid learned from being irresponsible?

What. What issues or things is he more prone to be irresponsible over? For instance, is it about homework? Library books? Chores? Personal possessions? Other people's property? Clothes? Sports equipment? Curfews? Appointments?

Who. Does he display the same attitude to everyone? Are there some individuals he is more likely to flaunt this attitude on—for instance, a teacher, coach, grandparents? Why do you think he flaunts it toward some people and not others?

When. Is there a particular time he is more prone to use this attitude: Right before school? Dinner? Chores? Homework time? Soccer game? If so, what might be the reason?

Where. Are there certain places he is more likely to be irresponsible (at school or day care, home, scouts, play group, Uncle Al's)? Why?

How. What is the typical way your kid displays his attitude when he is irresponsible? For instance, does he blame someone else? Make up an excuse? Lie? Con someone into doing it for him? Expect someone to take care of the problem he caused? Feign ignorance? Defy your requests? Appear not to care? Accuse you of being irresponsible (*you* didn't remind him, wake him up, put the item back)?

Now take a look at your answers. Are you seeing any predictable patterns? What is your best diagnosis of why your kid has learned this attitude? Confer with other adults who know your kid well to see if they agree. Keep one thing in mind: he uses the attitude because it works. What can you do to teach him it does not work? Now let's look at how you respond to your kid's attitude.

WHAT'S WRONG
WITH YOUR CURRENT RESPONSE?

How do you typically respond to your child's irresponsible actions? For instance, what was the last occasion your kid was irresponsible? Mentally photograph the irresponsible action. Now focus the image on you. What was your response? For instance, did you let him get away with it, or did you hold him accountable? Did you make an excuse for him, or make him apologize? Did you step in and do his assignment or job for him? Do any of these other parental responses to irresponsible attitudes fit you:

☐ *Rescuer.* You come to your kid's aid, and solve his quandaries for him.

☐ *Doer.* You find yourself doing or finishing most of your kid's responsibilities.

☐ *Excuser.* You make excuses for your kid's lack of follow-through or bad attitude.

☐ *Overexpecter.* You put too high or unrealistic expectations on your kid.

☐ *Low expectations.* You minimize the number of expectations you place on your kid.

☐ *Enabler.* You try to make things as easy as possible for your kid.

☐ *Reminder.* You always remind your kid of his assignments, jobs, and schedule.

☐ *Other:*_____

_____

_____

What is the one thing you have tried time after time that you should never do again?

I will not _____

_____

FACING YOUR OWN BAD ATTITUDES

Think about when you were growing up. Were you responsible for doing chores in your home? If so, which ones? Are you responsible now?

Studies have shown that kids a few decades ago were responsible for doing much more around the house than kids today. What has changed in our lifestyles that is causing the decline in kids' responsibilities? How is that affecting our kids' attitudes?

Your kid wasn't born with this attitude, so how did he develop this irresponsible attitude? Seriously consider whether he could be learning it from others—even you! Check ones that apply to you:

- [ ] Do you emphasize the importance of responsibility in your home?
- [ ] Do you blame others for problems and not take ownership for your own actions?
- [ ] Are you always late when picking up your child from school?
- [ ] Do you attend parent-teacher conferences and respond in a timely manner to notices that are brought home from school?
- [ ] Do you make excuses for your problems?
- [ ] Are bills, DVDs, and library books piling up on your table with overdue notices?
- [ ] When you make a mistake, do you admit it? And does your child hear you?
- [ ] Would others say they can count on you to do what you say?
- [ ] Do you take care of your possessions or see property as easily replaceable?

What is the first step you need to take in yourself to help your child deal with his or her irresponsible attitude? Write down changes you need to make.

I will _____

_____

_____

BAD ATTITUDE NEWS ALERT

A recent TIME/CNN poll found that 75 percent of people surveyed said kids today do fewer chores than in the past. There's no denying that today's families are different: most parents and kids are overscheduled and stressed to their limits, and home priorities have dramatically changed. The fact is that chores help kids develop responsibility. Studies also show that doing chores increases the likelihood that kids will become responsible, contributing family members who really do enjoy helping out around the house.

THE "DON'T GIVE ME THAT ATTITUDE" MAKEOVER

To squelch your child's irresponsible attitude, take the following steps.

Step 1. Give Your Kids a Clear Message About Responsible Attitudes

Take time to explain your beliefs and expectations about responsibilities. Consider developing a family motto about responsibility. A father in Atlanta told me that conveying this life message to his kids was so important that they spent an afternoon together brainstorming family anthems about responsibility such as: "We keep our word," "We always do our best," "We can be counted on." They wrote them on index cards, and his kids taped them on their bedroom walls. Develop your own family anthem as a reminder that your family code is always to be responsible and that you expect your kids to convey that belief in their daily actions and attitude.

To assess your kids' understanding of those beliefs, pose questions such as these:

"What are things a responsible person would say and do?"
"What responsibilities do you have in this house? Dad? Mom? The other kids?"
"What happens if you don't follow through on those responsibilities at home or school?"
"How would that affect others?"
"What if I didn't go to work every day? What if I didn't pay the bills on time or take you to the doctor to get your shots on time?"
"What if we didn't pay our taxes? What would happen then?"

Step 2. Expect and Require Responsibility

A big part of changing kids' irresponsible attitudes is to flat-out require responsibilities, and the easiest place to begin is right at home. First, think about the responsibilities you want to delegate to each child. You might even gather the troops and brainstorm together all the things they should be responsible for and additional ways they could help out at home. These might include household chores (watering plants, making beds, dusting), personal responsibilities (brushing teeth, showering), personal possessions (putting toys, bicycles, video games away), and school (do homework to the best of your ability, return library books). Then clearly spell out to each family member your expectations and the consequence for incompletes. (See Step 5.) Go through each responsibility step by step at least once with your kid so that she clearly knows how to do it. This is the time when you can correct any poor habits.

Most kids, especially younger ones, need reminders. Charts using words or pictures that list job assignments, responsibilities, and completion dates are helpful. Even non-readers can "read" their responsibilities on a chart with pictures of what they are expected to do. Kids can then off mark their responsibilities as they are completed.

Whatever you do, don't do any task your child can do for herself. She'll never learn to be responsible if she knows you'll finish the job for her. Recognize your role is helper, not doer. Once you get your role straight, your battles are half over. After all, the work responsibility rests in your kid's hands, not yours. So keep your role straight in your mind as well as in your kids' minds.

Step 3. Teach How to Make Responsible Decisions

A large part of being responsible is making good decisions. Kids toting irresponsible attitudes frequently don't own up to their poor choices, blame someone else for the outcome, or expect to be rescued. If those traits describe your kid, teaching decision-making skills should be a big part of his attitude makeover. Here are a few techniques:

- **Ask if-then questions.** To help narrow choices and think about possible outcomes, teach your kid to ask himself after each selection, "If I do that now, will I still feel okay about it tomorrow?" "What about next week?" Teach one decision-making rule: "Eliminate any choice that you may regret later."
- **Be a fortune-teller.** Tell a younger kid to pretend to be a fortune-teller: "How will I feel tomorrow if I chose that today?"
- **Weigh pros and cons.** To help an older child weigh the pros and cons of each possibility, have him ask himself: "What are all the good and bad things that might happen if I chose that?"

Step 4. Don't Excuse Excuses

Irresponsible kids often try to get out of their responsibilities by making excuses (or fibbing, inventing justifications, or lying). So set a new family policy: "We do not excuse excuses." Then the very next time your kid tries shirking his responsibilities with an attitude, enforce the policy, and help him find a solution to his problem so there is no excuse.

Suppose your kid makes an excuse for his misplaced library book: "How can I remember where it is? I can never find anything around this house!" Your response to the attitude is: "That's an excuse. We don't make those in this house. We're going to figure out right now what you can do so it won't happen again." One excuse-busting solution that a parent and child created was to have the child set aside a box near his bedroom door for his library books; then he taped a big card to the box with the due date plainly visible. The result: no more excuses or lost library books. Here are a few more examples of kid excuses turned into solutions:

- *"I was too busy to put my toys away."* A young child draws himself a picture of a box or shelf as a reminder that the rule is: "Not later but now" or "As soon as you stop playing, you put your toys away."
- *"I didn't know what time the game started."* Your kid writes his time schedule and posts it on the refrigerator or bedroom door. A young child can draw a clock face showing the time.
- *"I forgot to give the note to you."* Your child sets aside a basket near the front door. As soon as he walks in the house, he must empty his backpack and put any teacher notes in the basket.
- *"It got too late to do my homework."* The new house rule is: "Homework must be done (and done well) before play or entertainment."

Step 5. Set a Consequence
If the Bad Attitude Continues

If your kid continues displaying this attitude, it's time to set a consequence; your child must learn to be accountable for his actions. There should be a consequence, and the most effective ones always fit the crime, cause a bit of misery (so your kid will want to change his attitude), and are consistently enforced. Above all remember, no more excusing your child and no more "rescuing." Here are a few examples of logical consequences for being irresponsible:

- *Didn't clear up a food mess.* If your younger child has left her ice cream cone to melt on the counter, enforce the rule:"No more ice cream cone for two days."
- *Forgets to put dirty clothes in the hamper.* If your kid doesn't put her dirty clothes in the hamper, she won't have clean ones and must wait until the next wash cycle.
- *Failure to do chores.* If kids are paid for chores, withhold their allowances.
- *Destructiveness of property.* Anything that your kid broke, tore, or lost (whether the property belongs to your kid or another), he must replace or repair it. He also must pay for it by earning the money. If he has none, make a list of house chores he can do with an appropriate price value (vacuuming: $2.00; raking: $3.50) to pay off the damaged property.
- *Unfinished assignments.* If homework isn't finished by a predetermined time—ideally, the same time each night—your kid knows he will lose a desired privilege either that evening or the following day.
- *Forgets to bring lunch money.* She doesn't eat lunch that day, and she *will* survive. Chances are also high she *will* remember to bring money in the future, especially if she knows you won't be rescuing her.

Step 6: Reinforce Responsible Actions

Change is never easy, especially when kids have been using irresponsible attitudes for a while. So don't expect instant success in this makeover. Do also remember to acknowledge your kid's effort for trying every step of the way and celebrate improvements—for example:

"Jeremy, it took courage admitting you were responsible for breaking the neighbor's window. Thank you for your honesty."

"Kim, I noticed you finished your work before watching TV. That was being responsible."

The First 21 Days

It's time to carry out a Major Responsibility Campaign in your home. Give your child a really important job, and trust her to do it. If she's younger, it might be making her responsible for growing a little lima bean garden (or something else that she likes). Start by giving her a packet of seeds, and get her started in the planting process. Then trust her to water them every day until they grow to a height that's ready to transplant into your yard. Watch her face light up when her plants sprout, and the beans are ready to eat.

For an older kid, find a project that requires skill building, dedication, and perseverance—perhaps making a family Web site, researching and planning a family vacation, adopting an abandoned dog or cat from the animal shelter and taking care of it, or earning enough money to buy a cell phone or other electronic gadget of his choice.

ATTITUDE MAKEOVER PLEDGE

How will you use these six steps to help your child become less irresponsible and achieve long-term change? On the lines below, write exactly what you agree to do within the next twenty-four hours to begin changing your kid's attitude so he is more responsible.

_____

_____

_____

THE NEW ATTITUDE REVIEW

All attitude makeovers take hard work, constant practice, and parental reinforcement. Each step your child takes toward change may be a small one, so be sure to acknowledge and congratulate every one of them along the way. It takes a minimum of twenty-one days to see real results, so don't give up! And if one strategy doesn't work, try another. Write your child's weekly progress on the lines below. Keep track of daily progress in your Attitude Makeover Journal.

WEEK 1

_____

_____

_____

WEEK 2

_____

_____

_____

WEEK 3

_____

_____

_____

ONGOING ATTITUDE TUNE-UP

Where does your child's attitude still need improvement? What
work still needs to be done?

_____

_____

_____

ATTITUDE MAKEOVER RESOURCES

For Parents

_Didn't I Tell You to Take Out the Trash: Techniques for Getting Kids to Do
Chores Without Hassles,_ by Foster W. Cline and Jim Fay (Golden,
Colo.: Love and Logic Press, 1996). The importance of chores and
tools for getting kids to do them without hassles.

_Raising a Responsible Child: How Parents Can Avoid Overindulgent
Behavior and Nurture Healthy Children,_ by Elizabeth M. Ellis (New
York: Carol Publishing Group, 1995). Creative solutions to helping
kids take responsibility for their own actions and earn privileges—
without your stern looks and threats.

Teaching Children Responsibility, by Linda and Richard Eyre (New
York: Ballantine, 1984). A must-read: the classic in teaching kids
responsibility using practical and _real_ solutions.

_The Procrastinating Child: A Handbook for Adults to Help Children Stop
Putting Things Off,_ by Rita Emmett (Toronto: Anchor Canada, 2002).
A unique guide with dozens of practical ways to help your kid stop
putting off what they are responsible for doing _NOW._

Pick Up Your Socks . . . and Other Skills Growing Children Need, by Elizabeth Crary (Seattle, Wash.: Parenting Press, 1990). Well-structured content for parents to assist their kids in developing skills and then developing self-motivation.

For Kids

A Child's Book of Responsibilities, by Marjorie R. Nelsen (Longwood, Fla.: Partners in Learning, 1997). Ten child-centered categories illustrated in a clever book. Kids flip the cards themselves to the "I did it" pocket when they are finished. Ages 3 to 6.

Sam Who Never Forgets, by Eve Rice (New York: Greenwillow, 1977). Sam the zookeeper never forgets to feed the animals in his care. Ages 4 to 7.

How to Do Homework Without Throwing Up, by Trevor Romain and Elizabeth Verdick (Minneapolis, Minn.: Free Spirit Publishing, 1997). Hilarious cartoons and text provide helpful homework tips and insights. Ages 6 to 12.

Bad Attitude

13

Jealous
Antidote: Thankfulness, Trust, Forgiveness

"She's so pretty, I just hate her."

Dear Dr. Borba,
We are blessed to have four great daughters, but we're really con-
cerned about our youngest. She's so jealous of her friends and sisters
and is never satisfied with being herself. She always compares herself
to others and says she's just not pretty, smart, or plain good enough.
What can we do to help our daughter appreciate her own qualities
instead of always being so envious of others?

—Karen C., mother of four from Minneapolis, Minnesota

Bad Attitude Act Out
"Daddy, why can't I be rich like Tim?"
"You like my friends more than me!"
"Why bother: I'll never be as thin as her!"

EMERGENCY ATTITUDE

Focus on the one specific issue or individual who seems to get your kid's jealous streak boiling most. What turns your kid's eyes the greenest?

☐ Appearance: hair, weight, height?
☐ Abilities: musical talent, grades, athletic skills?
☐ Material possessions: cell, Barbie dolls, CD collection?
☐ Fashions: shoes, jewelry, hats, jeans?
☐ Peers: being included or even invited?

Pick one at a time only, and then find the true source of the issue. If it's an authentic need to be more competitive, then help your child do better at whatever it is. If it's math and you can help, spend some serious time going over her homework and preparing her for tests. If she is lagging behind her team-mates on the soccer field, buff up her endurance by going on a run with her every night. If you feel for any reason that you're unable to do this, then find a way to bring in outside help. If her jealousy is an unrealistic feeling based on insecurity, for attention or approval, materialistic greed, or lack of confidence, then address that issue on a more personal level. For example, if you just had a new baby, find more time to do things together; if he is too shy to make new friends, then coach him in social skills to overcome his shyness. Pick the worst aspect of your child's jealous attitude, and don't let up until you've found where it comes from and wiped it clean.

Jealous kids always wish they could be, do, or have the success, good fortune, possessions, or qualities of others. Never satisfied with who they are or what they have, they compare themselves to others: "She's smarter." "He's more popular." "They're wealthier." "She's prettier." And each longing to be "more like her" (or "him" or "them") strips a little more of gratitude for what they have, replacing it with resentment and self-centeredness.

There are many reasons kids become "green-eyed," but certainly a big contributor is today's popular culture, which intensely tries to convince kids how they "should look" and what they "must have" to be "popular" and "with it." Envying those peers who meet that tough criterion (at least in a kid's eyes) is bound to be inevitable for those who can't meet the standards. And today's advertisers take advantage of preadolescents' insecurities. Marketers spend billions on kid-directed commercials of "must-have" fashions, electronic gadgets, and toys. Oh, the envy if a kid gets one of those coveted items and they don't.

Then there are all those music videos, TV shows, films, magazines, and billboards constantly pushing the supposed ideal physical benchmark to our kids. The image for girls is super-thin (with no trace of body fat), a perfectly proportioned figure, flawless skin, and long, flowing hair. For guys, it is being tall, having a well-built muscular physique, and displaying a macho swagger and attitude. And, oh, the pain of being a kid and trying to fit in: for some, the only way to measure up is by wishing to be someone else.

Of course, misguided parenting also turns kids' eyes a darker emerald shade. For example, these days, fierce contests to see whose precious offspring can stockpile the most trophies (for higher grades, game scores, beauty competitions, school admissions) also fuel peer resentment big time. After all, in any contest, one kid always comes out "the winner" (kid translation: "He's better." "She's prettier." "He's smarter."), leaving others in the dust wishing they could have the same qualities. High hopes for our kids' success also ignite envy: "Why can't you get grades like Chelsea?" "Try kicking like Kevin. He *scores.*"

And don't ever forget that our own jealous desires are picked up by kids' radar: "How did the Levys afford that Lexus?" "Sally looks so good—it *must* be Botox." "Jim and Carol are invited to *everything.*" Hmmm.

So where is this coming from? Are kids with jealous attitudes just victims of the Big Brat Factor, the culture, the media, the peer group? Not necessarily. Many kids are expressing jealous attitudes because they're desperate for attention and appreciation. They may be feeling especially insecure, inadequate, or unable to live up to family or peer standards and expectations. You may need to read between the lines of their jealous words to find the true scared, lonely self hiding behind the envy and craving.

Of course, jealousy doesn't just pit peer against peer, classmate against classmate, and neighbor against neighbor; it invades our homes as well. Most parents would agree that one of the most frustrating forms of jealousy is sibling rivalry. Much as we try to make our kids feel loved, they accuse us of showing favoritism: "You love him more than me!" If not curtailed, those early envious sibling feelings can slowly damage family relationships and remain forever. It's just all the more reason we need to curb our kids' jealous attitudes, and the sooner the better. After all, envy wasn't named one of the Seven Deadly Sins for nothing. This sin damages our kids' moral growth, self-esteem, social relationships, and family harmony. It must be replaced by the virtues of thankfulness, trust, and forgiveness. So get moving on this makeover!

BAD ATTITUDE ALERT

Before you start altering your kid's jealous ways, tune into where this attitude is coming from, why it developed, and how your kid uses it.

Diagnosis

Answering these questions will help you pinpoint the cause of your kid's jealous streak so you can begin turning this bad attitude around.

Why. What is causing your kid to be so jealous? Does he lack self-esteem or self-confidence? Does he lack friends and social skills? Does he perceive he is being constantly compared to another peer or sibling? (And might he be correct?) Does he feel his relationship with you or the other parent is contingent on his achievement? Are scores, grades, or competition placements valued more than character in your home? Might your child feel as though his place in the family is somehow in jeopardy? For instance, is there a strain in your marriage, are there new stepsiblings, or are you engaged in a new relationship? Does your child feel resentful because he feels a lack of control or influence? Might he be hearing you or your spouse talk enviously about others? Pretend you are in the shoes of the child who feels jealous. How would you feel if you were your kid? How would you act? Be honest: Is his jealousy justified? Why?

What. Are there particular issues or things he is usually more jealous about? Are they about possessions (electronic gadgets, fashions, toys)? Popularity? Appearance (weight, height, hair, physique)? Capabilities (intelligence, athletic)? Sense of humor? Wanting the same amount of attention? Feeling privileges aren't equal with other kids? Perceiving unfair treatment (rules and discipline are not fair)? Are his jealous feelings justified?

Who. Who is your kid most jealous about: a friend, classmate, teammate, sibling, you? Why? What might be fueling that resentment? Does he display the same jealous behaviors toward everyone? Are there some individuals he is not jealous of? If so, who? Why not? How do you know he is jealous? Does she verbalize her jealousy, treat someone else unfairly, spread rumors, leave that person out, or act aggressively toward her?

When. Is there a particular time of day, week, or month when he is more jealous—for instance, when Dad comes home or when the game gets more competitive? Is there a reason? Might he need attention or reassurance? Is another sibling receiving more attention? Also, when did this attitude start? If you can identify the time, what might have triggered the jealousy: A new baby? A move? Your new relationship? Your new work schedule? A more competitive or difficult classroom?

Where. Are there certain places where or events when he is more likely to be jealous at school or day care, home, the store, Grandma's)? Why? What situations seem to escalate peer or sibling rivalry?

Now take a look at your answers. Are you seeing any predictable patterns? Do you have any better understanding of your kid's jealous attitude and where it's coming from?

WHAT'S WRONG
WITH YOUR CURRENT RESPONSE?

Think of the last time your kid displayed this attitude. What did you do? For instance, did you ignore it? Chastise or scold him? Confirm he was right? Criticize him? Tell him jealousy is "a sin"? Dismiss his feelings? Tell him "not to worry"? Humiliate him publicly? Agree with him? Is this how you typically respond to your child's jealousy?

And might you be doing anything to fuel this attitude? For instance, do you compare his grades to those of the kid next door? Spend time acknowledging your nephew's sports talents? Praise another child for being so thin? Push your kid to try playing that instrument because his brother excelled at it? Might you be responding in a way that is causing your kid to wish he were more like someone else?

What response have you learned does not succeed in stopping your kid's jealousy? Write down the one response you will never do again.

I will not _____

_____

FACING YOUR OWN BAD ATTITUDES

Think about when you grew up: Were you ever jealous? What was that about? How long did it last? Did you keep it in or display it? If so, how? Were your parents aware of your envy? Did they ever talk to you about it?

Would those who know you well say you are a jealous person? Whom are you most envious of: Your spouse? A sibling? A friend? A neighbor? Why? What kinds of things are you most prone to be jealous over? For instance, is it about appearance, money, weight, clothing? Abilities, talents, possessions, or status? Do you voice your envies to friends? Your family? Your colleagues? How often do your kids hear you verbalize your jealousies? Do you do anything to try to improve those areas in yourself?

Our kids are most prone to display jealousy with siblings. Of course, much as you'd hope you aren't showing favoritism toward one child, sometimes we do so quite unintentionally, and the seeds of sibling rivalry are sown. So take a good long look in the mirror, and see if any of *your* attitudes and behaviors might be triggering your kid's jealous streak. Here are a few questions to help you assess how well you're doing in making all your kids aware of their own unique qualities and feel special in your eyes. Mark any potential problem areas, and then make a pledge to improve them. Get into your child's shoes for a minute, and respond how you think your child would answer:

- [ ] Do you automatically expect more of your oldest child?
- [ ] Do you coddle your youngest?
- [ ] Does each kid feel like your favorite?
- [ ] Do you avoid comparing your kids in front of others?
- [ ] Do you provide opportunities for each child to nurture her special talents?
- [ ] Do you openly listen to each child's concerns?
- [ ] Do your eyes light up with the same intensity when you see each of your kids?
- [ ] Do you schedule equal one-on-one time with each child?
- [ ] Do you avoid taking sides whenever there's a conflict between your kids?
- [ ] Do you pay equal attention to each child's hobbies, friends, school, and interests?
- [ ] Do you set rules and expectations for each child that your other kids consider fair?
- [ ] Do you distribute chores, rewards, and opportunities fairly among your kids?

Next, ask yourself if you might be comparing your child to other kids. Could your child be feeling as though he is being measured against other kids, and might this be where he is picking up this jealous streak? For instance, when your child shows you his graded work, do you ask the grades of the other kids? Do you ask him what his friends are doing over the weekend? What invitations they received? Which camp, sports, and music lessons they are attending? The bottom line is whether your child might sometimes feel he is being compared to his peers. Do remember that the nonverbal messages you give out—a smirk, subtle shrug, frown, or raised eyebrow—are just as powerful as your verbal ones. Take a serious look in the mirror at nonverbal cues you might be sending your kid anytime involving a discussion about his peers.

If the jealousy issue is predominantly a sibling rivalry problem, talk to your kids individually, and find out what they enjoy most (and least) about each sibling. It might help you assess what's going on between them. Ask if they have any suggestions that might improve their relationship. Is there a suggestion you could use? If so, what will you do to begin to implement the idea? What will you do to change your relationship with this child so he feels just as special in your eyes?

What will you do to be a better example to your son or daughter? Write what you will do, and then commit to doing it.

I will _____

_____

_____

_____

BAD ATTITUDE NEWS ALERT

Many parents say that sibling rivalry is among the most frustrating form of jealousy. Renowned pediatric experts William Sears and Martha Sears cite four factors that affect the intensity of sibling rivalry: (1) each sibling's natural temperament, (2) how parents feel about and relate to each kid, (3) conditions parents create to encourage sibling harmony, and (4) how much sibling warfare parents allow. The Searses stress that while parents can't influence the first factor, they do affect the remaining three.

THE "DON'T GIVE ME THAT ATTITUDE" MAKEOVER

To help eliminate your child's jealousy, take the following steps.

Step 1. Identify the Cause

Here are a few of the most common causes of jealousy. Check the ones that may apply to your child:

☐ *She may need more attention.* Do you favor a sibling, or does she feel that you do? Are there other relationships or commitments that may interfere with your time with her?

☐ *She feels insecure.* Does she lack confidence or self-assuredness?

☐ *She wants peer approval.* Does she lack friends? Does she feel the way to gain entry or be popular is to be like others?

☐ *She feels the need to compete.* Is competitiveness (for grades, scores, popularity, status) emphasized in your home? Does she feel she must compete against others to gain your approval?

☐ *She craves the latest material possessions.* Does she feel that certain possessions are absolutely necessary to maintain status among peers?

☐ *She is compensating for a lack of control.* Has something happened at home that she can do nothing about (a divorce, an illness, a financial setback)?

☐ *She lacks self-esteem.* Is she jealous of another child's abilities, appearance, or qualities because she feels she isn't worthy, lovable, or likeable? Is she constantly compared to others and realizes she can never make the grade?

☐ *She feels things aren't fair.* Is one sibling treated differently? Is she experiencing harsher treatment? Are standards and expectations unequal? Is she correct in her view? Does a parent or teacher always come to the other child's defense and not hers?

Identifying the specific source of your kid's jealous attitude will help greatly in turning it around.

Step 2. Refrain from Comparisons

Never compare or praise one kid's behavior in contrast to that of a peer or sibling: it can create long-lasting strains. "Why aren't you organized like your friend?" All too easily, kids can interpret such comparisons as: "You think he's better than me." Here are other points to keep in mind:

- *Never compare work.* Kids should compare their schoolwork, test scores, and report cards only to *their own* previous work, never to the work of their siblings or friends. Instead of stimulating a child to work harder, comparisons are more likely to fuel resentment. Or they may say, "You love him more than me." It unfairly puts pressure on the child you praised and devalues your other child.
- *Refrain from comparing behaviors.* Never compare or praise one kid's behavior in contrast to a sibling: it can create long-lasting strains: "Why can't you be more like your sister?" "Why aren't you organized like your brother?" All too easily, kids can interpret such comparisons as, "You think he's better than me" or "You love him more." It unfairly puts pressure on the sibling you praised and devalues your other child.
- *Stop comparing appearances.* Telling your child that another child is thinner, more handsome, better groomed, or has nicer hair or dresses better can be devastating. "Maybe she could help you lose some weight." "I wish you had hair like he does."
- *Never complain about achievements.* Not every kid comes in first, so let your child know you're satisfied with her just doing her best. Do not say, "Why didn't you get a trophy, too?" or "How come you didn't get first prize in English?"

Step 3. Minimize Conditions That Cause Rivalry

Treating kids equally is unrealistic: they come packaged with different temperaments, interests, and needs. So don't drive yourself too crazy trying to make things always fair when your kid says you're not. It just isn't realistic. Besides, real life isn't fair. The trick is to minimize conditions that break down sibling or peer relationships and can cause long-lasting resentment. You can also do the same when your kids' friends come to visit. Use the following ideas to guide you in minimizing jealousy and disharmony among peers and siblings:

- *Listen openly.* Listening fairly to your kids is a powerful way to convey that you respect each child's thoughts and want to hear all sides: "Thanks for sharing. Now I want to hear your brother's side." The key is to build a fair relationship with each sibling so that he or she knows that you value each opinion and are an unbiased listener.

- *Don't take sides.* During conflicts among friends or siblings, stay neutral, and make suggestions only when your kids seem stuck. Taking sides builds resentments and feelings of favoritism.

- *Don't encourage complaints.* Make one rule stick: unless your child is reporting a peer or sibling problem that could lead to injury, don't buy into it. Doing so often leads to rivalry and jealousy. Once the rule is set, be consistent: "Is this something you can't work out yourself?" or "Is this helpful or unhelpful news?" The rule works wonders in curbing tattling, putting others down, and gossip.

- *Nurture together time.* If sibling rivalry is the issue, maybe it's time to rekindle your relationship with your child so she doesn't perceive favoritism. One of the easiest ways is by having your child spend more "alone time" with you. Capitalize on those individual moments as they arise: "Your brother's asleep. Let's read books together." Or make a date with each sibling to have special time with just you, and mark it on the calendar. Then enjoy each other without other siblings around.

Step 4. Nurture a Unique Skill or Quality

All kids can benefit from knowing what makes them unique. The more you can expand your child's awareness of his qualities, the greater the likelihood is that he will value his identity and not feel resentful and jealous about others. Here are the four keys to unlocking your child's awareness of his special qualities:

- *Identify strengths.* Choose one or two positive qualities you want your child to recognize about herself right away—for example, her artistic abilities, a sense of humor, kindness, grace, strength, flexibility. Make sure the strengths are already present in your child, not ones you wish were true about her.

- *Praise the quality.* Find opportunities to praise the talent or strength frequently. You can start out by giving one strength message a day, and gradually work your way up to two to four strength reminders. Be specific in your praise, so that your child knows exactly what she did to deserve recognition: "You're very open-minded; you always seem to listen to everyone's ideas before you form an opinion." "You're so caring. I noticed how you stopped to ask that older woman if she needed help crossing the street." "You always seem to have something upbeat and positive to say about people. It brightens everyone's day."

- *Develop the skill.* If your younger child is graceful, enroll her in ballet; if she is musically inclined, give her music lessons. If your teen has a flare for fashion, find a modeling class to join. Cultivate your child's talent so she can improve that special quality and boost her self-confidence.

- *Support the special quality.* Find ways for your child to demonstrate his qualities to others. If he is artistically inclined, he might design your family stationery. If she is athletic, enroll her in a sport so you can cheer her abilities at games.

Step 5. Show How to Deal with Jealousy

Jealousy doesn't always bring out the best in kids. They can wallow in self-pity and want our sympathy. They might mope around, making their lives as well as ours quite miserable, or diss the person they long to be most like with complaints, gossip, or put-downs. So what do you do when your kid turns into a green-eyed little critter? Here are a few points:

- *Target the issue.* Don't rush too quickly to sympathize. Your first goal is to find out what is really bothering her and triggering the issue: "You seem really jealous of Sally. Do you wonder why she was invited to Rosemary's party and you weren't?"
- *Clarify feelings.* Sometimes all that is needed is for someone to acknowledge the jealous child's feelings. Try it: "You're hurt because you think Jake is being treated more fairly than you are." "You're frustrated because you're not getting a turn at Nintendo."
- *See it from the other side.* Kids often get so caught up in jealousy or feeling they're being treated unfairly that they don't stop to think how the other person might be feeling. So ask, "See it from the other side now. How does your friend feel?" This also builds empathy.
- *Challenge the jealous view.* If your child says, "The coach likes Sam better. He always gets to play," question his view: "I know you're disappointed you don't get to play as much as Sam. But why do you think the coach lets Sam play more? Could it be Sam's a good player? Is that something you want? What can you do to improve your skills?" The trick is to get your kid to understand there may be something else to the issue; maybe the other child practices more or is a better sport, for example.
- *Point out past successes.* When your child's jealousy is directed toward another kid's success, point out past successes: "You're right, Bill did win the art award. You won the award last year."

- **Offer ways to cope.** "I know you're really disappointed right now that you weren't chosen for the team and Kara was. Unfortunately, there are going to be a lot of times we don't get things to go the way we want. Let's think of things you can do when you're feeling down to make yourself feel better."
- **Congratulate the winner.** "I know you're envious of Jennifer for placing. Even though you wish you could trade places, you can't. But you can congratulate her. People usually remember you more for how you handled defeat than how you won. How will you congratulate her success?"

The First 21 Days

Start a Family Gallery of Blessings Project. It's a simple way to document all the good things your child and family should be thankful for, such as their unique talents, strengths, and special qualities. Doing so will help your child refocus from what he doesn't have (and enviously covets in others) to what he does. Here are a few project ideas for kids of varying ages to rediscover the blessings right in front of them:

- **Photo collage.** Put together photo images showing each family member's unique strengths and contributions (for example, Dad's humor, Mom's warm smile, Noah's rock climbing, Brooke's riding skills).
- **Family Blessings scrapbook.** Log the developing talent of each family member in a bound scrapbook or a few stapled blank pieces of paper. It's best to track one or two talents only (such as "The Chronology of Ben's Tennis Skills") with updated notations about

---

the talent. For younger kids, consider photographing or drawing their talents and gluing them into their own personal scrapbook.

- *Accomplishment Journal.* Give each child a blank journal or composition notebook. Encourage them to record their accomplishments and successes in the journal on a regular basis.
- *Family Blessings Web site.* Put up your own family Web site displaying your family's talents and blessings. This is a fun way to get the whole extended family involved. Links to everyone's e-mails and the Web site can become a family newsletter as well.
- *Hall of Fame.* Put up a bulletin board for your kids to display their best work and talents.

ATTITUDE MAKEOVER PLEDGE

How will you use these steps to curb your kid's jealously and achieve long-term change? On the lines below, write exactly what you agree to do within the next twenty-four hours to begin changing your kid's attitude so he is less jealous and more appreciative of the differences of others.

_____

_____

_____

THE NEW ATTITUDE REVIEW

All attitude makeovers take hard work, constant practice, and parental reinforcement. Each step your child takes toward change may be a small one, so be sure to acknowledge and congratulate every one of them along the way. It takes a minimum of twenty-one days to see real results, so don't give up! And if one strategy doesn't work, try another. Write your child's weekly progress on the lines below. Keep track of daily progress in your Attitude Makeover Journal.

WEEK 1

_____
_____
_____

WEEK 2

_____
_____
_____

WEEK 3

_____
_____
_____

ONGOING ATTITUDE TUNE-UP

Where does your child's attitude still need improvement? What work still needs to be done?

_____
_____
_____

ATTITUDE MAKEOVER RESOURCES

For Parents

Envy: The Enemy Within, by Bob Sorge (Ventura, Calif.: Regal Books, 2003). A book to help adults explore the basis of their own green-eyed ways.

Overcoming Jealousy, by Wendy Dryden (London: SPCK and Triangle, 1999). A simple adult book with a Christian base that cuts right to the meat of the issue: Why are you jealous, and what can you do about it?

Siblings Without Rivalry: How to Help Your Children Live Together So You Can Too, by Adele Faber and Elaine Mazlish (New York: Avon, 1998). An absolute must parenting book that covers sibling jealousies and fighting, and intense rivalries.

Loving Each One Best: A Caring and Practical Approach to Raising Siblings, by Nancy Samalin (New York: Bantam, 1997). A guide for parents that offers advice on how to deal with competing demands, sibling rivalry, stress, and feelings of guilt and inadequacy.

For Kids

Katie Did It, by Becky Bring McDaniel (Danbury, Conn.: Children's Press, 1994). The youngest sibling always gets blamed for all her siblings' mishaps until one day she takes credit by doing something wonderful all by herself. Ages 4 to 8.

7 × 9 = Trouble, by Claudia Mills (New York: Farrar Straus Giroux, 2002). A third-grade boy struggles learning his multiplication facts. If only he were as smart as Laura or as quick as his brother. Wilson learns he doesn't have to be jealous; if he keeps on trying, he'll succeed at his own speed. Ages 7 to 10.

Losers, Inc., by Claudia Mills (New York: Scholastic, 1997). Always comparing himself to others, the boy considers himself a loser—that is, until he finally learns to find worth in himself. Ages 8 to 12.

The Pain and the Great One, by Judy Blume (New York: Simon & Schuster, 1984). An eight-year-old sister and six-year-old brother tell all about each other and the contest to see whom Mom and Dad loves most. Ages 5 to 10.

Behind My Back: Girls Write About Bullies, Cliques, Popularity, and Jealousy, by Rachel Simmons (New York: Harvest Books, 2004). Bestselling author of *Odd Girl Out* writes a powerful book. For preteen and teen girls.

14

Judgmental
Antidote: Tolerance, Fairness, Compassion

"You're stupid!"

Dear Dr. Borba,
My ten year old is so judgmental that I'm starting to be concerned.
He's constantly putting others down with critical comments like,
"You're such a dummy," or "Can't you do anything right?" His
brothers don't want to be around him; who knows when he'll start
doing the same to his friends? I'm hoping you can tell me how to
turn his attitude around (or if it's even possible to do so). I'm even
wondering if something else is going on that's making him so difficult.

—Joan R., a mom of three from Little Rock, Arkansas

Bad Attitude Act Out

"None of the boys in my class are good artists."

"This family sucks! Everyone always says the same ol'
crappy stuff."

> "Why go? I'm sure it's going to be a dumb movie and everyone going is dumb."

EMERGENCY ATTITUDE ℞

Stifle your own judgmental or critical comments. It's okay for parents to be teachers and guides, but that doesn't give you a license to condemn your kids' activities, trash their choice of friends, or dismiss their opinions. So stop making those sarcastic comments, critical observations, and barbed remarks. This kind of negative attitude can quickly become a household epidemic. Remember that quick and nasty judgments can sting and really cause emotional damage. You're the model for demonstrating constructive criticism, so start tuning into what you're saying so you can model and pass on a less judgmental attitude right away.

"Books suck." "You're a dummy." "She needs a brain transplant." Judgmental kids tend to find only the inadequacies in themselves and others, and put everything and everyone down. Beneath their judgmental attitudes can be arrogance, a feeling of inadequacy, hostility, anger, or resentment. They are hypercritical and enormously frustrating, and can turn almost any event into "not fun" for one and all. Although negative attitudes used to be confined to the middle school set, even younger kids are now adopting them and can be part of the Big Brat Factor.

Make no mistake: this attitude is also rude and self-centered. That's because judgmental kids don't usually care how their criticism affects others. They are concerned only about *their* sense of superiority or inferiority, and *their* opinions, and they make sure everyone knows.

Keep in mind that kids aren't born critical: research clearly shows this attitude is learned. And today's culture bombards our youth with negative messages. Need evidence? Tune into popular musical lyrics, and notice how often you hear criticism and despair. Eavesdrop on kids' conversations, and count the number of negative comments you hear. Listen to TV sitcoms and hear the steady onslaught of put-downs. Is it any wonder that many kids are negative?

Granted, changing negative ways isn't easy, but left unchecked, this attitude will seep slowly and steadily into every arena of kids' lives and often serves to derail them from developing solid character. Judgmental attitudes are contagious and can spread quickly throughout your household. What your child needs is to replace these bad attitudes with the virtues of tolerance, fairness, and compassion. The time to start this attitude makeover is now!

BAD ATTITUDE ALERT

The key to unlocking your child's judgmental mind-set is discovering it's true source. So check out the diagnosis process below and follow it step-by-step.

Diagnosis

You can develop a specific plan to help change your kid's judgmental attitude by answering these Five W's of Attitude Awareness.

Why. What is your best guess as to why your kid is so critical? Is he mimicking the attitude of others in the family? Looking for attention? Seeking to provoke a reaction? Wanting revenge? Overexposed to negative messages? Think what might be provoking his judgmental attitude. Next, eliminate more serious causes. For instance, could your child be anxious about something or suffering from low self-esteem? Talk to other adults who know your child well. Ask them if they think any of these factors could be provoking negativity.

What. Is there any particular thing your child expresses negativity about? Is there a pattern? For instance, is he more negative when it comes to schoolwork? Any particular subject? A teacher? A sport?

Who. Who are the primary recipients of his negative barbs: a sibling, cousin, friend, teacher, coach, babysitter? You? Why? Are there some individuals he does not use his negative ways on? If so, who? Why not? Are there particular situations or people who cause the negative behavior to flare up? Or is he mostly negative toward himself? Why?

When. When did the attitude start? Were there any new events that happened around the same time—a new teacher, school difficulties, relationship frictions, a hectic schedule, a family change—that might have triggered the attitude? Are there times of the day or circumstances where you don't see negativity? Why or why not? Write down any patterns you notice.

Where. Are there certain places he is more likely to be negative (at school, home, the store, Grandma's)? Why? Are there particular situations or places that cause the attitude to flare up?

Now take a look at your answers. Are you seeing any predictable patterns? Do you have any better understanding of your kid's judgmental attitude and where it's coming from?

WHAT'S WRONG
WITH YOUR CURRENT RESPONSE?

First, ask yourself how you respond to your child's highly judgmental attitude. Could your response be stoking his negativity?

Typical parental responses that provoke a judgmental attitude in kids often end in "-ing": insulting, judging, criticizing, scolding, humiliating, threatening, and yelling. If any of these fit your parenting style, how will you change your response?

Think of the last time your kid displayed his negative ways toward you. How did the episode begin? What did your kid say or do? What did you do? How did this episode end? Did any of those "-ing" parental responses enter into your interaction with your kid? Even one small change can make a big difference. Write one thing you will never do when your kid flaunts his negativity.

I will not _____

_____

FACING YOUR OWN BAD ATTITUDES

Reflect on your own childhood. Did you think of yourself as a critical or constructive kind of person? Did you use words to get even, express anger, or put down others in a spiteful or arrogant way? How did your parents respond? Did it help curb your bad attitude?

How about now? Judgmental attitudes are learned. Your kid forms much of his attitude from absorbing and mimicking others. Tune into the kinds of language used in your family. Are the interactions on the whole more positive or negative? Would your family assess your household atmosphere as warm, accepting, and positive or more critical and negative? Take an honest look at family members to make sure that isn't the source. What about his friends? Neighbors? Cousins? TV? Peers? Music? Coach?

Now make a serious appraisal of your attitude and what you might be modeling to your kid. For instance, do others think of you as more affirmative or more critical? Are you moody? Occasionally cranky or hostile? Do you tend to see the good or the bad things in people? How often do you verbalize those critical messages to your kids? On the whole, do you say more positive or negative comments? What about how you interact with your kids on a day-to-day basis? Do you typically dish out more criticism or praise? Would your kids agree with your estimation?

It's time to make a commitment to replace your kid's negativity, and the starting place is by changing your own behavior. What is the first step you need to take in yourself to be a better example to your sons or daughters in dealing with their negative behavior? Write down changes you need to make.

I will _____

_____

BAD ATTITUDE NEWS ALERT

A national survey cited by the National Parent-Teacher Organization found that the average parent makes eighteen critical, negative comments to his child for every one positive comment. Are you becoming a negative role model for your kids?

THE "DON'T GIVE ME THAT ATTITUDE" MAKEOVER

To eliminate your kid's judgmental attitude, take the following steps.

Step 1. Dig Deeper

There may be a number of reasons for a judgmental attitude. Here are a few:

☐ A kid may really feel confident that he knows better and is smarter than anyone else. This may be a by-product of youthful arrogance or the fact that you've made this little critter feel as though he's the center of the universe and every word from his lips is gold.

☐ He may be overcompensating for a sense of inferiority or lack of confidence. He cuts and slashes as a defense against feeling he's inadequate.

☐ He may be retaliating in a hostile or aggressive manner to the critical abuse he's been getting at home or in school.

☐ He may somehow have learned to be intolerant of diverse perspectives and identities or may be unable to handle complexity or ambiguity.

☐ He may be a part of peer culture where it is "cool" to be negative, to put down everything and everyone.

Before beginning your campaign to reverse your kid's bad attitude, take a hard look at where it's coming from.

Step 2. Accentuate the Positive

The first step to squelching your kid's negative attitude is captured in the lines of a great old song: "You have to accentuate the positive to eliminate the negative." After all, the best way to learn any new attitude is by experiencing it, so begin your kid's makeover by intentionally stressing a more positive outlook in your home so he does. Here are a few ways to do so:

• *Model positive self-talk.* Kids often learn negativity from listening to others, so deliberately say more positive messages out loud so your kid overhears them—for example, "I love the recipe I used today. I really liked how it turned out." "I'm proud of myself: I stuck to my 'to-do' list today and finished everything I'd planned." You may feel strange affirming yourself at first, but once you notice your kid copying the positive comments, you will overcome any hesitancy.

- **Create a family covenant.** One way to curb critical comments that members say to themselves or each other is to establish a moratorium against them. Gather everyone together and say, "In this family, put-downs are not allowed. They tear people down on the inside, and our job in this family is to build people up." Take a vow as a family to squelch them by creating a family care covenant that clearly spells out in writing that critical comments are not permissible in your family. After all members sign it, post it in a visible place as a concrete reminder.

- **Monitor negative consumption.** Tune in closer to what your kids listen to and watch: TV shows, Internet, musical lyrics, video games, and movies. How much of it is providing a negative outlook on life? Are any changes needed? If so, turn off any media that might be contributing to your kid's negativity.

- **Bury put-downs.** Many teachers have shared with me an activity they say is powerful in reducing classroom negativity called a "put-down funeral." The ceremony begins with the teacher asking students to write as many negative comments as they can think of on slips of paper. The comments are placed in a shoebox, and the students march solemnly to the playground, where they bury the box. The symbolic gesture clearly conveys to the class that those negative comments are buried and never to be used again. They are dead. Consider holding a put-down funeral in your back yard.

Step 3. Teach Positive, Appropriate Alternatives

Negative kids often say so many critical comments that positive ones are temporarily misplaced, forgotten, or even lost. Sometimes kids don't feel comfortable saying positive comments because they haven't practiced them enough. Don't overlook that you might actually have to teach or reteach your kid how to be positive:

- **Teach encouraging words.** Start by explaining to your kid that one of the easiest ways to make the world a kinder place is by saying encouraging, caring words. You might ask, "What are words you say or you hear others say that make people smile and feel good?" Then make a poster of ideas and display it. Here are a few to get you started: "Tell me what I can do." "I enjoyed that." "Hope you feel better." "Do you need anything?" "Are you all right?"
- **Institute the Two Positive Rule.** Launch a strategy called the Two Positive Rule: the child must say at least two positive comments during a specified time period. You might begin in the safety of home by challenging your family every night for a week: "Everyone must say at least two positive comments before they leave the dinner table."
- **Say positive comments.** Encourage your kid when his friend comes over: "Remember to tell your friend at least two positive comments before he leaves." Finally, when your kid leaves your house, gently remind him of the rule: "Remember to say two positive comments today."
- **Practice positive attitudes.** Continue finding practice opportunities for your kid to use the rule until positive comments become a natural part of his daily speech replacing negative ones.

Step 4. Challenge the Judgment

If your child has a consistently judgmental attitude, you may be able to temper it by confronting the content of what he's saying. Every time he makes a sweeping carte blanche judgmental statement, challenge him to prove it. At first (or with younger kids) you'll have to guide him through the process. But once he understands he must prove what he says, he'll start speaking less judgmentally.

Stage 1

Kid: All jocks are stupid.

Parent: The facts show that a number of athletes in many
sports are downright brilliant.

Stage 2

Kid: Kevin is really a wimp.

Parent: So give me an instance when he's not. I can think of
a few.

Kid: Okay, he swims ten laps a day.

Stage 3

Kid: I hate hip-hop music. Wait a minute, I actually like a
lot of it. There's good hip-hop and bad, but the last one
I bought really sucks.

Step 5. Penalize Put-Downs

If you've consistently tried other strategies and you're still
hearing a steady blast of judgmental comments coming from
your kid's mouth, it is time to take matters up a notch. She
needs to know that a judgmental attitude can hurt. Here are
three consequences appropriate for varying ages. Choose one
consequence, and then *consistently enforce it.* Your kid must
know you mean business:

- *Turn negatives into positives.* A great rule to combat negativity is called: "One negative = One positive." Whenever a
family member says a negative comment, the sender must
turn it into something positive. If your kid says, "This is stupid. Why do we have to do this?", encourage him to turn the
statement into something positive: "Okay, if I clean my closet,
I'll have some room." Enforcing the rule gradually dimin-
ishes negative statements—but you must be consistent.
- *Issue a sincere apology.* Enforce a household rule: anytime
you say a hurtful, put-down comment, you must sincerely
apologize to the recipient. The apology must state (1) why

you are sorry, (2) how you think the recipient feels, and (3) what you will do to make amends. An example is: "I'm sorry I said you were stupid. I know it made you feel bad. I'll try not to say it again, but if I slip, I'll do your chores for a day." The apology may also be written, or young kids can draw it.

- **Use a put-down jar.** Create a new house rule: "Any family member who says a put-down comment must put twenty-five cents of his or her money in the jar for each offense—parents included! If you're short of money, you must work it off." Then set aside a jar and post a list of twenty-five-cent chores. When the jar fills up, the family brings it to their favorite charity.

The First 21 Days

Start a Negative Comment Count-down Plan by keeping track of every critical comment family members make around the house each day. You may be surprised at just how many put-downs, sarcastic or cynical slams, or judgmental statements are uttered on a regular basis. Then for the next twenty-one days, everyone must commit to reducing their negative messages. At first, each time anyone says a critical comment, he or she has to say a positive one. Slowly the ratio of negative to positive comments will start to change. Ideally, set a goal that by the end of the twenty-one days, everyone says at least two positive comments for every negative one. You may be surprised how this strategy alone changes your family dynamics and may dramatically decrease your kid's judgmental attitude.

ATTITUDE MAKEOVER PLEDGE

How will you use these steps to help your kid become less negative and judgmental and achieve long-term change? On the lines below, write exactly what you agree to do within the next twenty-four hours to begin changing your kid's attitude so he is more positive and upbeat.

_____

_____

_____

THE NEW ATTITUDE REVIEW

All attitude makeovers take hard work, constant practice, and parental reinforcement. Each step your child takes toward change may be a small one, so be sure to acknowledge and congratulate every one of them along the way. It takes a minimum of twenty-one days to see real results, so don't give up! And if one strategy doesn't work, try another. Write your child's weekly progress on the lines below. Keep track of daily progress in your Attitude Makeover Journal.

WEEK 1

_____

_____

_____

WEEK 2

_____

_____

_____

WEEK 3

_____

_____

_____

ONGOING ATTITUDE TUNE-UP

Where does your child's attitude still need improvement? What work still needs to be done?

_____

_____

_____

ATTITUDE MAKEOVER RESOURCES

For Parents

Positive Self-Talk for Children: Teaching Self-Esteem Through Affirmations, by Douglas Blouch (New York: Bantam Books, 1993). A wonderful guide that instructs parents, step-by-step, how to help toddlers to teens turn off the negative voice within and activate the powerful "yes" voice.

Raising Positive Kids in a Negative World, by Zig Ziglar (New York: Ballantine Books, 1996). Written by the popular motivational speaker Ziglar, this book offers sensible guidelines on raising positive, happy kids.

For Kids

Chrysanthemum, by Kevin Henkes (Hew York: Harper Trophy, 1996). Chrysanthemum always thought her name was perfect—until she started kindergarten and the kids made fun of it. A perfect book for young kids about name-calling and put-downs. Ages 4 to 8.

Positively Mother Goose, by Diane Loomans, Karen Kolberg, and Julia Loomans (New York: H. J. Kramer, 1991). These rhymes are a delightful twist on the traditional Mother Goose tales. The authors have turned the old rhymes into new positive, affirming ones. For young ones.

The Pushcart War, by Jean Merrill (New York: Dell, 1984). A satire on the garbage strike in New York City and how negativity began to spread to all. Ages 10 to 13.

The Meanest Thing to Say: Little Bill Books for Beginning Readers, by Bill Cosby (New York: Scholastic Trade, 1997). A plain wonderful way to help kids learn a lesson of a prosocial way to combat meanness and name-calling. Ages 4 to 8.

Lord of the Flies, by William Golding (Upper Saddle River, N.J.: Prentice Hall, 1959). The classic novel about a group of English schoolboys stuck on a deserted island and the destructiveness of put-downs. Ages 12 to 15.

Bad Attitude **15**

Lazy
Antidote: Industriousness, Perseverance, Productivity

"Can you make my bed, Mom?"

Dear Dr. Borba,
I can't believe I'm admitting this, but my nine-year-old son is so lazy. I don't know where he gets this attitude: my husband and I work our tails off and have four jobs between us just to make ends meet. Our other two kids have such a strong work ethic that I have to tell them not to study so hard. But our youngest kid somehow has the notion that he's privileged and doesn't have to work as hard. Just getting him do his homework is a nightly battle. Any ideas as to how we can turn his attitude around?

—Jaynie B., a mom of three from San Diego, California

Bad Attitude Act Out
"Yeah, I know I'm supposed to water the plants, Mommy, but I just like to lie here and watch TV."

"Come on, I raked the leaves last week."

"All the teacher told us was copy the words. Why should I study them too?"

EMERGENCY ATTITUDE R

Be lazy yourself, and see how your kid likes it. Most kids don't have the foggiest idea of how exhausting it is when you have to do for them what they've been too lazy to do for themselves. Go further: stop doing what they ordinarily expect. See how they feel when you don't do their laundry, make their beds, pick up their toys, clean their bathrooms. Once they understand that everyone has a job to do and there are consequences if they are not done and done well, they will have taken the first step in changing their lazy ways.

"If only he'd apply himself!" "She always takes the easy way out." "I've never seen anybody so good at wasting time!" If you've had any of those thoughts about your kid, you may have the makings of a spoiled, brat "work-a-phobic" on your hands. Rest assured, you are not alone: the ailment is spreading. Lazy kids want to take the easy road, and so they take shortcuts, put out minimum effort, and certainly don't work up to their potential. The end result is always predictable for anyone affected with the disease: their feelings of accomplishment are greatly undermined, and their character is diminished.

Often laziness is just a symptom or strongly related to other bad attitudes like irresponsibility, insensitivity, and self-centeredness. It may also be a result of avoiding the pain of failure or depression or some long-term or recent trauma. Or it could be you're putting so much pressure on your kid that he's stressed out about meeting your expectations and may not have the necessary skills or natural talent to fulfill your goals. In some cases, kids who appear to be lazy are in fact suffering from a lingering, low-level chronic illness. Be sure to have your child's health evaluated.

Do keep in mind that willfully lazy kids shortchange not just themselves but others as well. Because they don't do their fair share, fail to get their jobs done, or just plain expect someone else to do their work for them, their attitude is selfish. Don't think for a second that lazy kids stop to consider how their attitude affects others. My best advice is to curb this attitude and do so quickly! Being labeled lazy is deadly to any kid's reputation. Need proof? Would you hire a lazy kid as an employee, pick one for your team, or choose her as a friend? Exactly! What everyone wants is an individual who is industrious, perseverant, and productive. So get busy with this makeover.

BAD ATTITUDE ALERT

Prior to expecting an end to your kid's lazy attitude, try to discover whether this is really a sign of irresponsibility or something deeper like a fear of failure or a sense of hopelessness.

Diagnosis
Ask yourself these questions.

Why. Why does your kid have this attitude? Here are a few questions: Is he expected to work? Is his work load realistic? Are there set chores or work expectations? Does he see others working? Are things such as TV, video games, or friends too much of a distraction from work? Is he capable of doing the work? Is he spoiled and expects someone else to do the work for him? What is your best guess as to why your kid is lazy or why he can't remember, has low energy, seems over-whelmed, has poor time management, is easily distracted, or is discouraged? Might he have some chronic illness or health problem? Might he be smoking marijuana or abusing alcohol? Have you considered his mental state? Could he be depressed or feeling powerless?

What. What particular issues usually bring out your kid's lazy ways: homework, reading, exercise, putting away toys, feeding pets, practicing an instrument, cleaning his room? What about competition? For example, does he always feel he couldn't make the team even if he tried out, that he wouldn't be elected anyway, or that he would never be admitted to that college? It helps to make a list of issues that usually cause frictions. List also things that do not cause problems. For instance, maybe you don't see this attitude emerge when it comes to cleaning his bike, working on the computer, playing the drum, or practicing basketball. Reread your list: Do you see any pattern? For example, you may discern that he is laziest about school-related issues but quite industrious when it comes to practicing his swimming strokes. You can then ask the key question: Why? For instance, if a kid is lazy predominantly about school-related issues, then he might have problems organizing, prioritizing, concentrating, handling complex tasks, or even knowing how to study. What is your best guess?

Who. Does he display the same lazy attitude to everyone? Are there some individuals he does not use his lazy ways on? If so, who? Why not? Are they responding differently? Expecting more or less? Modeling how to do the task? Reinforcing his efforts? Not being so critical? Also, does he demonstrate this attitude only around his friends? Why? Is this peer pressure where he doesn't want to be seen as a "kiss-up," nerd, or goody-goody? Do his friends label him lazy? Or does he pull this attitude only around siblings? If so, is there a jealousy or rivalry issue?

When. Is there a particular time of day, week, or month he is lazier than at other times? If so, what might be the reason? For instance, might he be tired, overscheduled, overwhelmed, or stressed? Or is it that it's homework, music lesson, or chore time? Is this kid of yours always lazy or lazy during certain times? What's the pattern here? What's the reason?

Where. Are there certain places he is more likely to be lazy (at school or day care, home, on the baseball field)? Why? Now get even more specific. If school is the place where your kid is most lazy, where in school does this show up: during spelling or math, practicing handwriting, or during physical education? Why? Is it that he doesn't want to do the work or that he has trouble doing the work? That is a huge difference. If it's the latter, then this is not a "lazy" issue; it's an academic issue and your kid is using his lazy attitude as perhaps a way to cover up for humiliation, shame, self-consciousness, or failure. Don't overlook what might be triggering the attitude.

Now take a look at your answers. Are you seeing any predictable patterns? Do you have any better understanding of this attitude and where it's coming from?

WHAT'S WRONG
WITH YOUR CURRENT RESPONSE?

Your next task is to reflect on how you typically respond to your child's laziness. For instance, are you more likely to criticize, scold, yell, lecture, plead, coax, threaten, bribe, help him, do it for him, give up, or something else? Would your kid agree with your analysis? Are you really taking the time to get into your kid's shoes and figure out if her lazy attitude could be covering up a deeper problem?

Now think of the last time your kid displayed her lazy ways toward you. What was the task? How did the episode begin? What was your kid doing at the time? How did you announce your expectations? How did your kid respond to you? How did the episode end? Did your response alter your kid's attitude in any way? If not, what is the one thing you will never try again?

I will not _____

_____

_____

FACING YOUR OWN BAD ATTITUDES

Kids are not born lazy, so where is your kid learning this attitude: Siblings? Friends? Neighbors? Relatives? You? For instance, do you take the easy way out, side-skirt your duties and hope someone else will pick up the pieces, minimize your effort on tasks that you don't enjoy? Do you sit back and expect your family or hired help to do your work for you? How often do you finish what you set out to accomplish? Would your kids see that you aim to finish what you start—without procrastinating—and you put your best effort into those tasks?

Here's another way of looking at it. Have you ever been accused of being lazy when really it was that you weren't feeling well or you were preoccupied with some problem in your life? Have you ever neglected daily responsibilities because you were so distracted by a crucial life decision or were developing a relationship?

Seriously reflect on your work ethic and the example it sends to your kids. What would your kids say is your daily example and attitude about work? Would their perception of you match your picture of yourself?

What is the first step you need to take in yourself to be a better example to your sons or daughters of dealing with their lazy attitude? Write down changes you need to make.

I will _____

_____

_____

BAD ATTITUDE NEWS ALERT

Researchers discovered that people who don't sense they are moving toward their goals are five times more likely to quit and three times less likely to feel content with their lives. That's just one of the reasons that we have to help our kids set goals and then put effort toward achieving them so they feel productive and satisfied with themselves. How satisfied is your daughter with the kind of life she is carving with her own productivity?

THE "DON'T GIVE ME THAT ATTITUDE" MAKEOVER

To eliminate your child's lazy attitude, take the following steps.

Step 1. Evaluate Your Kid's Physical and Mental Health

Be sure that your couch potato isn't suffering from some kind of illness or chronic fatigue. When was the last time you took him to the pediatrician for a checkup and blood work? And could this lazy attitude be part of a mood swing? Think if anything distressing has happened lately to cause your kid to be distracted or withdrawn. Could this be normal adolescent development, or could his hormones be acting up? Has there been any unusual pressure or stress on him lately? Have you moved? Is he at a new school? Has he been harassed by a bully? Are his classmates overly competitive? Is he over-scheduled? What about a change at home: a divorce, death, or illness? Is he depressed? Did you know that adolescent depression has increased 1,000 percent in the past three decades? Could your older kid be experimenting with drugs or drinking, which leaves him tired and debilitated? You may discover that your child's lazy attitude is not simply irre-sponsible or selfish but rather the result of a deeper under-lying issue.

Step 2. Model Productivity

Take a pledge, especially this month, to show your kids that you don't give up on a task even when things get difficult. Before starting a new task, make sure your child overhears you say, "I'm going to *work hard* until I am successful." Modeling the trait is always the number one teaching method, so con-sciously tune up productivity in your behavior. Your kids need to see examples of serious work both in your house and out of it. This is the best way for them to understand that life isn't all fun; sacrifice and hard work are part of it too. And it's the best way to get ahead. Here are a few other ways you can set an example for your kids:

- *Work when your kids work.* When your kids do their homework, make a point of doing productive tasks such as reading, writing your correspondence, finishing financial business, or organizing to-do lists, *not* watching TV.
- *Model organization.* Get your kids to go through the cal-endar and make priorities and lists with you.
- *Show your responsibilities.* Take the kids to your office or other workplace, or enlist them to help you in your house-hold tasks (grocery shop, clean, make lists) so your kids see you work and understand what your day is about.
- *Discuss work.* Talk with your kids about work and how your day was.

- *Talk about work responsibilities.* Turn off the car radio, and talk about your day and theirs.
- *Set a clear routine.* Make a clear policy at home: work first, then play.
- *Organize your chaos.* Develop work space so your kids have their own "office space."
- *Show interest in your kid's work.* Take an interest in what your kid is working on and doing.

Step 3. Teach the Value of Effort and Hard Work

I walked into a classroom at William F. Davidson School in British Columbia and instantly knew the teacher was emphasizing perseverance. A large hand-printed sign greeted her students with Thomas Edison's quotation, "Genius is one percent inspiration and ninety-nine percent perspiration." The teacher told me, "I put it up weeks ago and told my students the best way to guarantee their success is not by being lazy, making excuses, and procrastinating but by working hard. I never realized how effective that poster could be: my students are not only quoting it—but also modeling it!" By continually emphasizing the importance of productivity and hard work, her students "caught" her message and incorporated it into their own lives. Here are a few ways to help kids understand how critical industriousness is to achieving success:

- *Discuss industriousness.* Take time to explain that *industriousness* means working hard and hanging in there until you complete the task you started. Then use the word frequently to help your kids understand how important the trait is in their lives.
- *Reinforce productivity.* When your kids work hard and stick to a task, point it out: "There's industriousness for you. You hung in there with your work even though it was hard."
- *Teach "Don't Give Up" words.* Help your children tune into the language of persevering individuals so they can learn to use the terms in their own life. Ask, "What are the

kinds of things you hear people who don't give up say?" Write a list of phrases such as: *I can do it! I'll try again. Don't give up! I won't quit! This is hard, but I'll keep going. I'll give it the best I have.* Hang up the poster with the heading, "Don't Give Up Words," and encourage everyone to say at least one phrase a day.

- **Establish a family motto.** If you haven't already, begin a family motto that emphasizes the attitude of productivity, such as: "Try, try, and try again, and then you will win." "In this family, we finish what we start." "Quitters never win." "It's not good enough just to start. You have to finish." You might even write your motto on index cards and tape them on the refrigerator or kids' bedroom walls.

Step 4. Teach Organization to Curb Procrastination

Lazy kids are often disorganized and can't find things in their messy spaces. Their bedrooms, closets, backpack, and notebooks are often in disarray. If you open their lockers, you better be wearing a hard hat. So teach them how to eliminate clutter and chaos from their lives. The goal is not to turn your kids into neatniks, but to clear a space in their physical environment, and consequently their minds, so their life can be more organized.

Purchase simple "getting organized" equipment. Help your younger child organize toys and clothing with special boxes, storage bins, drawers, and hangers. For older children, invest in more sophisticated tools and equipment like Day Timers, file cabinets, and electronic organizers.

Step 5. Emphasize Prioritizing

Some kids are overwhelmed with tasks because it seems that they will never be able to complete them. "There's too much work on the page." "How can I do all this at once?" So help them to break up the task into more manageable pieces. Here are a few possibilities:

- Divide your child's homework into smaller pieces, and tell her to do "one chunk at a time." She could even take a short break after completing each chunk. Chunking assignments is often helpful for kids who have difficulty sticking to a task, have shorter attention spans, or are overly concerned with making sure "everything's right!"
- Increase the size of each chunk after your child has completed a few assignments successfully.
- Older children can start a calendar daily, weekly, or monthly, and parcel out tasks as to when they need to be completed.
- Help your child create a list of things to do numbered in order of importance. An older child should be taught to update the list on a regular basis. A young child can draw reminders of a few tasks that need to be done daily.

Step 6. Reinforce Effort and Productivity

Once your child has begun to make a real effort to overcome his lazy attitude, stay with him every step of the way with continuing support, reinforcement, and appreciation. Regular praise can make work seem less like work. Pride in accomplishment can go a long way. Here are some ways to reinforce your kid's productivity and effort:

- *Appreciating effort.* "Every time you play that piece, it's sounding a little bit better. Keep up the good practice."
- *Praising the product.* "Nice job on making your bed. The quilt looks so much better on the bed than on the floor."
- *Expressing pride in front another adult.* "Hey, Norma, doesn't the car look great? Eddie did such a good job on the hub caps."

The First 21 Days

Turn your whole family around. Launch an Anti-Laziness Campaign before this bad attitude starts to dominate every aspect of your household life. Laziness can become habit forming before you know it. First, identify two or three crucial areas needing improvement. Is everyone in your family getting fat from eating too much junk food? Is everyone becoming sluggish from a lack of exercise? Is your house such a mess you're praying for no visitors? Are you watching too much TV? Has your family stopped going to church, taking family hikes, or eating dinner together?

Pick one of these problems and replace your current passive approach with a proactive day-by-day campaign. For instance, institute a daily exercise routine; put a moratorium on TV (or at least set a maximum viewing time per day); plan a big neighborhood party so you have to clean up the house and yard; start saying a blessing before every meal. The important thing is to be aggressive about sticking to whatever routine you've chosen and make sure everyone is on board.

ATTITUDE MAKEOVER PLEDGE

How will you use these steps to help your kid become less lazy and achieve long-term change? On the lines below, write exactly what you agree to do within the next twenty-four hours to begin changing your kid's attitude so he is more industrious and productive.

_____

_____

_____

THE NEW ATTITUDE REVIEW

All attitude makeovers take hard work, constant practice, and parental reinforcement. Each step your child takes toward change may be a small one, so be sure to acknowledge and congratulate every one of them along the way. It takes a minimum of twenty-one days to see real results, so don't give up! And if one strategy doesn't work, try another. Write your child's weekly progress on the lines below. Keep track of daily progress in your Attitude Makeover Journal.

WEEK 1

_____

_____

_____

WEEK 2

_____

_____

_____

WEEK 3

_____

_____

_____

ONGOING ATTITUDE TUNE-UP

Where does your child's attitude still need improvement? What work still needs to be done?

_____

_____

_____

ATTITUDE MAKEOVER RESOURCES

For Parents

The Myth of Laziness, by Mel Levine (New York: Simon & Schuster 2002). Written by an acclaimed pediatrician, put this on your must-read list if you have any concerns about your kid touting a lazy attitude. Packed with research, case studies, and helpful solutions.

The Procrastinator's Handbook: Mastering the Art of Doing It Now, by Rita Emmett (Toronto: Doubleday Canada, 2000). If you're noticing that laziness and procrastination may be an attitude plaguing you as well as your kid, here's the perfect book offering great solutions that inspire you to get started. For teens as well as adults.

Put Your Rear into Gear: Understanding and Breaking Free from Procrastination, by Jeanine Reiss (Kelwona, B.C.: Lifeworks Publishing, 2000). A simple format offering situations and solutions dealing with procrastination. For teens as well as adults.

The Procrastinating Child: A Handbook for Adults to Help Children Stop Putting Things Off, by Rita Emmett (New York: Random House, 2002). Practical tips for tackling youthful procrastination.

For Kids

Rudy (Columbia Tristar Home Video, 1992). Based on a true story of a working-class boy whose goal is to play football at Notre Dame despite a mediocre academic record and athletic ability. Well, he makes it! PG.

The Journey of Natty Gann (Walt Disney Home Video, 1985). A young girl during the depression of the 1930s journeys to join her father who is logging in the Pacific Northwest. It's a story of hope, courage, tenacity, industriousness, and not giving up. Rated PG.

16

Manipulative
Antidote: Truthfulness, Integrity, Trustworthiness

"If you give it to me, I'll be your best friend!"

Dear Dr. Borba,
We have an absolutely charming eleven year old. He's intelligent, good looking, and a fabulous athlete. Our concern is that he's so darn manipulative about trying to get his way. Every issue turns into a battle of wits, and it's us against him: he twists our words, pretends he's helpless, blames others, and basically wears us down until he wins. He's so good at coming up with excuses that we can't figure out when he's telling the truth. We're beginning to feel as if we're on one of those reality survival shows, and we're losing! Any tips?

—Manuel B., a father from Phoenix, Arizona

Bad Attitude Act Out
"Daddy would let me stay up late. Why are you so mean?"

262

> "I'll do it for five bucks—but that's my last offer."
> "That teacher has it in for me. She's to blame, and it's not my fault."

EMERGENCY ATTITUDE ℞

From this moment on, change *your* behavior, call the manipulation for what it is, and absolutely refuse to give in, regardless of what your kid is trying to obtain or accomplish. You're right, it won't be easy; in fact, it could be exhausting. But remember one thing: *manipulators must rely on someone else for their ploys to win.* It takes two for a manipulation to occur. For his scheme to succeed, another person must believe his fib or his make-believe helplessness, write his excuse, accept the blame, buy into the guilt, or just plain wear down and acquiesce. Take a solid vow that you will not be used as a pawn in your child's manipulative games. Then pass that message onto anyone and everyone he's been taking advantage of so you're all on board together and his attitude stops.

"Dad said I could." "The teacher didn't tell me." "You don't love me." "I *promise* I'll do it tomorrow." "My stomach hurts: I can't go to school." Manipulative kids have only one objective: to get things to go *their* way. And they will stop at almost nothing to maintain their candidacy in the Big Brat Factor Hall of Fame. Excusing, blaming, fibbing, threatening, and guilt tripping are just a few of the devices they resort to. And can they wear you out!

Manipulative **263**

But what's really going on here? Are these manipulative critters just young psychopaths in the making? At times you may think so. But do keep in mind one key point: these kids were not born scheming, plotting, lying, and strategizing. They learned those devices as ways to get what they want. And once their ploy succeeds, look out! It is stored in their growing arsenal of manipulative tactics with almost one certain guarantee: it will be used again . . . and again . . . and again—*but only, only, only if you allow it to.*

Learning the craft of manipulation is never acquired overnight, and a manipulator's tactics do not start out so cunning, sophisticated, and devious. In fact, first attempts are often quite crude and usually unintentional. They pretend to be sick, they claim to be helpless, or they hold out for some unreasonable reward—and much to their surprise, it works! Through trial and error, even the youngest cherub learns what buttons to push on each loved one and figures out who are the easy marks.

For instance, a three year old learns that meltdowns are amazingly effective in getting Mom to buy her a toy. A five year old quickly recognizes that affectionate embraces and sugarcoated charm work wonders to get Dad to say yes. A seven year old realizes that comments like "You don't love me" slung just at the right moment are fabulous for spinning Mom's parental guilt into acquiescence. They beg Dad to please, please, please do their science project, and what do you know, he does it. So their little fibs become bigger lies; off-the-cuff excuses turn into devious explanations; blame games become more elaborate; and the web of deception grows bigger and wider. Meanwhile, the kid becomes better skilled and proficient as a con artist. Ah, just what you always dreamed of raising.

In fact, let's give these kids some credit: manipulators are very ingenious at finding ways to get what they want. They alter rules to go *their* way, bend values to fit *their* schema, take advantage of situations to meet *their* needs, and depend on you or anyone else to take on *their* responsibilities. They can stop at nothing to make the world turn the way they want it to, and so they are also selfish, rude, and very self-centered.

These kids are difficult and tough to live with. They can turn your words into mush, exhaust you to tears, and make you wonder if there's an ounce of intelligence left in your head. They're that good in their manipulative ways! But letting them win is disastrous, and for a number of reasons. For starters, manipulative attitudes squelch kids' ability to manage life's ups and downs. That's because they take great pains to avoid whatever ails them (be it frustrations, fear, work, relationships). So instead of learning ways to cope, they take the easier path and shirk their troubles. Doing so stifles their potential for developing self-reliance, resilience, and self-esteem. Nor do devious, dishonest, scheming tactics enhance kids' ethical development. In fact, manipulative attitudes are absolutely lethal to a kid's character. Each deception rips a little more from their conscience and moral growth. Finally, there's the obvious: a manipulative kid can destroy family harmony, a parent's trust, and everyone's peace of mind.

Where is this behavior coming from? Start by looking at your own reaction to your child. You may have brought up your kid to depend on bribes, assume you'll jump in to do all the heavy lifting, blame everyone else when something goes wrong. He may also have observed your own manipulative behavior, like breaking promises to him or acting in an insincere or devious way yourself. Or he may have watched family friends and peers being manipulative at home, in school, or at work. Or it may even arise from his deep feelings of insecurity, distrust, shame, or fear of failure.

So stop being manipulated. In fact, what are you waiting for? Begin the campaign to replace this bad attitude with truthfulness, integrity, and trustworthiness. Start this makeover *now.*

BAD ATTITUDE ALERT

Gear up for this makeover by contemplating why your kid is manipulative, and how it plays out in your home.

Diagnosis

Answer these questions to help you consider why your child is using this manipulative attitude and what he is gaining from it.

Why. There are many reasons that kids may be manipulative, dependent, and blaming others, but the central issue usually revolves around trying to avoid something or someone. What could your child be trying to avoid: work, humiliation, fear or pain, possible failure, jeopardizing a relationship, punishment, losing your approval or love, coping with an insecurity or anxiety, taking responsibility? What is your best guess as to why your kid is manipulative?

What. Are there particular issues or things about which he usually is more prone to using manipulative ways: doing his chores or homework; taking a bath, eating dinner, or brushing his teeth; going to bed alone or on time; practicing violin or a sport; going to school, day care, or the babysitter's; or going to the dentist or doctor?

Who. Manipulative kids are great at figuring out who will cave in to their devices. So who are the individuals most likely to fall under your kid's manipulative ways? The babysitter? Day care worker? Teacher? A relative: cousin, aunt or uncle, grandparent? Coach? A friend, classmate, or peer? A sibling? You? Your spouse? And who are those he doesn't use his manipulative antics around, and why not? A big clue is how those individuals respond to your kid's ploys.

When. Is there a particular time of day, week, or month he is more manipulative? Is there a reason? For instance, does it show up every Saturday morning at ten o'clock when, coincidentally, it's the time that family chores are to be done? Or does it show up almost like clockwork every night around eight o'clock when she gets clingy and demanding (and it's also bedtime)? You might even want to track his manipulative ploys on a calendar; usually there is a pattern. Maybe report cards are due, the piano recital is coming up, or it's her turn to stay at Dad's. Look for a pattern.

Where. Are there certain places he is more likely to be manipulative (at school or day care, home, the store, piano lessons, on the soccer field)? Why? Does she tend to win at certain places? Does she pull out the charm at the store, so you will buy her the toy? Does he throw a fit at hockey practice because he wants you to take him home? Does she fake a stomachache during the piano lesson because she hates it? There is a reason, so try to discern it. What might your kid be trying to avoid?

Review your answers carefully. It also helps to compare notes with others who know your child well. Are you seeing any predictable patterns? Do you have any better awareness of this attitude and where your child's manipulative attitude is coming from? Is there anything you can do to remedy it? Write down any thoughts.

WHAT'S WRONG WITH YOUR CURRENT RESPONSE?

Think about the last few times your kid employed his manipulative schemes on you. What tactic did he use? What was the issue about? And most important, how did you respond? Did you threaten or scold? Argue? Plead, coax, or bribe him to act right? Ignore him and hope the attitude would go away? Tell another adult to deal with it?

Did you address his manipulative attitude at all and make him accountable? If so, how did that happen? Did you make him apologize? Did you encourage him to admit he was quite capable of doing whatever it was himself? Make him do what he was trying to avoid? Ground him or remove a privilege? Was it effective in squelching his attitude or not? Why? Or did you give in to his manipulative tactic and let him win? If so: Did you write an excuse? Do his responsibility? Blame the person? Let him off the hook? Sympathize? Why did you give in? What did your kid learn from your giving in?

Manipulative kids are great at recognizing what works so the manipulated parent gives up and once again they get their way. So what has your kid learned about you? How is he able to push your buttons so you finally acquiesce? Does he play on your impatience? Your desire to pump up his confidence? Has he learned your weakness for his self-pity, his charm, or his posture of helplessness? Might it be that he can recognize when you're on overload: if he keeps it up a little longer, he figures he'll just wear you out? You just don't have the energy to deal with it? Or do you believe him (or want to believe him)? Could it be that you want to save face before he pulls his antics in front of others? You're afraid you'll harm his self-esteem? You don't think it's worth jeopardizing your relationship with your kid?

What is the one response you know does not work? Write it so you will remember to never use it again.

I will not _____

_____

FACING YOUR OWN BAD ATTITUDES

Did you ever manipulate your parents? Of course, you did, but how much and over what issues? For example, was it over a missed curfew, a bad grade, going somewhere without permission, blaming your little sister for something you did, or avoiding a music lesson, schoolwork, recital, or doing chores? What tactics did you use? For instance, did you fib, use your charm, debate them to death, feign helplessness, play one parent against the other, aim for their sympathy? Did they ever call your bluff? Which parent was the easier mark? Which parent was tougher to manipulate? Why? What were their hot buttons that if you pushed enough, they'd give in?

What about now? Do you ever try manipulating a situation at home or work so it comes out in your favor? Who are you most likely to try to manipulate? Your kids? Spouse? Colleagues? Friends? Relatives? What tactics are you most likely to use? Bribe or threaten your kids to comply? Blame your boss? Tell white lies? Fake illness, a headache, or fatigue to get out of something? Use anger, threats, or guilt? Do the targets ever see through you? How far will you carry out your deception?

What kind of manipulative interactions are you noticing between yourself and others? What about between your spouse and you? Between your children and you? Make a list of those interactions. Next, try to identify what the real issue is that you are trying to hide from in each situation. Is it work, change, pain, loss of power, or a confrontation? What are you really trying to avoid that is causing you to use manipulation tactics? Which of those fears are legitimate? Which ones should you be facing instead of avoiding?

And just why are you allowing your kid to manipulate you? Are you thinking it is just a phase (that your kid will grow out of)? Might your kid be learning to be manipulative because you are afraid to take charge and say no? If so, why? Do you want to minimize your kid's stress? Think it might hinder his self-esteem? Fear your relationship with your child might be jeopardized? Feel guilty because you don't always have the time you wish to spend with your child? Worry that it may somehow taint his childhood memories? When you realize you're being manipulated, do you say nothing for fear of confronting a difficult situation, hurting your kid's feelings, spoiling your best-pals relationship, or embarrassing your kid by telling the painful truth? Well don't feel alone; lots of parents do this all the time. The key to change is that first honest admission and then committing yourself to that change.

What is the first step you need to take in yourself to be a better example to your kids? Write it down, and then commit yourself to doing it.

I will _____

_____

BAD ATTITUDE NEWS ALERT

E. W. Swihart Jr., a pediatrician and professor of pediatrics at the University of Minnesota, and Patrick Cotter, a pediatric psychologist, authors of *The Manipulative Child,* share the belief that highly manipulative kids inevitably develop poor self-esteem. What's more, these kids are prime candidates for developing other social maladies, such as eating disorders, substance abuse, and suicide. Two decades of observations of their young clients and their parents have also led these experts to conclude that the central cause of these kids' manipulative attitudes is their well-meaning, successful, well-read, motivated parents who have raised their kids to learn to adapt to life in a dependent fashion by getting their way through manipulation. They contend that's because parents today are afraid to take charge of their kids and concerned that saying no may somehow jeopardize their kids' emotional development or relationships. And parental guilt is their biggest reason for doing so. Could this be a big reason for your kid's manipulative attitude?

THE "DON'T GIVE ME THAT ATTITUDE" MAKEOVER

Take the following steps to squelch your child's manipulative attitude.

Step 1. Recognize Your Kid's Manipulative Tactics

Here are a few of the most common manipulation tactics kids use to get their way. Check ones that apply to your child:

- [ ] *Lies.* "I left it on the bus." "I did it already." "My friend borrowed it."
- [ ] *Plays one adult off the other.* "Dad would let me." "But Mom said it was okay."
- [ ] *Makes excuses.* "The teacher didn't tell me." "I thought it was Sally's job."
- [ ] *Shifts blame.* "How am I supposed to get a good grade—my teacher is bad." "Go yell at the coach, not me. It's not my fault." "Don't blame me. You should have told me you were going to ground me."
- [ ] *Uses affection or charm.* "I love you so much, Mom. I really will try harder." "Sorry Dad, I forgot. How about a hug?"
- [ ] *Pretends to be helpless.* "I just can't do it, Dad. Pleeeeease can you help me?"
- [ ] *Uses guilt.* "If you were around more to help, I'd be getting better grades." "You're the worst parent in the whole world." "All the other parents let their kids do it."
- [ ] *Fakes a physical ailment.* "I have a stomachache . . . headache." "I'm so tired . . . sick."
- [ ] *Uses self-pity.* "I can't do it!" "It's too hard!" "Everyone will laugh at me."
- [ ] *Employs blackmail.* "If you let me stay out late tonight, I'll do it." "What'll I get?"
- [ ] *Gives the silent treatment.* Is moody, mopes, pouts, doesn't smile, withdraws.

☐ *Exploits emotions.* Uses tears, hysterical crying; trembles, clings, pleads.

☐ *Verbally threatens.* "If you don't, I'll . . . [tell Dad, run away, not love you anymore, never do my work] as long as I live."

☐ *Verbal tirades.* Wears you down with arguments and verbal battles.

☐ *Uses aggressive behaviors.* Has tantrums, bites, hits, rants, punches, or has other outbursts.

☐ *Knows your hot buttons.* Waits until you're exhausted to ask. Knows when you're so busy you don't have time to talk things through.

☐ *Other:* _____

_____

_____

Once you recognize the most common tactics your kid uses to get his way, you will be able to spot it each time and stop it in its tracks. Be sure to pass on your findings to those other important caregivers in your kid's life so you are all on board in curbing his manipulative ways.

Step 2. Get to the Real Purpose of the Attitude

There are two parts to the next makeover step. First, you must discover what's really behind your kid's manipulative attitude and why she needs to be deceptive. The best way to figure this out is by reviewing which boxes you checked in Step 1. Next, ask yourself if there is any pattern. There are many reasons kids are manipulative, but the usual cause is to escape from something unpleasant. Another possibility is that the child is just plain selfish and manipulates others to get what she wants. Check possibilities that apply to your kid:

☐ *Avoiding humiliation.* She is saving face from possible failure or embarrassment.

☐ *Fear of jeopardizing a relationship.* She is concerned about her image with peers.

☐ *Avoiding punishment.* She is escaping possible punishment if her actions are discovered.

☐ *Not wanting to lose approval.* She is afraid of losing the approval or love of someone she cares about.

☐ *Authentic lack of skills and experience.* You've been doing so much for this little sucker that now she hasn't the ability to do it on her own.

☐ *Insecurity, fear, or anxiety.* The situation causes her anxiety, so she is avoiding it.

☐ *Avoiding responsibility.* She is avoiding taking responsibility or being accountable for her actions.

☐ *Not wanting to work.* She is avoiding work, chores, or practice that she doesn't want to do.

☐ *Being selfish.* This is the way to get what he wants or have things go his way.

☐ *Other:* _____

_____

_____

Compare your notes with others who know your kid well, and then write down your best guess as to the real purpose of her deceptive attitude. You will use it in the next step. Meanwhile, from this moment on, any time your kid tries to sway you with this or any other manipulative tactic, immediately stop her in her tracks. That means in public as well as in your home. The next step shows you how. *Her attitude cannot be allowed for any reason.*

Step 3. Expose the Underlying Deception

Once you recognize your kid's manipulative tactics and underlying purpose, let him know you're onto him. As soon as you see him starting to be manipulative, stop him on the spot (and that means anywhere you are—in a restaurant, on a soccer field, in a supermarket, or in your family room). If he is agitated or losing control, do wait until he is calm enough to talk. For a younger kid, this might mean sitting him next to you for a brief period or putting him in a quiet area until he can settle down. For an older kid, ask him to go to his room a few minutes, or tell him you will wait in another room until he is in control. Only then should you confront your kid with his deception and your theory as to why he is using it. Use a calm, firm voice, and stick to the facts. Cut out judgments, lengthy sermons, and admonitions ("You keep this up, you'll end up in juvenile detention"): they are never helpful. Here are a few examples:

"I've noticed that every time it's your turn for sharing, you say you have a headache. Do you feel a little scared about talking in front of your class?"

"I saw how you pulled that tantrum as soon as we got to the toy section and you saw those cars. You did the same thing with Dad last week." A young kid will not be able to explain, so just jump to the chase: "Throwing a fit to get what you want will not work."

"Every time Mrs. Castro carpools, you can't seem to find your backpack so I end up driving you. What's going on so you don't want to be in Mrs. Castro's car?"

"You've been pretending that you can't lift your toy box to that upper shelf. But I've seen you stand on a chair to get down that heavy box of video games. I don't want to hear any more about being so helpless."

"Each time you get red-carded by the umpire for your poor sportsmanship, you blame someone else. How can your teammate be the cause of your tripping an opponent? You are responsible for your own actions, and you are the one getting red-carded."

A few words of caution: First, don't ask your kid to explain why he is deceptive. He honestly may not know.

Manipulators (especially younger ones) usually don't calculate their attitudes; they just respond to the situation. Older kids often act out of a habit that just kicks in automatically. Also, don't expect a profound ethical discussion to take place between the two of you. It would be nice, but chances are it won't happen. After all, you are confronting your kid about his devious, dishonest ways, so he is likely to be embarrassed, deny the charges, or flat-out refuse to listen. Your goal here is to have your kid hear you out and let him know in no uncertain terms that the attitude will not be tolerated. Do make sure other potential manipulated victims are aware of your kid's tactics and the new policy so you're on board together.

Step 4. Help Kids Face Their Fears, Not Avoid Them Through Manipulation

If your child is using manipulation to avoid something causing anxiety or fear, don't be too quick to let her off the hook. First, think things through. If she is capable of the task and the expectation is fair and reachable, *then do not give in*. That would be a huge mistake. Instead, insist that she face her fear. A big part of life is learning how to cope, and childhood is the best time to learn how.

Do not dismiss your child's fear or punish her for it. The fear is very real. Instead, comfort her by acknowledging that you understand how she feels. Then let her know you believe in her and are confident she can succeed. Be very clear that you will not rescue her, but will help her cope until she prevails. Here are a few ideas to help her face her fears without manipulating her way out:

- *Recognize feelings.* "I know it seems hard, but you can do it." "I know how apprehensive you feel, but I'm here for you."
- *Teach coping skills.* Teach her a few healthy ways to deal with her anxiety, such as saying a statement inside her head to help her handle the stress: "Chill out, calm down." "I can do this." "It's nothing I can't handle." Teach her to close her

eyes and slowly breathe in and out three times. Or ask her to think of a place she has been where she feels calm—for instance, the beach, her bed, the park. When anxiety kicks in, tell her to close her eyes and imagine that spot, while breathing slowly.

- *Model accepting blame.* Help your kid learn how to accept blame for her actions. Start by admitting your own shortcomings so your kids have a model to copy—for example: "This was all my fault: I should have read the movie section before dragging you here to find out the show started thirty minutes ago." Then expect your family to take ownership for their mistakes and not pass the blame onto others.
- *Arrange tutoring.* Does she need special help to improve? If so, arrange it.
- *Rehearse the skill.* New skills take lots of practice, so rehearse them over and over until your child gains the confidence to demonstrate the skill in front of others.
- *Celebrate little steps.* Acknowledge each little effort your child makes along the way, and then celebrate her successes both big and little.

Step 5. Set a Consequence
That Enforces Honesty and Ethics

Beware: Confronting kids with their deceptions long after the fact ("Your teacher last year said you had cheated" or "Remember when you lied to me about your chores last month?") is useless. For consequences to be effective in curbing bad attitudes, they must be enforced immediately and fit the crime. I always think the best consequences are ones that also *right the kid's wrong.* With that said, here are some consequences that help kids tune up their moral attitudes, face their wrongdoing, as well as learn that manipulation is not acceptable:

"If you take something, you will return it to the owner with an apology."

"If you break something, you will pay for it out of your earned money."

"If you are dishonest, you owe the person a sincere apology as an admission of your wrongdoing."

"If you got out of a responsibility through deception [such as practice or a chore], you owe that time by doing that practice or chore."

Don't expect your manipulator to immediately get the connection between the enforced consequence and the moral message you're trying to instill. He will in time. Right now, a manipulator needs to recognize that any time he commits an ethical infraction (such as a dishonest, manipulative act), he must make face his wrong and try to make things right. If he doesn't get it at first, he will eventually because you will continue to hold him accountable.

The First 21 Days

Immediately begin a No Excuse, No Blame Policy in your home. Manipulators rarely accept responsibility—it's always someone else's fault, they think, and so they make up excuses and fault others for their oversights. "How am I supposed to remember? It's *your* fault." "The coach didn't tell me." "The teacher should have reminded me." Don't allow it. Instead announce that the new operating premise in your home will always be honesty and accountability. Here's how to begin:

1. Gather the masses and state your policy: "From this moment on, no excuses or blaming others are

allowed. Everyone is responsible for his or her own actions, duties, work, and schedule." Be really clear on this one: you will not rescue, write an excuse, or do their tasks.

2. Brainstorm the most common issues that cause you, your partner, or the kids to make up excuses and blame others for. A typical list might include: "forgotten" dentist appointments, chores, video rentals, oboe practice, school testing days, home-work, and money for lunches.

3. Make a chart, checklist, or schedule so everyone is clear on their responsibilities, and kids (and parents) can't use manipulative tactics like excuses or blaming others if they "forgot." Post it on the refrigerator so everyone sees it, and you can refer to it as "proof" when needed. Picture charts can be substituted for younger manipulators. Here are a few ideas:

Charts. List chores, expectations, and rules.

Calendars. Write personal schedules (appoint-ments, homework schedules, practices, recitals, parties, events, library book due notices). Con-sider purchasing a weekly or monthly calendar printed on a white board. You can then write on it again and again with washable pens.

Contracts. Put behavior agreements and conse-quences for manipulation infractions in writ-ing. All relevant parties should sign it.

Refrigerator magnets. Purchase one magnet per family member. Any special events, notices, or reminders are then clipped to the magnet and remain visibly on the refrigerator. *Hint:* Sometimes the best reminder is a single word written on a note card and attached to the magnet: "Chores." "Homework."

The key to a successful No Excuse, No Blame Policy is simple: *don't accept any excuses, guilt, or pass-the-buck tactics from your kids.* Manipulation works only if you let it work. So don't let it.

ATTITUDE MAKEOVER PLEDGE

How will you use these steps to stop your kid's manipulative attitude and achieve long-term change? On the lines below, write exactly what you agree to do within the next twenty-four hours to begin changing your kid's attitude so he is less manipulative and more honest and forthright.

_____

_____

_____

_____

THE NEW ATTITUDE REVIEW

All attitude makeovers take hard work, constant practice, and parental reinforcement. Each step your child takes toward change may be a small one, so be sure to acknowledge and congratulate every one of them along the way. It takes a minimum of twenty-one days to see real results, so don't give up! And if one strategy doesn't work, try another. Write your child's weekly progress on the lines that follow. Keep track of daily progress in your Attitude Makeover Journal.

WEEK 1

WEEK 2

WEEK 3

ONGOING ATTITUDE TUNE-UP

Where does your child's attitude still need improvement? What work still needs to be done?

ATTITUDE MAKEOVER RESOURCES

For Parents

The Manipulative Child: How to Regain Control and Raise Resilient, Resourceful, and Independent Kids, by E. W. Swihart Jr. and Patrick Cotter (New York: Bantam Books, 1998). If your kid is ruling your household, this is the book for you. A pediatrician and a child psychologist offer effective tools from their clinically proven program for blocking manipulative behavior and getting kids back on track.

In Sheep's Clothing: Understanding and Dealing with Manipulative People, by George K. Simon Jr. (Little Rock, Ark.: A. J. Christopher, 1996). Simon reveals the common tactics manipulators like to use and tells you how to respond to them.

Stop Negotiating with Your Teen: Strategies for Parenting Your Angry, Manipulative, Moody, or Depressed Adolescent, by Janet Sasson Edgette (New York: Perigee Books, 2002). A therapist offers practical strategies for parents who don't know where to turn when dealing with a sullen, withdrawn, or sarcastic and manipulative teen.

"Trust Me, Mom—Everyone Else Is Going!" The New Rules for Mothering Adolescent Girls, by Roni Cohen-Sandler (New York: Penguin Books, 2002). Great sound advice when your adolescent (or preadolescent) wants to put a manipulative guilt trip on you.

For Kids

It's Not My Fault, by Franz Brandenburg (New York: Morrow, 1980). Although the mice siblings quarrel and blame each other, they miss each other terribly when apart. Ages 3 to 7.

Sam, Bangs, and Moonshine, by Evaline Ness (Austin, Tex.: Holt, Rinehart and Winston, 1966). "Mistruths" get out of hand. The main character must deal with her manipulative deceptions and their harmful consequences. Ages 3 to 7.

One-Eyed Cat, by Paula Fox (New York: Bradbury, 1984). Disobeying his father, a boy takes a rifle and shoots a stray cat. Though he tries at first to wheedle his way out of taking responsibility for his actions, guilt finally sets in, and he tells the truth. Ages 8 to 12.

Narrow-Minded
Antidote: Tolerance, Open-Mindedness, Flexibility

"All boys are stupid."

Dear Dr. Borba,
My wife and I have always prided ourselves on being tolerant and open-minded. But somehow our ten year old has turned out very narrow-minded. Once he forms an opinion (and heaven knows where he gets them), he just won't listen. He thinks he's right, and there's no way we can change his thinking. The problem is that his views are often quite ignorant and biased. What can we do to help him become more open-minded?

—Leon L., a father of two from Atlanta, Georgia

Bad Attitude Act Out
"I'm only going to play with white kids, and no one else ever."

"You can't trust girls. They'll cheat on you every time."

"I'm never going into business—*everyone* is so unethical!"

EMERGENCY ATTITUDE

Identify something your kid is narrow-minded and closed-viewed about—for example, gender ("Girls are dumb"), race ("Chinese are sneaky"), religion ("Muslims are all terrorists"), or age ("The elderly are all senile"). Then institute a plan to give him face-to-face evidence that his view is not only unfair but also incorrect. For instance, if a young child is prejudiced against a certain ethnicity, you might find a day care that has diversity, or expose him to positive images of the group using toys, music, literature, videos, and public role models. A plan for a teen biased about physical disabilities might be for him to help out in the Special Olympics or expose him to examples in literature, film, and the real world of successful people who have lived with their disabilities: the deaf composer Ludwig van Beethoven; the disabled physicist Stephen Hawking; the author who battled depression Virginia Woolf; the deaf and blind advocate Helen Keller; the schizophrenic mathematician John Nash, subject of the best-selling biography and film *A Beautiful Mind*; or the one-handed pitcher Jim Abbott. Ignorance and lack of experience are two of the most common reasons that kids develop biased views. Providing your kid with an experience putting him in direct confrontation with his bias is one of the best ways to help him recognize that his attitude is not only narrow but also wrong.

"Adults are so out of touch they don't have a clue!" "You can't trust any of the news.""If I were Asian, I'd have a much better chance of getting into college: all of them do." Narrow-minded kids are tough to live with: they are set in their ways, think their views are always right, and are usually quite unreceptive to new opinions. They are dead certain that their way is not only the right way but also the only way. Trying to convince them their views are wrong can be exhausting. Kids with these attitudes see things only from their side and hear only what they want to hear, and that's usually only the views that fit their beliefs or help them get their way. And so narrow-minded kids are also self-centered.

It's as though they want to close the door to ideas that counter theirs and seem almost afraid to let new opinions in. But they are shutting out the potential for stretching their knowledge and their awareness of others' feelings and thoughts. And there's a bigger danger: it jeopardizes their growth of character as well. By keeping their minds locked to new perspectives, they are robbed of developing the very virtues that can strengthen their moral growth and activate their concern for others.

Five virtues in particular are on the endangered list of narrow-minded kids:

- Empathy—identifying with and feeling other people's concerns
- Respect—valuing others
- Kindness—concern about the welfare of others
- Fairness—choosing to be open-minded and to act in a just way
- Tolerance—respecting the dignity and rights of all persons, even those whose beliefs and behaviors differ from our own

But there's something else going on that should also be a big warning: not only are these kids narrow-minded, they can also be very bigoted. The whole matter of your child's tolerance his ability to respect the rights of all persons, even those whose beliefs and behaviors differ from his own—is at stake. Since narrow-minded kids are willing to hear only what they want to believe and don't take the time to listen, they run the risk of forming views far too quickly. And often they are based not on facts but on broad categorical judgments. Those stereotypes can have deadly outcomes because they plant the seeds of prejudice and hate. After all, how can you possibly learn to be accepting of different beliefs, genders, abilities, cultures, and religions unless you are willing to be open to those differences? Sadly, narrow-minded kids are robbed of those opportunities because their close-minded views don't allow new beliefs to enter into their close-minded outlooks on life.

There are several factors that might contribute to children's being narrow-minded and prejudiced. They may be picking up on attitudes from you or other members of your family when they hear racist or sexist language, jokes, or casual remarks, whether they are conscious or not. They may be getting it from their peers or the media. For example, they might be part of a group that shapes their value and identity by opposing another group or type of person. They may have had a bad experience at school or in the community that you may not even know about that has left them with a profound bias or misunderstanding. They may have never been exposed to various points of view, cultures, and individuals. Or they may have deep unresolved fears and insecurities, which they're projecting on to others as scapegoats for their own problems.

To help our kids live in a more harmonious world, we must teach them to be more open-minded and tolerant. Their world is growing more diverse every day. Many communities today have large populations of what used to be known as minority groups (such as African Americans, Latinos, Asians, and Muslims) but are now in fact the majority. Whereas some kids are responding to this change with fear, prejudice, and hate, others are learning to accept and respect differences. The more open-minded and tolerant your kids are, the more open they will be to learning about other people. The more they learn, the less they will be uncomfortable or fearful in any kind of situation, with any kind of person. Although it's certainly never too late, the sooner we instill the virtues of tolerance, open-mindedness, and flexibility, the better the chance we have of preventing insidious, intolerant attitudes from taking hold.

BAD ATTITUDE ALERT

Prod deep down to find the roots of this attitude to figure out why it took hold.

Diagnosis

Answer these questions to reflect on how your kid developed her narrow-minded biased ways in the first place, as well as why she is continuing to use them.

Why. Your first step is to try to determine why your kid is so narrow-minded and biased and what he is gaining from using this attitude. Here are a few reasons kids are prejudiced. Check ones that may apply to your kid:

- [ ] Lacks empathy for those who are different
- [ ] Is anxious toward a certain group due to a previous negative experience
- [ ] Is around others who make frequent comments or jokes putting another group down
- [ ] Is part of a peer culture that seems to focus on the negative traits of others or considers active conflict with another group to be an essential part of their identity
- [ ] Is seeking attention or approval from others who think his biased comments are cute, clever, or funny
- [ ] Has been allowed to be biased; no one counters his views

- [ ] Lives in a family where only one point of view is tolerated
- [ ] Is self-centered: has been made to believe his views are always correct
- [ ] Has been raised in an authoritarian home where dialogue and debate are not encouraged
- [ ] Is underexposed to diversity: raised in a homogeneous environment
- [ ] Lacks knowledge: his views are biased due to limited information
- [ ] Other: _____
  _____
  _____

What. Are there particular issues or things he is usually more biased about: certain races, cultures, nationalities, religions, gender, age, sexual orientation, appearance, abilities, or disabilities? How does he display his bias? Does he show disrespect toward people because of their differences? Does she make comments that put another person down, focus only on the negative traits of a particular group, tell derogatory jokes about another group, or refuse to listen to any other point of view but her own?

Who. Does he display the same biased attitude to everyone? Why? Are there a few individuals who help fuel his biased beliefs? Who are they? A cousin? Neighbor? Sibling? Peer? What about an adult? A coach? Teacher? Your friends? Are there some individuals he does not use his narrow-minded ways on? If so, who? Why does he spare them?

When. Is there a particular time of day, week, or month that might be inspired by a TV show, a racist uncle's visit, or a particular holiday (like Martin Luther King Jr.'s birthday) that provokes your kid's narrow-minded attitude? Is there a reason? For instance, he might be seeking attention or peer approval, or he might be in the company of peers, relatives, or friends who are also biased.

Where. Are there certain places where he is more likely to voice his biased views (at school or day care, home, the soccer field, one of your friend's homes, Aunt Em's)? Why?

Finally, think seriously about your answers. Are you seeing any predictable patterns? Do you have any better understanding of your kid's narrow-minded attitude and how it got started?

WHAT'S WRONG
WITH YOUR CURRENT RESPONSE?

Now reflect on how you typically respond to your child's narrow-minded attitude. Start by reviewing the last few times your kid was narrow-minded. Now replay the scene in your mind. What was the issue about, and, more important, how did you respond to her attitude? If she made a biased comment or joke, did you laugh or let her know you thought it was "cute"? What about your nonverbal messages? Did she see you smile, quietly chuckle, or nod your head in agreement? Did you respond with another biased comment or joke? Or did you ignore her comment, pretend you didn't hear it, and let it slide?

Did you feel uncomfortable about her comment and express your discomfort? Did you tell her why you were uncomfortable? If you didn't say anything, did she see your uneasiness in your body language? For instance, did you frown, roll your eyes, shake your head, or frown?

Did you agree or disagree with her view? Did you let her know your opinion? If so, how? For instance, did you debate the issue with her and point out why the comment was narrow-minded or offer evidence to support your view? Did you ask her to defend her opinion? Listen to her side carefully? Ask her where she obtained the information? Ask why she feels the way she does? If you didn't disagree with her, how will she learn a different view?

If your kid said a prejudicial, biased comment directed at someone, did you hold her accountable? For instance, did you ask her to reflect on how the victim felt? Demand that she apologize or do something toward the person to try and remove the hurt? Did your kid comply with your requests?

What is the one response you know does not work in stopping her narrow-minded, prejudicial attitude? Write it down so you will remember never to use it again.

I will not _____

_____

FACING YOUR OWN BAD ATTITUDES

Were you raised in a home where everyone was expected to follow a strict party line, or were you exposed to a variety of points of views? Were you allowed to express your feelings and beliefs? What if your beliefs differed from those of your parents? How did your parents respond if someone made a prejudicial comment or joke in their presence? Can you think of instances in which your parents demonstrated intolerance toward anyone? What were they about?

What were some of your parents' political biases and personal prejudices? Do any of those remain with you today? Do you feel you are passing any of these on to your child? If so, which ones? Take time to reflect on how you might be projecting those outdated ideas to your child.

Take a serious look at yourself. Do you consider yourself tolerant and unbiased, or intolerant and prejudiced? Would your kids, colleagues, spouse, and friends agree with your self-appraisal? What are your secret, even embarrassing attitudes that you hate to admit even to yourself? How many friends of other ethnicities or cultures do you invite to your home or include in your family activities? What response, if any, do you make if you hear a prejudicial comment in your presence? What if your kid is in your presence and hears the comment as well?

Do you allow discussion, dissension, and debates in your home? What if the views of your kids (or spouse, friends, or colleagues) differ from your views? Do you listen openly to where they come from? How receptive are you to hearing all sides of an issue before forming your views? Do your kids feel you listen fairly to their opinions, or are they more prone to stay tight-lipped, figuring you already are set in your views? Is there anything you can do to cultivate more open-ended discussions among your family?

What can you do temper your own narrow-minded attitudes so that they don't become your child's views? What is the first step you need to take to be a better example of openness and acceptance to your children? Write it, and then commit to doing it.

I will _____

_____

BAD ATTITUDE NEWS ALERT

Figures show that American youth are displaying intolerant actions at alarming rates and at younger and younger ages. Researchers say that most hate crimes are committed by youth younger than age nineteen, and youthful hatred has become all too common in our schools. Consider these troubling facts:

- Researchers from Northeastern University surveyed thirty Massachusetts high schools and found that one-third of students reported that they had been victims of one or more hate-based crimes.
- The Review of Higher Education estimated that each year, at least 1 million bias-motivated incidents take place on American college campuses.

THE "DON'T GIVE ME THAT ATTITUDE" MAKEOVER

To help eliminate your child's biased, narrow-minded attitude, take the following steps.

Step 1. Clean Your Own House

Kids aren't born intolerant, biased, narrow-minded, bigoted, and prejudiced. They learn those lethal attitudes, and one of the places they learn them best is right underneath our own noses: from us! The first step to tempering your kid's narrow-minded ways is by realizing your own biases. Here are a few assumptions that can be so deeply seated that you may not be aware they are there. But our kids sure are! And chances are that you are communicating those attitudes to your child. Check ones that apply to you:

☐ *Loyalty.* "My kid can do no wrong."
☐ *Wealth.* Because you work hard, you're entitled to certain privileges.
☐ *Education.* You can be educated only if you go to college. You can get a good education only at an Ivy League school.
☐ *Sexual orientation.* Homosexuality is a choice. Gays will go to hell.

- [ ] *Race and culture.* The Chinese are sneaky. Asian kids are all great students. All blacks have rhythm. All Jews are rich. Latinos make great lovers. Italians are all members of the Mafia. All the Irish do is drink.
- [ ] *Politics.* My party, right or wrong. All Democrats do is tax and spend. Republicans always favor the rich.
- [ ] *Sex roles.* Women should be seen and not heard. Blondes are dumb. Women will claw their way to the top. Men are superior. Football players are stupid. Boys who don't play sports are wimpy.
- [ ] *Groups.* Police officers are racists. The homeless could get jobs if they tried.
- [ ] *Age.* The elderly are all senile. Teens care only about themselves.

Once you discover which narrow-minded views you may be spreading to your kid (and usually quite unconsciously), make a conscious effort to temper them so that they don't become your child's prejudices.

Step 2. Cultivate Listening Skills

Narrow-minded kids only want to hear what they want to hear, and rarely tune in to what the other person is saying. The result: they will continue to be narrow-minded. Cultivate your kid's listening skills so that he not only hears new information but becomes more receptive to fresh ideas. Here are ways to do so:

- *Model listening.* Kids learn listening best not through our lectures but by copying others. Use natural opportunities to really listen to your child so he has a good model to copy. Stop what you're doing, give him your full attention, and then model good listening skills: look him eye to eye, nod and smile, and lean in slightly toward him so he feels your presence.
- *Teach listening behaviors.* SOLER is a simple acronym representing the five behaviors good listeners demonstrate.

Teach it to your kid, and then help him practice it until he masters it: S: sit upright; O: be open and show your interest; L: lean in; E: look eye to eye at the speaker and nod; and R: review in your mind: "What did I hear?" You may want to make a large poster of the acronym and put it on your refrigerator as a reminder.

- *Learn paraphrasing.* Help your kid listen more attentively to a speaker around your dinner table or any other times you're together. Here's how. Each family member takes a turn briefly describing something that's happened to him or her during the day. The next speaker must correctly restate the previous talker's ideas before contributing his experience. For fun, after everyone has had a turn, see if anyone can identify one important idea from each person's conversation.

- *Find a new fact.* When a natural opportunity arises (for example, when members of your family are listening to a speaker, reading a book, listening to the news, or watching a documentary), encourage everyone to listen for one fact that is new to him or her and then report it to the group. To make it challenging, no one may replicate another person's fact.

- *Provide new knowledge.* Once your kid is more open to listening, educate her about the issues she is most narrow-minded about. After all, an enormous amount of prejudice, hate, and narrow-mindedness comes from sheer ignorance. So provide her with more appropriate information about the topic she is so closed about. Take her to museums, help her find Web sites, and select movies or books about the subject so she sees a different side.

Step 3. Take a Stand Against Biased, Judgmental Statements

All kids are bound to make occasional biased comments, state narrow-minded opinions, or repeat discriminatory jokes. How you react has a lot to do with whether they will try to again. You also send your kids a clear message about your own attitudes. So if or when you hear a biased statement, do express your displeasure: "That's a biased comment, and I don't want to hear it." Your child needs to hear your discomfort so that she understands your values. You also model a response she could imitate if prejudicial, narrow-minded statements are made in her presence. Here are two others:

"I know you think Eminem is a great musician, but I strongly object to how disrespectfully he refers to women. It's hurtful and incorrect."

"I was very uncomfortable when Uncle Jake was talking about how absurd it was for a Latino to become president. That is such a narrow-minded view."

Step 4. Teach How to Recognize Stereotypes and Biases

Before your kid is willing to change his narrow-minded attitude, he must understand what a stereotype is, how to recognize one, and why they can be harmful. These next ideas help your kid learn those important three parts:

- *Define stereotypes.* You might say, "A stereotype is a big sweeping idea we believe about a whole group of people or subject area. Usually the beliefs are wrong because they are not true about every member of the group or every instance about the subject. They are also unfair because the person believing the stereotype makes a judgment without getting all the facts." Point out that if the comment has words such as "You always . . .," "You never . . .," "They always . . .," or "They're all . . .," chances are that what follows is a biased stereotype.
- *Listen for stereotypes.* A fun way to help your kid recognize stereotypes is by listening for them together on tele-

vision. Turn it into a game by trying to count how many biased statements you hear in a set time. As soon as one is detected, yell out, "Stereotype!" The biased comment must then be repeated: "The reporter said: 'All teachers in Los Angeles schools are bad.' Stereotype!"

- *Give examples of harmful biases.* Our culture is saturated with biased views that can erode our kids' attitudes and perpetuate narrow-minded views. Provide your kid with a few examples, and then discuss that although they seem harmless, they can be quite hurtful and cloud our views. Here are a few: Teenagers only about care themselves. Adults are out of it. Boys who play football are stupid. The Polish are dumb. Cheerleaders are "easy." Girls are poor at math. Then ask your child to give evidence of why it isn't completely true—for example, "Jenna and Kara are really good at math."

- *Play, "Prove it!"* Encourage family members that whenever anyone in your household utters a sweeping stereotype, another member should gently counter the person's view by responding, "Prove it!" For example, if your kid says, "Jocks are so stupid," a sibling could retort, "I beg to differ: I know five guys on my football team who are in all the accelerated classes."

- *Use the media.* Film, advertising, music, television, literature, and jokes are major perpetrators of stereotypes. Asking your child questions that point out biases as they occur is often beneficial in helping him recognize the misrepresentation. Here are a few examples that show how:

  Newspapers: "I've read a number of stories lately about police brutality. Do you think people might get the impression that all police are unfair and beat up minorities? What do you think?"

  Nightly news: "The news always seems to be showing blacks as aggressive and caught doing bad things. Do you think they are reporting the news fairly?"

Literature: "This is another story in which the stepmother is wicked. Is that true for all stepmothers? If a kid keeps reading stories like this, what do you think her attitude about stepmoms will be?"

Step 5. Challenge Biased Views

One thing is certain: if you don't challenge your kid's narrow-minded view, his attitude will continue. The most important thing is not to overreact or be too quick to criticize; that response will stop his comment but not his attitude. Your goal is to change his attitude, and the only way to do that is by listening carefully to your child's words and why he feels that way. Only then can you give him evidence to counter his view. Here are a few ideas that will help your challenge his biased attitude:

- *Listen first.* When you hear your child make a prejudicial, narrow-minded comment, the first step is always the hardest: listen without judging or interrupting. You want to gather as many facts as you can to find out why she feels the way she does and what gave rise to her words. That way you can help her change it before it turns into a long-lasting prejudice. Suppose your child says, "Kids who don't speak English shouldn't be allowed in our school." You might say, "I want to hear why you said that" or "You sound as if you feel very strongly about that. Why is that?" or "Where did you hear that?"
- *Challenge the view.* When you're clear as to why your child expresses such a biased attitude, challenge her opinion with more accurate information and point out where she is incorrect. It's always best to try to give examples that dispel her view. For example, if your child says, "Homeless people should get jobs and sleep in their own houses," you might counter: "There are many reasons homeless people don't work or have houses. Some of them are ill. Some can't

find jobs. Houses cost money, and not everyone can pay for a house or an apartment."

- **Demand proof.** In some cases, ask your child to provide proof of her claim. For instance, if she adamantly states that old people are all senile, put her on the Internet to find examples that counter his view ("What about Grandma Moses?"). "If you're diagnosed with cancer, you'll die" ("What about Lance Armstrong?"). "If you have asthma, you can't be a runner" ("What about Jackie Joyner-Kersee?").

Step 6. Enforce Moral Consequences for Hurtful Comments

Let your child know that any comment that is insulting to someone else will not be allowed. In addition to being painful to the victim, such prejudicial comments breed hate. If your child does make a comment, then she must apologize. Most important, the apology *must* be genuine and delivered sincerely. You may need to spend time talking to your child about the victim's pain. Ask, "How would you feel if someone said that to you?" so that your son or daughter really understands the ramifications. Your message is, *What you did caused someone else to hurt. So what will you do to make up for that pain?* Children must realize that although they cannot take back the hurt caused from stinging words or deeds, they are responsible for their actions. Even the youngest child can apologize, draw a picture, or phone the victim to say, "I'm sorry." Here are some examples for helping them understand:

"Telling Maria she talks weird is hurtful. She speaks a different language at home and is just learning to speak English. You need to apologize to her."
"The joke you told Josh is not funny because it made fun of his religion. It's wrong. I can't allow you to hurt other people's feelings. What do you plan to do to let him know you are sorry?"

The First 21 Days

Organize a Formal Family Debate Night, a great way to contest common problems in a supportive atmosphere. It is also a way for kids to practice communication skills and hear different points of view. Not only will your narrow-minded kid get a chance to hear a different side to his biased attitude, but he may just change his opinion. Do remember that each member's opinion is considered equally important, and everyone has a right to be heard. That also means your kids do not have to agree with *your* opinion, and *you* must respectfully listen to your kids' views as well. Use these tips to make your debates fun, as well as provide the opportunity to help change your kid's biased attitude:

- *Set Fair Fighting rules.* Five rules must be enforced: (1) Everyone is listened to. (2) No put-downs are allowed. (3) You may disagree, but do so respectfully. (4) Talk calmly. (5) Everyone gets a turn.
- *Create a suggestion box.* Many families set aside a small box for members to suggest family issues or topics they'd like to address at the next debate. Young kids can draw pictures of ideas.
- *Use current events.* Search the news for debate topics that might pique your kids' interests. Possibilities for younger kids are not protecting bears in the forest, not being allowed to ride bikes or skateboards on the sidewalk, and not funding art or music in school. Possibilities for older kids are lowering the drinking age, raising the driving age, legalizing marijuana,

abortion, the Iraq War, legalization of gambling, resti-
tution to black Americans, and the death penalty.

- **Debate family issues.** Topics can also be hot button
  issues in your home. For younger kids, they can
  cover rules, sibling conflicts, chores, privileges,
  allowances, and TV choices. For older kids, consider
  quality time with parents, curfews, computer access,
  R-rated movies, car use, choice of peers, and dating
  and romance.

ATTITUDE MAKEOVER PLEDGE

How will you use these steps to help your kid become less
biased and narrow-minded and achieve long-term change?
On the lines below, write exactly what you agree to do within
the next twenty-four hours to begin changing your kid's attitude so he is more tolerant and accepting.

_____

_____

_____

THE NEW ATTITUDE REVIEW

All attitude makeovers take hard work, constant practice, and
parental reinforcement. Each step your child takes toward
change may be a small one, so be sure to acknowledge and
congratulate every one of them along the way. It takes a minimum of twenty-one days to see real results, so don't give up!
And if one strategy doesn't work, try another. Write your
child's weekly progress on the lines that follow. Keep track of
daily progress in your Attitude Makeover Journal.

WEEK 1

_____
_____
_____

WEEK 2

_____
_____
_____

WEEK 3

_____
_____
_____

ONGOING ATTITUDE TUNE-UP

Where does your child's attitude still need improvement? What work still needs to be done?

_____
_____
_____

ATTITUDE MAKEOVER RESOURCES

For Parents

Does Anybody Else Look Like Me? A Parent's Guide for Raising Multiracial Children, by Donna Jackson Nakazawa (Cambridge, Mass.: Perseus, 2003). The author is of European descent, and her husband is Japanese American. They had hoped to raise their kids to be color-blind but found they couldn't ignore the stares and curious comments about their children's appearance. Nakazawa offers parents ideas on how to cope. Although the book is written for multiracial parents, her ideas work for all parents.

I'm Chocolate, You're Vanilla, by Marguerite Wright (San Francisco: Jossey-Bass, 1998). Great tips on how kids, who are born color-blind, can be protected from learning prejudice and intolerance.

40 Ways to Raise a Nonracist Child, by Barbara Mathias and Mary Ann French (New York: HarperPerennial, 1996). A simple guide for helping parents talk openly with their kids about racism and respect for racial differences.

Teaching Peace: How to Raise Children to Live in Harmony—Without Fear, Without Prejudice, Without Violence, by Jan Arnow (New York: Perigee Books, 1995). Ways to encourage tolerance and respect in kids.

Teaching Tolerance, by Sara Bullard (New York: Doubleday, 1996). Solid research-based suggestions for raising more open-minded, tolerant, and empathetic children.

For Kids

Angel Child, Dragon Child, by Michele Maria Surat (New York: Scholastic, 1983). A young Vietnamese girl arrives at her new American school and faces taunts by her classmates for her cultural differences. Wonderful for ages 5 to 8.

My Dream of Martin Luther King, by Faith Ringgold (New York: Crown, 1995). An interpretation of Martin Luther King's legacy and the civil rights movement that poignantly urges that intolerance, hatred, and prejudice be replaced by love, tolerance, and dreams. Glorious! Ages 7 to 12.

Hana's Suitcase: A True Story, by Karen Levine (Morton Grove, Ill.: Albert Whitman, 2003). This unusual story from the Holocaust begins with a persistent curator's quest to find a girl named Hana whose name is printed on a suitcase donated to the Auschwitz Museum by the Holocaust Center in Tokyo. The family photographs supplied by

Hana's surviving brother make this a deeply moving account of the horrors of intolerance. Ages 10 and up.

Focus (Paramount, 2002). The film adaptation of Arthur Miller's story of a man and wife mistakenly ostracized due to narrow-minded community members during World War II. Excellent for discussion among teens.

18

Noncompliant
Antidote: Respect, Obedience, Dependability

"Try and make me!"

Dear Dr. Borba,

Our youngest son has always been difficult, but lately he's become an absolute nightmare. He's disobedient, debates everything, and usually refuses to do what we ask. We've tried everything to get him to shape up—grounding, rule charts, bribing—but nothing seems to work. Somehow he thinks he can call the shots in our house. Meanwhile, I feel as if I'm a contestant on one of those survival shows— and I'm losing! I can't believe I'm asking this, but what can I do to get my kid to obey?

—Carol C., a mom of three from Auburn, New York

Bad Attitude Act Out

"I'm not going to, Daddy, and you can't make me."

"Why should I do what you want?"

"Yeah, right, as if I'd listen to you."

EMERGENCY ATTITUDE ℞

Decide which issues really matter and are worth fighting over and which you can let slide for the time being. One of our biggest problems as parents is feeling overwhelmed with all the different issues and conflicts going on with our defiant kids. Right now, your child is probably not doing anything you want him to do. By getting him to comply with one just crucial thing, you're starting on the right path toward a big attitude change. For a younger child, playing without hitting might be your important goal, and picking up all her toys isn't as vital right now. For an older kid, completing homework might be the essential task, while making his bed isn't such a big deal after all. The key is to pick your battles wisely by choosing ones that are most crucial. Then stick to those, and let go of the others for now. Once your kid starts complying, you can gradually add more requests. Meanwhile, you'll save your sanity, your household harmony, and your relationship with your child, and you will be more likely to start turning your kid's defiant attitude around.

"I'm not going to: you're a bad, bad Mommy." "Why should I?" "Yeah, right. Let's see if you can make me." Heard a few defiant words uttered from your charming offspring lately? Of course, kids will disobey Mom and Dad—as well as teacher, coach, Grandma, and the babysitter—every once in a while. Usually a stern look or a firm reprimand is all that is required to shape them up and put them back in their place. But when kids consistently disobey us, they've gone way over the line. Defiance is at the extreme of the Big Brat Factor bad attitude spectrum, and it's time for immediate triage.

Defiant kids put themselves in charge, basically stripping their parents' authority and demoting them to second-class citizens. This attitude is all about control and disrespect to the maximum: it's kids pushing adults—and as far as they can push—to do what *they* want. The battle for power between parent and kid can be long, gruesome, and utterly draining. To ensure they win, defiant kids will stop at nothing. World War III can result from the simplest parental request to take out the trash or walk the dog. And if you happen to be in public when your kid pulls one of his all-out control quests, my sympathies are with you. The experience can be so humiliating that you'll go to any length to avoid friends as well as any witnesses for weeks.

Defiant kids are way above average self-centered and rude. But let's go further: surliness, contempt, and complete disrespect for adults are also part of this attitude. After all, non-compliant kids want *their* needs met, and to do so means to flat-out refuse to comply with anyone else's requests (let alone listen to them). These kids are so set in their quest for control that they are blind to anyone else's feelings or concerns. It should also be evident that that attitude is highly lethal to the child's moral character as well as the family's harmony.

Defiant, disrespectful, rude attitudes should never be tolerated. But that doesn't mean we shouldn't try to understand why our kid is acting this way. Yes, defiant kids are *extremely* taxing and frustrating (okay, obnoxious), but keep in mind that they may well be using their attitude because their own needs for structure, boundaries, limitations, and rules are not being met; they may have a short fuse based on temperament; the hard-wiring of their nervous system may be prone to defiance; they may be chemically imbalanced or depressed; or they simply don't know another way of getting the attention they crave. That's why to really change a defiant kid's ways, a major overhaul is needed in not only the kid's attitude but how we relate to her as well. So consider every cause, and then once you have the best treatment plan in mind, be relentless until you replace her defiance with respect, obedience, and dependability.

BAD ATTITUDE ALERT

Take comfort: though a defiant, noncompliant attitude is one of the most difficult to turn around, it *can* be done. Your first step is to reflect on how this attitude started.

Diagnosis

Consider how and why your child has such a defiant, disobedient attitude.

Why. What do you think is at the root of your kid's noncompliance? Does the cause lie in your day-to-day family dynamics? Is he subconsciously or even explicitly asking for boundaries, rules, and limitations? Does he really just want you to be more of the executive authority, the boss of the family? Or is he copying the attitude from someone else? Has he learned that using the attitude works so handily that he continues doing so? Or do you think it lies primarily in the temperament or hard-wiring of your kid? Is he depressed or traumatized? Could he be using drugs or self-medicating himself? Could he be reacting to tyrannical or abusive parenting? Just why does your kid have such a need of being in charge? Could she really be craving attention or love? Is she resentful of another sibling or someone in your relationships? Are family members rarely listening to or treating her respectfully? Does she know another way of getting her needs met? Of course, she may also be defiant because she's been allowed to be disrespectful, self-centered, and rude. So what's your best guess as to why your kid is resorting to this attitude?

What. Does your kid refuse to do everything you ask or just some things? To help you figure this out, fold a paper in half and make two lists. On one side, list issues that usually cause home-front wars: homework, chores, curfew, TV, getting up, use of the computer, hanging out with certain kids. Then list items that she will at least sometimes comply with (or produce less heated debates). Maybe your list includes going to soccer, coming to dinner, and feeding the dog. Finally, review your lists. Kids usually comply with requests they enjoy, feel less threatened by, or feel less likely to fail at. Do you see any pattern that might fit your kid? If so, what?

Who. Does he display the same defiant attitudes to everyone? Are there some people whom he is more compliant toward? If they are doing something that works, what is it? Talk to them to seek out their advice or watch how they respond to your kid. You might try copying their technique.

When. Do you see an increase in the attitude at a particular time of day? After his bath because bedtime comes next? Following dinner when it's time for homework? Saturday morning when it's time to get ready for gymnastics? Thursday morning when it's time to go to the babysitter? What might be the reason? Has he just been with some friends? Is there a new odor around him (cigarette smoke or alcohol, perhaps)? Also, when did you first notice this attitude emerge? Was anything going on about the same time that might have triggered it? A new babysitter? A difficult teacher? Bullying? Peer problems? A change at home (a move, a divorce, an illness, a new job, a new baby)? Or was it always a problem? ("Even when he was two he was having tantrums when I told him it was bedtime." "She even refused to do what her preschool teacher asked.")

Where. Are there certain places he is more likely to be defiant (at school or day care, home, in the carpool, at a friend's home, during swimming practice)? What might be the reason?

Now review your answers. Are there any predictable patterns you might have missed? Talk to those who know your child well to help you uncover the pattern. Do you have any better understanding of why your kid is using this attitude and how it developed? Write your thoughts.

WHAT'S WRONG
WITH YOUR CURRENT RESPONSE?

How are you responding to your kid's defiant attitude? For instance, the last time your kid disobeyed or refused to comply with your request, what did you do? Yell? Chastise? Debate? Threaten? Or do you report his attitude to others (teacher, nanny, other parent, the police) and have them deal with your kid's defiance? Are other adults usually with you when your kid is defiant? If so, what do they typically do? Support you? Scold him also? Ignore it? Yell at you? Do they help or hinder the situation?

Do you discipline him for his attitude in any way? If so, how? Ground him? Use time-out? Spank? Slap? Lecture? Remove a privilege? Demand an apology? If you discipline, how does your kid respond? What discipline doesn't work?

Here's another possible response: Do you ignore his defiance altogether? If so, why? Is it just easier? You hope it's just a phase? You don't have the energy? You're too busy to deal with it? His debates and tirades last so long you know you will be late? You feel threatened? You're concerned about the emotional health or even physical safety of siblings or other kids watching?

What is the one response that is guaranteed not to work in stopping your kid's defiant, noncompliant attitude? Write it down so you will remember never to use it again.

I will not _____

_____

FACING YOUR OWN BAD ATTITUDES

Many parents say kids today are far more defiant and disrespectful toward parents than when they were growing up. Do you agree? What might be the cause? Now think about when you were a kid. Did you defy your parents? How often and over what? What about your siblings? If you or they did, how did your parents react? How did your parents' discipline affect your own parenting style?

Next, consider how your kid became so defiant. Might she be modeling this attitude from you or another parent? A relative? Cousin? Sibling? Peers? Or could she be responding to how she is treated? Tune into the attitudes of those closest to your child, and watch for clues.

Now take a close look at your own attitudes. Could your kid be learning his defiant ways from you? For instance, do you insist that things go your way with your friends? At home? At work? Do you pay attention to family requests or flat-out refuse? Do you expect all family rules and expectations to be obeyed instantly? What about with colleagues? Your partner? Do you allow for negotiation or compromise or even listen to reasonable requests? Or are you too laissez-faire and loose with your kids? Do you have few or inconsistent rules in your family and no expectations of cooperation, respect, discipline, and responsibility? Are you just trying to be your kid's best friend instead of assuming the normal role of a parent—the one with the ultimate responsibility, the grown-up?

How is your relationship with your partner or your child's biological parent? What do your kids see? Are you overly demanding and controlling? Do they see you engage in yelling matches? Refusing to comply or even bother to listen? Give the "silent treatment"? Walk away or even out the door? Do you ever scream, slam doors, hit the person, or throw things? Would your kids say you are more of a dictator, compromiser, wishy-washy, or easy-going? How would you describe your daily style with your kids, spouse, friends, and colleagues? Bottom line: Are you presenting a model you'd like your kids to copy?

How do you typically relate with that defiant kid of yours? Be honest. How do you make your requests known to your child? Do you say them in a calm and respectful tone, or are you quick-tempered? Are you polite or disrespectful (or even a tad sarcastic)? How are your nonverbal cues? Do you roll your eyes, shrug, or smirk, or do you wait politely? Do you flat-out demand compliance or listen to his requests? Would your kid agree with your self-assessment? Put yourself in your kid's shoes. Would you want to be talked to and treated in the manner he is by you?

What is the first step you need to take in yourself to be a better example to your child?

I will _____

_____

BAD ATTITUDE NEWS ALERT

Defiant kids don't wake up one day with that attitude. It develops gradually and almost always starts with the breakdown of respect. Could this be an issue in your household? Studies suggest it clearly is a problem with many families. Consider these facts:

- Dr. Thomas Lickona, a renowned educator and the author of *Educating for Character*, cites large numbers of children showing attitudes of defiance for authority as one of the ten most troubling youth trends and warns it is a clear a sign of moral decline.
- A nationwide survey published in the *New York Times* showed that 93 percent of responding adults believed parents have failed to teach children honesty, respect, and responsibility.

- Louisiana lawmakers were so concerned with the breakdown of basic civility in school kids that they recently passed legislation making the saying of "Yes, ma'am" and "Yes, sir" expected student behavior. Failure to address a teacher respectfully is now considered an offense that can bring detention.

THE "DON'T GIVE ME THAT ATTITUDE" MAKEOVER

To make over your child's defiant bad attitude, take the following steps.

Step 1. Look Inside the Volcano

There are many reasons for a defiant attitude, but here are a few of the most typical. Check ones that apply to your child:

☐ *Faulty discipline.* Is your discipline so harsh that your kid rebels, so lenient that he is allowed to get away with this defiant attitude, or inconsistent so he doesn't know what to expect?

☐ *Relationship fallout.* Is there friction with a particular parent? Is there a lack of time with a parent? Does the child feel unloved or unappreciated?

☐ *A feeling of resentment.* Could he be jealous of a sibling, peer, or your relationships?

☐ *A feeling of inadequacy.* Might he be compensating for low self-esteem, inadequacy, or feeling that he's not good enough?

☐ *Explosive or quick-tempered.* Does your child have difficulties controlling his anger? Is he short-fused?

☐ *Undue anxiety or stress.* Are there heavy pressures on him to succeed (academically, socially, athletically)? Is competition to achieve a big commodity around your house? Is he so scheduled that he has no downtime?

☐ *Learning disability.* What about a learning disability causing difficulties in processing what he hears? If so, are you seeking professional help? If not, why not?

☐ *Depression.* Is he suffering from an emotional problem, depression, or trauma that is triggering this attitude?

☐ *Unfair expectations.* Might your expectations be unrealistic or unfair? Are they within your kid's developmental level?

☐ *Alcohol or substance abuse.* Could your older kid be indulging in alcohol or drugs?

☐ *Abusive treatment.* Is your child treated disrespectfully? Has he now or in the past been verbally or physically abused?

☐ *Other:* _____

_____

_____

There are many reasons for a defiant, noncompliant attitude. The key is to get at the root so you can deal with the real cause. Once you do, make sure you get the help you need to remedy it.

Step 2. Spell Out Your Expectations

At a time when both you and your child are calm, explain that from this point on, you expect her compliance with your requests. Be very clear so that there can be no doubt what you mean. You might say: "If I sound serious or say 'I'm serious,' I mean it." Then make sure your kid clearly knows your "serious tone" by modeling it. Explain that if she doesn't do what you ask, there will be a consequence. (Review Step 4 so you can tell your child what the consequence is if noncompliance continues.) You might even consider letting your child participate in creating her own consequence. Just remember that you don't have to agree to her suggestions; it's a way to involve her in the process. To make sure she understands your agreement, have her repeat what you said. You might even put the consequence in writing, and then have your kid sign it so there's absolutely no doubt. A young kid can draw the contract. Put it in a safe place so you can rely on it later if needed.

In case your child really does have a genuine reason for not complying with your request (the possibility does exist), hear her out but demand respect. You might say, "If you really have a legitimate excuse why you can't do what I'm asking, please tell me right now. Maybe you have a spelling test the next day and need a reprieve from your chores so you can study. But you *must* tell me your reason in a respectful tone." To be clear your child knows what kind of tone you require, model it to her. She needs to understand that you won't be granting too many reprieves. There really should be a very good reason for her not to do what you ask.

Step 3. State Your Request Respectfully

Now the time comes when you want your kid to do something. First, make sure you have his attention and then state your request firmly, calmly, and respectfully. Also, try lowering your voice instead of raising it. Nothing turns a kid off faster than yelling, so do the opposite. When you talk more softly, not louder, the tone usually catches the kid off-guard, and he stops to listen. Your kid may try every trick in the book to wear you down. Don't let him.

The following strategies are also helpful in reducing verbal power struggles with kids:

- *Limit words.* The fewer words you say the better: "Homework" or "Bed." Keep your requests short, sweet, and specific.
- *Use the Ten-Second Rule.* Stop your directions (threats, coaxing, pleading) at the end of ten seconds. If you need to talk beyond ten seconds, you're saying too much.

- *Give a warning.* It is difficult for some kids to shift gears, especially if they're in the middle of something interesting. So give a time limit: "I'll need your assistance in three minutes" or "I have to talk to you in two minutes."
- *Use the Review Method.* To ensure your kid understands your requests, use the Review Method: state the request (the fewer words the better) and then your kid "reviews" (repeats) what you just said back to you.
- *Try the Broken Record Technique.* Tell why you want your kid to comply, and then state your position: "Ms. Ling is coming in five minutes: you need to be at the door now." Calmly repeat your request word for word each time your kid tries to argue.
- *Offer choices.* Just a bit of leeway sometimes breaks down a resister. "You need to study for your spelling today. Would you like to do so before dinner or after?"
- *Compromise.* "Your chores are supposed to be done now, but you're working so hard on your throwing. Do you agree to do your chores in half an hour?" Don't ever let your kid force you into a compromise you don't think is fair or appropriate.

If your kid doesn't obey your request within seconds, then you must follow through on the agreed consequence. So go to Step 4, stay thick-skinned, and enforce it.

Step 4. If Defiance Continues, Enforce a Consequence

If you've been clear with your expectations yet your kid continues to defy you, it's time to set a consequence. Effective consequences are clear to the child, have a specified time, directly relate to the offensive attitude, and fit the kid's age and temperament. They must also cause a bit of misery so the child is more willing to change his behavior than suffer the consequence. Once you set it, consistently enforce it, *and don't back down*! Also, do not negotiate, plead, yell, coax, or bribe. One of the hardest parts of dealing with a defiant kid is remaining calm. But you must; stick to your word and enforce the consequence. Your kid has to learn you mean business. Here are a few consequences suitable for defiant attitudes for different aged kids:

- *Time-out.* For kids generally up to age eight, time-out may be appropriate. This is when a child is immediately removed from an activity for defiance and asked to sit alone quietly for a specified time to think about his actions. The simplest rule for determining the time length is one minute for each year of the child's age (four years equals four minutes, eight years equals eight minutes, and so on). Customize depending on the age of your child, his temperament and personality, and the severity of the offense. For some kids, it's an unendurable cruelty, and for others it's no fun but not a big deal. Make sure that when your child completes time-out (and the time starts the second he complies with your time-out rules), he must still comply with your requests.
- *Loss of privileges.* Any continued display of the targeted misbehavior can result in your kid's losing certain specified privileges. Make sure it's something you have control over. Losses could include watching TV; using his favorite skateboard, scooter, or bike; playing video or computer games; talking on the phone; listening to music; or even using a common family area.
- *Grounding.* Other than school or church time, your child must stay on the house premises for a specified length of time—generally a few hours for young kids and one to five days for older kids—and lose all social privileges except for education or church-related purposes. This should be spelled out ahead.
- *Code red.* If the offense is particularly egregious or defiance continues, some parents pull some or all home entertainment privileges (TV, video games, and phone), in addition to grounding. The reason is simple: unless the attitude stops,

it will continue to spiral out of control. This is especially true with preadolescents.

- **Boot camp.** Find a service project your child can do (with an adult to oversee it), and then require duty for a set period. Maybe it's working in a soup kitchen, helping underprivileged kids, or tutoring second-language children.

The first few times you enforce consequences will not be easy with a defiant kid who is used to getting his way. At times, you may really think it's a heck of a lot easier to give in to your kid. Don't. Once your kid wins again, things will only get worse. Be prepared for your kid to resist your consequences big time and do anything, including an Exorcist-type tantrum, calling you every name in the book, and basically making your life miserable. The trick is for you to stay calm (I know, I know—easier said than done) and above all: *do not back down*.

Step 5. Nurture and Expect Respect

Kids with defiant attitudes are clearly also disrespectful. So while part of your makeover is to no longer tolerate a defiant attitude and to expect compliance, the other part is to rebuild respect in your child. Here are four strategies to enhance this critical virtue:

- **Define respect.** Take time to explain clearly what you mean by acting respectfully. You might say, "Respect means that you value or admire someone or something by treating them in a considerate, courteous, and polite manner. How you treat people can let them know you think they are special. It can also let them know you don't value them. I expect you to act respectfully because it's one way to make our world a better place." Once your child understands, then expect respect.
- **Ask the Golden Rule question.** Emphasize the Golden Rule in your family: "Treat others as you want to be treated."

Explain that a simple way to determine if you are acting respectfully is to always ask yourself before you act, "Would I want someone to treat me like that?" Once your child understands the meaning of the question, use it any time her attitude is disrespectful: "Are you using the Golden Rule?" It will help her think about her attitude and its consequences to other people's feelings.

- *Reinforce respect.* Don't overlook one of the easiest ways to tune up respect: acknowledge your kid when he acts respectfully. Remember that attitudes that are reinforced are ones that kids will continue to use. "You told Dad using a respectful voice why you couldn't take out the trash because Grandma was calling any minute."

- *Create new family rules.* Many families develop a set of rules based on respect that everyone agrees will govern how they treat one another. Though they are almost always ones you would choose yourself, because the kids have a voice in determining them, they become "their rules," not "yours" (so they're much easier to enforce). Begin by brainstorming together, "What rules should guide how we treat one another in our family?" Write all suggestions on paper, and then use the democratic process and vote. The top suggestions become the family constitution. Here are a few family guidelines:

Don't borrow without asking.
Listen to one another.
Don't pass on to others what is said in confidence.
Treat one another as you'd like to be treated.
Be considerate of one another.
Use a calm, pleasant voice.
Say only things that build people.
Respect each other's privacy.

Many families make their final version into a chart, have all members sign it, and post it as a visible reminder.

The First 21 Days

For the next twenty-one days, put your kid in charge of a major but age-appropriate Personal Responsibility Project that would benefit the entire family. For example, for a young child, organize the family games and sports equipment into bins or weed the flower patch. For older kids, possibilities are organizing the family photos, painting the steps down to the basement, or alphabetizing the family videos, books, and DVDs. Agree on a list of requirements and goals for the twenty-one-day time frame, and let your kid figure out how to get to the finish line on time. Also build in a consequence for failure, like loss of privilege. Don't help, and don't monitor. This kind of responsibility and respect can go a long way toward building self-confidence, creating independence, and ultimately teaching a spirit of willingness and cooperation, to replace the noncompliance and defiance of recent attitudes.

ATTITUDE MAKEOVER PLEDGE

How will you use these steps to help your kid become less defiant, rebellious, and disobedient and achieve long-term change? On the lines below, write exactly what you agree to do within the next twenty-four hours to begin changing your kid's attitude so he is more compliant.

_____

_____

_____

THE NEW ATTITUDE REVIEW

All attitude makeovers take hard work, constant practice, and parental reinforcement. Each step your child takes toward change may be a small one, so be sure to acknowledge and congratulate every one of them along the way. It takes a minimum of twenty-one days to see real results, so don't give up! And if one strategy doesn't work, try another. Write your child's weekly progress on the lines below. Keep track of daily progress in your Attitude Makeover Journal.

WEEK 1

_____

_____

_____

WEEK 2

_____

_____

_____

WEEK 3

_____

_____

_____

ONGOING ATTITUDE TUNE-UP

Where does your child's attitude still need improvement? What work still needs to be done?

_____

_____

_____

ATTITUDE MAKEOVER RESOURCES

For Parents

Children Who Say No When You Want Them to Say Yes, by James Windell (New York: Macmillan, 1996). A parent tool for handling stubborn, oppositional kids through adolescence.

From Defiance to Cooperation: Real Solutions for Transforming the Angry, Defiant, Discouraged Child, by John F. Taylor (Roseville, Calif.: Prima Publishing, 2001). Constructive ways to channel defiant, oppositional energy and determination with easy-to-implement suggestions.

Parent in Control, by Gregory Bodenhamer (New York: Fireside, 1995). Using common scenarios to demonstrate specific parenting techniques, a one-time probation officer offers a straightforward tested program for maintaining control over adolescents without harsh discipline.

Parenting Your Out-of-Control Teenager: 7 Steps to Restate Authority and Reclaim Love, by Scott P. Sells (New York: St. Martin's Press, 2001). Comforting advice and solid steps to reclaim your control over a defiant kid.

The Explosive Child, by Ross W. Greene (New York: HarperCollins, 1998). Sound parenting suggestions for dealing with easily frustrated, "chronically inflexible" kids.

Treating the Unmanageable Adolescent: A Guide to Oppositional Defiant and Conduct Disorders, by Neil Bernstein (Northvale, N.J.: Jason Aronson, 1996). Though aimed at clinicians, this guide offers invaluable suggestions for dealing with the out-of-control teen.

19

Pessimistic
Antidote: Optimism, Hopefulness, Joyfulness

"What's the point of trying?"

Dear Dr. Borba,
My wife and I are becoming increasingly concerned about our eight-year-old daughter. She's such a pessimist. No matter what the activity, she assumes she'll do miserably. It's almost as though she sets herself up for failure. It doesn't seem to make much difference what her mom and I say or how hard we try to convince her otherwise. Jenna just focuses on the doom and gloom. What can we do to help her be more optimistic and hopeful about life?

—Jerry K., dad from Ottawa, Canada

Bad Attitude Act Out

"Why should I care? We're all going to blow up anyway."

"My new school sucks—nobody's going to like me here either."

"What's the point of practicing? I'll never make the band."

EMERGENCY ATTITUDE ℞

A pessimistic attitude can be devastating and requires an immediate grasp of where it's coming from. Is your child suffering from reflecting some peer culture or media trend on the street that says it's cool to be down? Is your kid freaking out from watching terrifying news on CNN twelve hours a day? Have there been any recent tragic events in your family or community that may have traumatized her? Has he been having a series of repeated frustrating, disappointing, or distressing experiences at school lately? Does he have a diagnosed (or undiagnosed) health condition that might be affecting his mood? Is he anxious or depressed?

Some of these factors are controllable, and some aren't. Start the triage by a process of elimination. First, cut the ones that have no bearing on your child. Second, put aside the ones you can't control. Finally, focus on the single potential reason that is the easiest to change, like reducing negative media input, preventing him from hanging around with kids who bum him out, or taking him out of that accelerated class if it's causing him so much stress.

"Nothing I do matters." "Why should I bother?" "It isn't going to work, ya know!" Unlike kids with a judgmental attitude, these kids have a general doom-and-gloom outlook about the whole world. It's not that they are critical; it's that they feel hopeless.

Kids with pessimistic attitudes are among the most frustrating breeds. They give up easily, believe anything they do won't make a difference, and assume they won't succeed. Then when they do achieve or do something well, they discount the accomplishment: "It wasn't that great." "It was just luck." Sadly, they rarely see the good, wonderful things of life. These kids dwell instead on the negative bad parts, and often those parts are themselves. Instead of being optimistic, they find only the inadequacies in themselves: "I'm so dumb, why should I study?" "Nobody's going to like me, so why bother?" "I'm not trying out. Who would pick me for their team?" Because they engage in huge doses of self-pity, pessimistic kids are also self-centered. If left unchecked, this attitude can spiral into cynicism, criticism, and selfishness. Worse yet, it can plant the seeds of underachievement and even depression.

Kids aren't born pessimistic. Research shows a large part of this attitude is picked up along the way, and today's world is fertile for growing cynicism. Need evidence? Just tune in to popular musical lyrics, and listen to the despair. The nightly news and newspapers cement in kids' minds that the world is a bad, hopeless place. More and more kids are succumbing to the "mean world syndrome," and for good reason. Where once those tragic and terrifying world events seemed so far away or only printed words in the newspaper, they are now 24/7 on TV and the Internet. It's no wonder that many kids are pessimistic.

And don't forget how your interpretation of world events affects your kids. After all, many of our kids' views are formed from listening to ours. Sadly, too often kids hear a pessimistic, cynical outlook of life instead of an upbeat or positive one. Take heart: research at Penn State University concludes that parents can teach kids the virtues of optimism, hopefulness, and joyfulness, which dramatically reduces their pessimistic attitudes, improves their character, and increases the likelihood of long-term happiness. The sooner you start, the easier it will be.

BAD ATTITUDE ALERT

By now we realize that before we can eliminate pessimistic attitudes, we really need to know where, when, and how this state of mind evolved.

Diagnosis

Asking these questions is the way to start your makeover campaign.

Why. Why is your kid such a pessimist? Does she hear only dismal views of the world at home? Is she experiencing frequent frustrations or failures? Does she listen to despairing CD lyrics? Has anything fueled such a negative view—for instance, a traumatic event that could be triggering pessimistic feelings about the world, a change in your family, a divorce, a world event, the death of a loved one, a move, or a class or school change? What about a new teacher, school difficulties, relationship frictions, or a hectic schedule that might have triggered the attitude? Pessimism can also be a sign of more serious issues such as physical health, anxiety, low self-esteem, trauma, or depression. For your older child, could substance abuse be a possibility for her pessimism? If you think any of these more deeply engrained issues could be provoking pessimism, seek help from a trained professional. Talk to other adults who know your child well. What will you do?

What. Are there particular issues or things he usually expresses more pessimism about? For instance, is he pessimistic about the world in general or more specific things, such as his ability to succeed in an athletic endeavor, learn a particular subject (spelling, history, math), get along with friends, cope with a new teacher, coach, or stepparent, or be able to try any new experience?

Who. Does he express the same pessimistic attitude to everyone? Are there some individuals she does not use this attitude on? If so, who? Why are they spared?

When. Is there a particular time of day, week, or month she is more pessimistic? Might there be a reason? For example, is it in evidence following the nightly news, a family discussion, or visiting an elderly acquaintance? Can you identify when your kid became more pessimistic? Was there a particular event or incident that might have triggered or intensified her pessimistic views? If so, what do you think it was?

Where. Are there certain places she is more likely to express pessimism (at school, the babysitter's house, an athletic event, a particular teacher, a visit to a certain relative)? Why?

Now take a look at your answers. Are you seeing any predictable patterns? Do you have any better understanding of this attitude and where it's coming from? Talk to others who know your child well. Write down your thoughts.

WHAT'S WRONG
WITH YOUR CURRENT RESPONSE?

Now reflect on how you typically respond to your child's pessimism. Think of the last time your kid displayed this attitude. Where were the two of you? How did the incident start? What did your child say? How did you respond? Be specific. What did you say and do? Did you ignore it by walking away, dismiss it ("That's not true!"), belittle it ("Why would you say that?"), or agree with him ("You're right, you probably won't do well. You didn't study")? Were you insulting, judging, criticizing, humiliating, threatening, or yelling? What about your nonverbal cues. Do you smirk, smile, shrug your shoulders, shake your head, or raise your eyebrows?

Now think of your kid's reaction. How did he react to your response? What did he say or do? What about his facial expressions? After your response, did he appear more relieved? More stressed? Perplexed? Irritated? Frustrated? Get into his shoes. How would you feel if you just heard that response? What is one response you know never helps your kid to be less pessimistic? Write it.

I will not _____

_____

_____

FACING YOUR OWN BAD ATTITUDES

Have you ever been depressed or felt hopeless? Do you consider yourself an optimistic, positive individual or more pessimistic and cynical? Would your closest friends agree with your verdict? What about your kids? For instance, do you generally look for the good or bad in a bleak situation? How do you typically deal with setbacks and failures?

Kids are not born pessimistic, so where is your kid acquiring this attitude? From siblings, friends, neighbors, relatives, or you? Kids listen to, watch, and copy our reactions. What might your kid be copying? Here are a few situations to help you consider if you are more optimistic or pessimistic:

- A tragic world event is flashed on TV. Do you say that there may well be a catastrophic outcome—or express your view that world leaders will be able to solve it?
- You have been dealt a financial setback. Do you express your concerns that you will suffer severe losses that you might never recoup—or offer encouragement that you'll be able to make ends meet?
- You and your best friend had a tiff. Do you blame your friend for causing the friction—or convey that the two of you will work things through and remain friends?
- Your kid comes home with a bad report card in math. Do you tell her not to worry because women in your family were never good in math—or brainstorm a plan to help your daughter improve her grade because you know she's capable?
- An elderly friend is seriously ill. Do you express your concerns that your friend may never recover—or state your

326   *Twenty-Four Attitude Makeovers*

belief that she'll improve because of her tough spirit and the excellent medical care she is receiving?

What is the first step you need to take in yourself to be a better example to your sons or daughters of dealing with their pessimistic behavior? Write down changes you need to make.

I will _____

_____

_____

_____

BAD ATTITUDE NEWS ALERT

A child today is ten times more likely to be seriously depressed compared to a child born in the first third of this century. Martin Seligman, author of *The Optimistic Child*, found that helping kids become more optimistic and less cynical not only helps protect them from depression but also to be less frequently depressed, more successful at school and on the job, better able to bounce back from adversity, and even physically healthier than cynical people. His work also found that optimism can be nurtured and pessimism can be reduced.

THE "DON'T GIVE ME THAT ATTITUDE" MAKEOVER

To eliminate your child's pessimism, take the following six steps.

Step 1. Look for the Positive

Begin your kid's attitude makeover by stressing an optimistic outlook in your home so she sees the good parts of life instead of just the downside. A good first step is to monitor what your kid watches and reads. After all, a constant onslaught of gloomy news can have an impact on a kid's outlook. Focus instead on the good news happening in the world and share what you learn. Here are a few ways to look for the positive as a family:

- *Start Good News Reports.* Consider starting your dinner with a Good News Report in which each member reports something good that happened during the day.
- *Share optimistic stories.* The world is filled with examples of individuals who suffered enormous obstacles but didn't cave into pessimistic thinking. Instead, they remained optimistic, and kept at their dreams until they succeeded. So look for examples to share with your kids. Here are a few: Beethoven's music teacher told him he was hopeless as a composer; author Louisa May Alcott was told by countless publishers that no one would ever read *Little Women*; Michael Jordan was cut from his high school basketball team; Walt Disney was fired by a newspaper editor for lacking great ideas. He went bankrupt and had nervous breakdowns.
- *Institute goodness reviews.* Start a nighttime tradition of reviewing with your child the good parts about her day. Be sure to share your highlights as well. This is a precious way to spend the last waking hours with your kid, as well as instilling in her a habit of looking for the good in life.

Step 2. Confront Pessimistic Thinking

Many kids don't change their pessimistic ways because they are unaware of how often they are pessimistic. Psychologists teach clients to track their cynical thoughts using tokens such as marbles or poker chips. They instruct them to put the tokens in their left pocket, and then transfer a token to the right pocket for each negative comment stated either inside or outside their heads. They now have evidence of how often they are pessimistic and are more receptive to changing. Here are ways to help kids tune into their more pessimistic, cynical thoughts and then help them learn to confront the pessimism:

- *Point out cynicism.* Create a code, such as pulling on your ear or touching your elbow, that only you and your kid are aware of. The code means he's uttered a cynical comment.
- *Tune into it.* Encourage your kid to listen to his own cynical comments. Suggest an older kid wear a watch or bracelet as a reminder of negative thinking. Glancing at the watch is a visual cue that reminds her to tune into how often she is pessimistic.
- *Count negative thoughts.* Help your kid count his pessimistic comments for a set time period: "Listen for the next five minutes [or other brief time] to track how many times you say downbeat things out loud or inside your head." A young kid can count pessimistic comments on his fingers. An older kid can use coins, moving one from his left to right pocket for each pessimistic statement. Kids can also count them making tally marks on a piece of paper.
- *Confront "stinkin' thinking."* Teach your kid to "talk back to the pessimistic voice" so he doesn't listen to it. A great way to explain how is by using yourself as an example. Feel free to fictionalize the story, just as long as your kid gets the point: "I remember when I was your age. Right before I'd take a test, a voice inside me would say, 'You're not going to do well.' I learned to talk back to it. I'd tell it: 'I'm going to try my best. If I try my best, I'll do okay.' Pretty soon the voice faded away because I refused to listen to it. When you hear that voice, talk to it and say it's wrong."

Step 3. Balance Pessimistic Talk

Cynical kids can seem as if they're trapped in pessimistic thinking patterns and can see only the downward side of any situation. As the habit becomes more prominent, they often blow negative happenings out of proportion and downplay the importance of positive ones. One way to thwart your child's pessimistic thinking is by providing a more balanced perspective. If you use the strategy enough, your kid will use it to help counter his own inner pessimistic talk. Here are three examples that show you how:

- Your younger child won't go to her friend's birthday party because she thinks no one likes her. Offer a more balanced view: "If Sunny didn't like you, you'd never have been invited."
- Your older kid didn't make the soccer team and believes "everyone" thinks she's a bad player. Counter her comment: "I know you're disappointed, but remember that at least half of those kids know you're a good athlete in other sports such as skiing and roller-blading."
- Your daughter blows her first math exam exclaiming that she's stupid and can never do anything right. You say: "I see how upset you are, but nobody can be good at everything. You're good in history and art. Meanwhile, let's figure out a way to help improve your math."

Step 4. Deal with Mistakes Optimistically

Pessimistic kids often give up at the first sign of difficulty, never recognizing that mistakes are a fact of life and a big part of how we learn. Of course, one of the quickest ways kids will learn to erase thinking that mistakes are fatal is feeling our accepting response to their errors, so make sure you do. Here are a few more ways to help your kids keep a more optimistic outlook about setbacks:

- *Stress that it's okay to make mistakes.* The first step in helping kids realize errors don't have to fatal is to simply say: "It's okay to make a mistake." Make sure you do.
- *Admit your mistakes.* Obviously, we make mistakes, but too often we keep them to ourselves. So admit your own errors to your kids: it helps them recognize that mistake making

happens to *everyone*. When you make a mistake, tell your child not only your error, but also what you learned from it because you will be sending a more optimistic message: "I was late for work because I couldn't find my keys. I learned to put my keys in the same place every time so I can find them."

- **Call it by another name.** A common trait of optimistic kids is that they often call mistakes by other names: glitch, bug, a setback. Renaming helps curb any pessimistic, discouraging thoughts in the middle of their learning. Help your child come up with a word to say inside his head whenever he encounters a mistake. Any word will do—just make sure to help him practice saying it over and over so he'll remember to use it when he has a setback.

Step 5. Encourage Positive Speculation

Pessimistic kids often think of the gloomy outcome and bad possibilities to any situation. As a result, they can greatly short-change their potential for succeeding. Here are ways to help your kid think through the possible outcomes of circumstances. He will then be more likely to have a realistic appraisal before making any decision:

- **Ask "what if?"** Help your kid think about potential consequences of any situation by asking "what-if" kinds of questions. "What might happen if you tried that?" "What might happen if you didn't try?"
- **List pros and cons.** Another way to help kids decide on the best choice is by helping them weigh the pros and cons of possible choices. "What are all the good things that might happen if you choose that? What are the bad things? Now weigh the good with the bad. Are there more good or bad outcomes?"
- **Name the worst thing.** Ask your child to think of the absolute worst thing that could happen if he followed through with his intention. Then help him weigh if the outcome really is all that bad, as well as ways to deal with it.

Step 6. Acknowledge a Positive Attitude

Change is always difficult, especially when you are trying to alter an attitude that is a well-used habit. Be on the alert for those times your child does utter optimism. If you're not looking for the behavior, you may well miss those moments when your child is trying a new approach. Whenever you do hear optimism, acknowledge your child's effort. Just make sure to remind him what he said that was optimistic and why you appreciate the comment:

"Kara, I know how difficult your spelling tests have been. But saying you think you'll do better was being so optimistic. I'm sure you'll do better because you've been studying so hard."

"Sam, it pleases me that you said you'll try your best to tie your shoes by yourself. Way to be positive!"

 **The First 21 Days**

Initiate a Power of Positive Thinking Campaign in your family so everyone, and especially your kid with the pessimistic attitude, can learn positive statements to say inside their head to counter negative thoughts. This campaign will build confidence, and help everyone handle adversity as well. Here are a few positive thoughts to try—or ask your kid to create his own:

"It doesn't have to be perfect."
"No big deal; everyone makes mistakes."
"I can do it."

"Believe, believe, and you will achieve."
"Don't worry; it'll turn out okay."
"I'll never know unless I try."
"I can be calm and in control."

You might write the one or two most effective ones on a card so your kid can carry it in his pocket, make a tape recording of the phrase to play over and over, or turn it into a song for a young child to sing. If your kid keeps practicing for twenty-one days, he will acquire a new habit to curb pessimism, and that will last a lifetime.

ATTITUDE MAKEOVER PLEDGE

How will you use these steps to help your kid become less pessimistic and achieve long-term change? On the lines below, write exactly what you agree to do within the next twenty-four hours to begin changing your kid's attitude so he is more optimistic and upbeat about life.

_____

_____

_____

THE NEW ATTITUDE REVIEW

All attitude makeovers take hard work, constant practice, and parental reinforcement. Each step your child takes toward change may be a small one, so be sure to acknowledge and congratulate every one of them along the way. It takes a minimum of twenty-one days to see real results, so don't give up!

And if one strategy doesn't work, try another. Write your child's weekly progress on the lines below. Keep track of daily progress in your Attitude Makeover Journal.

WEEK 1

_____

_____

_____

WEEK 2

_____

_____

_____

WEEK 3

_____

_____

_____

ONGOING ATTITUDE TUNE-UP

Where does your child's attitude still need improvement? What work still needs to be done?

_____

_____

_____

_____

_____

ATTITUDE MAKEOVER RESOURCES

For Parents

Positive Self-Talk for Children: Teaching Self-Esteem Through Affirmations, by Douglas Blouch (New York: Bantam Books, 1993). A wonderful guide that instructs parents, step-by-step, how to help toddlers to teens turn off the negative voice within and activate the powerful "yes" voice.

Raising Positive Kids in a Negative World, by Zig Ziglar (New York: Ballantine Books, 1996). Written by the popular motivational speaker Ziglar, this book offers sensible guidelines on raising optimistic kids.

The Optimistic Child, by Martin E. P. Seligman (Boston: Houghton Mifflin, 1995). A wonderful guide offering parents specific tools to teach kids of all ages life skills that transform helplessness and negativity into mastery and bolster genuine self-esteem.

"I Think I Can, I Know I Can!" by Susan Isaacs and Wendy Ritchey (New York: St. Martin's Press, 1989). A guide to helping kids learn to replace pessimistic thinking patterns with positive self-talk.

Raising Resilient Children: Foster Strength, Hope and Optimism in Your Child, by Robert Brooks and Sam Goldstein (New York: Contemporary Books 2001). A unique, wise guide that helps parent focus on their children's strengths, not weaknesses, in overcoming obstacles.

Nurturing Resilience in Our Children: Answers to the Most Important Parenting Questions, by Robert Brooks and Sam Goldstein (New York: Contemporary Books, 2003). Two foremost experts on resilience answer parents' pressing questions about resilience and helping children overcome pessimistic thinking.

For Kids

Fortunately, by Remy Charlip (New York: Macmillan, 1987). An absolute must for young readers. It's a model on changing your unfortunates into fortunates. Ages 4 to 10.

My Mama Says There Aren't Any Zombies, Ghosts, Vampires, Creatures, Demons, Monsters, Fiends, Goblins, or Things, by Judith Viorst (New

York: Aladdin Paperbacks, 1988). A young boy discovers that adults—even his mother—can make mistakes. Ages 3 to 8.

Comeback! Four True Stories, by Jim O'Connor. (New York: Random House, 1992). The tale of four famous athletes who overcame serious injuries or debilitating conditions through effort, perseverance, and an optimistic outlook. Ages 7 to 11.

Mistakes That Worked, by Charlotte Foltz Jones. (New York: Doubleday, 1991). A series of short stories that describe over forty inventions that were all discovered by accident, including Silly Putty, ice cream cones, pizza, chocolate chip cookies, Velcro, aspirin, Frisbees, and even X-rays. Ages 8 to 13.

The Giraffe Project. [http;//www.giraffe.org/giraffe/]. A nonprofit organization that recognizes people for sticking their necks out for the common good and not giving up. The project's "Standing Tall" curriculum helps teachers and youth leaders build courage, caring, and responsibility in kids 6 to 18 years old.

Bad Attitude

20

Poor Loser
Antidote: Good Sportsmanship, Fairness, Forgiveness

"I should have won."

Dear Dr. Borba,
My wife and I are really concerned about our son's attitude: he's such a poor loser, and I don't mean about just sports but everything at home, school, among his friends. If something goes wrong for him, he just can't accept it! Instead he makes excuses or blames everyone (us, the teacher, his friends, the coach). At this rate, nobody's going to want him in their class or on a team. How can I turn around this bad attitude?

—Bill D., a father of four from Louisville, Kentucky

Bad Attitude Act Out

"You cheated, Dad! I never lose at Candyland."

"The teacher never gave me a chance. I could have gotten the answer right."

"They ought to fire the coach. He never lets me play."

EMERGENCY ATTITUDE ℞

Identify the most typical way your kid shows his poor response to losing. Does he blame other people? Make excuses? Cry or lose his temper? Does he cheat or lie? Does he quit in the middle or seek revenge? Then focus intentionally on replacing this bad attitude with a more appropriate and constructive response to losing. For example, if he blames his teacher or coach, tell him that response is no longer acceptable. Instead, help him to take responsibility for what happened. Challenge his view of the facts, and help him understand why it was nobody's fault but his own. Then help him do an instant replay with the scenario in a responsible and more mature way.

Watching any kid be a poor loser is embarrassing, but when the kid is yours, it's downright humiliating. Sure, the kid may be the best bassoonist in the orchestra, have the highest grade-point average in the class, be the best cheerleader on the squad, or be the greatest runner in town, but the moment she starts arguing, making excuses, cheating, blaming others, or booing, her skills no longer matter. What everyone sees instead is a poor loser, and that's a tough image to erase.

One big reason we may have such an epidemic of poor losers is that we aren't doing such a great job of modeling how to win or lose ourselves. Besides poor modeling, the parental emphasis too often these days seems bent on raising the "trophy kid"—that is, producing offspring with the most awards, highest test scores, and longest resumés. The payoff can be deadly to our kids' character.

A "win at any cost" mentality often means putting everything aside, including homespun values like consideration, camaraderie, and humility, and letting selfish, egocentric ways take over. It's all the more reason to help your kid learn to win as well as lose gracefully in all areas of life. Tuning up this attitude is about how to help our kids play the game called life—and how to play it well. We must replace a poor losing attitude with the virtues of good sportsmanship, fairness, and forgiveness.

BAD ATTITUDE ALERT

Being a poor loser is more than just about good sportsmanship. It may be an indication of deeper issues like fear of failure or inadequacy, extreme parental pressure, or vicious competition. So be sure to know where your child's bad attitude originated before beginning the makeover campaign.

Diagnosis
Start with these five questions.

Why. Is he a poor loser because he hasn't learned good sportsmanship? Is he trying to prove himself to others? Does he lack friends? Does he have a thin skin when it comes to teasing? Is he devastated if a friend lets him down in any way? Does he have trouble with the stress of competition, poor skills or ability, or low self-esteem? Is he afraid of losing or making a mistake? Is he afraid of lowering himself in your eyes? Doesn't he enjoy the game or classroom competition? Is it something you want him to do, rather than something he wants to do? Is there an overemphasis on winning (from parents, kid, or coach)? Once you determine the contributors, think through what you'll do to remedy the problem.

What. Next, observe your kid in some kind of competition. This could be competing against her previous grade on a term paper, playing checkers with a friend, engaging in a spelling bee, or swimming in an event. *Hint:* Do so without her knowing you're watching. What does she do that concerns you? Here are a few behaviors of a poor loser. Check ones that apply to your kid, and jot down the behaviors you notice need improving:

- ☐ Makes excuses
- ☐ Blames others for the loss
- ☐ Can't accept criticism
- ☐ Criticizes peers: their errors or abilities
- ☐ Negative: cheers others' mistakes or boos
- ☐ Argues with referee, music director, teacher, other adults or peers
- ☐ Fails to congratulate opponents
- ☐ Changes rules midstream for his advantage
- ☐ Cheats or lies
- ☐ Quits midstream or leaves when bored or tired
- ☐ Can't accept defeat gracefully; cries or complains
- ☐ Wants to quit or give up instead of work to improve performance
- ☐ Other: _____
  _____
  _____

Who. Does he display the same attitude toward everyone? Are there some individuals he does not use his poor loser attitude on? If so, who? Why are they spared? Does he display the attitude when he is competing against others, against siblings, or only when he competes against himself?

When. Is there a particular time of day, week, or month he displays the attitude? Is there a reason? For instance, might he be tired, more anxious, frustrated, concerned about final grades, insecure, needing attention, or concerned about who might be watching or who he is with?

Where. Are there certain places he is more likely to use the attitude (at school, home, band practice, in math class, on the baseball field, during choir practice, at a particular kid's house)? Why?

Now take a look at your answers. Are you seeing any predictable patterns? Do you have any better understanding of this attitude and why he's using it?

WHAT'S WRONG
WITH YOUR CURRENT RESPONSE?

How do you respond when your kid loses a sporting event or other competition or gets a poor grade? Do you ask him, "Why didn't you do as well as last time?" "Were the other kids upset with you?" "How about the teacher [or coach]?" "What did you get?" "Why didn't you score?" "Why didn't you get more playing time?" "How much longer do you have to have that coach?" "Why did you get such a bad grade?" "What did the other kids get?" "Was your teacher mad?"

Do you get mad? Blame your kid? Blame the teacher or coach? Plan to retaliate? Threaten to sue? What message is your kid picking up from your response? What response do you now realize you should never repeat?

I will not _____

_____

_____

FACING YOUR OWN BAD ATTITUDES

How did you handle defeat and failure when you were growing up? Do you see any of those same behaviors in your child? Kids love to hear that their parents made mistakes when they were growing up. If you haven't shared your pain of failure with your child, consider doing so. Did you learn any coping strategies that helped you bounce back? What were they? Where did you learn them? Have you modeled any of those strategies to your child? If not, think about how you might teach them to your child. Write down your reflections and plan.

Kids are not born poor losers, so where might she be learning this behavior? Siblings? Friends? Neighbors? Relatives? You? Think about where your kid might be learning this attitude. How well are you and your partner modeling how to win and lose gracefully? Do you make excuses for your own difficulties? Do you blame your boss or colleagues when something goes wrong for you at work? Are you always complaining that were it not for some unfair rule, law, or authority, your whole life would be better? Do you yell at the coach or referee? Do you criticize your kids' teachers in front of them? Do you blame the coach? Do you cheer when your kid's opponent gets hurt? What about when you watch a sports or a game show with your kid? Does he see you booing, criticizing, or blaming the coach or opponent? Might the example of the adults or other kids be influencing his attitude? Or when playing games as your children were growing up, did you always let them win? Did you let them learn how to lose gracefully and be a good sport about it? How do you react to the winners and losers when you watch reality TV, a sporting event, or a game show?

What can you do to create a better example for your kid? What is the first step you need to take in yourself to help your son or daughter lose with poise, bounce back from defeat, or be a better teammate? For instance, you could stop making excuses, criticizing, or blaming others for your defeats. You could take the time to thank or compliment the officials, teacher, or coach at your kid's events, cheer and encourage your kid's opponents or teammates, or model how to handle defeat. Write down changes you need to make.

I will _____

_____

BAD ATTITUDE NEWS ALERT

The National Association of Sports Officials told the Associated Press recently that it receives two to three calls a week from an umpire or referee who has been assaulted by a parent or spectator. The complaints range from verbal abuse to the official's having his car run off the road by an irate parent. Youth sports programs in at least 163 cities are so concerned about the trend of poor parent sportsmanship that they now require parents to sign a pledge of proper conduct before attending their kids' games. How do adults display poor loser attitudes around your kid?

THE "DON'T GIVE ME THAT ATTITUDE" MAKEOVER

To curb your child's bad attitude toward losing, take the following steps.

Step 1. Call Your Kid on the First Hint of a Bad Attitude

Any time your kid exhibits a poor loser attitude (for example, he makes an excuse, blames others, can't accept criticism, boos the other team, or criticizes his coach, teacher, sibling, or parent), call him on it and let him know that kind of attitude isn't allowed. If he exhibits the attitude with others, take him aside and tell him what you observed: "I heard you blaming others for your mistake," "You're fighting with the coach," or "You're criticizing others." Then let him know that if he doesn't stop the attitude on the spot or apologize, he leaves the game, field, or play group. Explain that he must be considerate of other people's feelings, and if he is not, he may not participate. And if your kid displays any aggressive or uncivil behavior—such as booing, hitting, or cheating—remove him immediately from the activity. A high school soccer coach once told me that the most effective way poor losers on his team got turned around was when their teammates told them to "get a life" and wouldn't tolerate their bad attitudes.

Step 2. Emphasize Good Sportsmanship

The only way your kid will learn that winning isn't everything (especially when people remember only that you were a lousy loser) is by your stressing sportsmanship over victory. Some families have a personal motto that represents their attitude, for example, "It doesn't matter if you win or lose, it's how you play the game," "If you can't play nicely, you don't play," "Winning isn't everything," or "What people remember most is how you play the game." You might suggest a few to your kids, choose the family favorite, and then intentionally repeat it again and again until kids can recite it without reminders.

Look for those teachable moments to do so, and then point out both the right and wrong way to handle defeat. It's one way to help him recognize that everyone suffers defeats and setbacks as well as victories, and sensitize him to others' feelings:

- While watching the Oscars, a quiz or reality TV show, the Olympics, or some other sporting event on television, say, "They've worked for years for this. They've just lost. Let's watch to see if we can tell how they feel. They're shaking hands with their opponents."
- Following your kid's band competition, say, "Congratulations, your school won! Did you notice how some of the kids acted who lost? They were complaining that the event wasn't fair. It sure didn't seem as if they were being good sports. Better that they kept those thoughts to themselves."

Step 3. Teach How to Encourage

Good sports *and* good losers support and encourage each other. One way to help your kid be more encouraging is to teach the Two Praise Rule. The rule is simple: you must praise your peers at least twice before the event ends. Discuss a few encouraging comments or actions so he has a beginning repertoire—for example, "Great song," "Super," "Smart answer," "Good argument," "Good performance," and giving high fives. Continue to expand the list as opportunities materialize. Then suggest he practice the rule at any group activity—a team game, a scout meeting, a friend's house, school, as well as at home.

Step 4. Teach How to Lose Gracefully

Everyone makes mistakes; it's how we learn. But some kids don't know how to handle their defeat and lose gracefully. And because they lack that skill, they often look like poor losers. Here are a few strategies that help kids bounce back from defeat and fail gracefully. Do remember that whenever your kid makes a mistake, show your support with both your words and your nonverbal reactions. The quickest way your kid will learn to handle defeat gracefully is feeling your acceptance of his errors:

- *Model how to cope.* Show how you cope with error so your kid can model your example. First say your mistake and then what you learned. Here's the formula: "My mistake was. . . . I learned . . . from my mistake." Example: "I had to redo a whole report today at work because I forgot to save the document on my hard drive. Next time, I'll save as I go along."
- *Teach positive self-talk.* Help your kid learn a statement to say to himself to bounce back from defeat. Some examples are, "It doesn't have to be perfect." "It's okay to make a mistake." "I can turn it around." "Everybody makes mistakes." Once you select one, help your kid practice saying the same

statement out loud several times for a few days. The more he hears it, the greater the chance is he'll remember it and use it.

- **Don't call it a mistake!** Kids who bounce back often call mistakes by other names—a glitch, a bug, or a setback—so they won't discourage themselves in the middle of their learning. Help your kid come up with a word to say inside his head whenever he encounters a mistake. Any word will do. Just make sure to help him practice saying it over and over so he'll remember to use it when he really makes a mistake. And he'll be less likely to make excuses, blame, or criticize others.

- **Handle defeat with grace.** Brainstorm together phrases your kid could say when she errs or suffers a defeat so she sounds like a graceful loser—for example: "Good debate!" "That was close." "Let's do it again." "I gave it my best." "Let's try again tomorrow." "You game for a rematch?" Help him practice at home so he can confidently say them to his peers.

 ## The First 21 Days

Start up a Family Game Night. Dust off your chess set, checkers, or Monopoly board or treat yourself to one of those amazing new video games, and play them as a family. It's one of the best ways to help your kid learn to lose gracefully and change that bad loser attitude. Start by reviewing the rules, and then remind your kid he must stick by them: "No arguing about rules. We agree to them at the beginning and don't change them unless everyone agrees to. No criticizing or excuses." As you play, deliberately allow yourself a few mistakes. Instead of making excuses, blaming, and criticizing, model how to handle defeat: "Wow, I wasn't thinking that time," or "You got me there!" You might even lose the game—on purpose, of course—but be subtle enough not to let your kid know. Show him how to lose gracefully: "Good game. Let's play again tomorrow," and then shake hands.

ATTITUDE MAKEOVER PLEDGE

How will you use these steps to help your kid handle defeat and be a better sport both on and off the field? On the lines below, write exactly what you agree to do within the next twenty-four hours to begin changing your kid's attitude.

_____

_____

_____

THE NEW ATTITUDE REVIEW

All attitude makeovers take hard work, constant practice, and parental reinforcement. Each step your child takes toward change may be a small one, so be sure to acknowledge and congratulate every one of them along the way. It takes a minimum of twenty-one days to see real results, so don't give up! And if one strategy doesn't work, try another. Write your child's weekly progress on the lines below. Keep track of daily progress in your Attitude Makeover Journal.

WEEK 1

_____

_____

_____

WEEK 2

_____

_____

_____

WEEK 3

_____

_____

_____

ONGOING ATTITUDE TUNE-UP

Where does your child's attitude still need improvement? What work still needs to be done?

_____

_____

_____

ATTITUDE MAKEOVER RESOURCES

For Parents

How to Win at Sports Parenting: Maximizing the Sports Experience for You and Your Child, by Jim Sundberg and Janet Sundberg (Colorado Springs: WaterBrook Press, 2000). How to help your kids enjoy the sports they play, deal with game day emotions in a healthy manner, and learn valuable sports-to-life lessons. A Christian perspective.

Learning to Play, Playing to Learn: Games and Activities to Teach Sharing, Caring, and Compromise, by Charlie Steffens and Spencer Gorin (Los Angeles: Lowell House, 1997). Over sixty entertaining kid activities that will help to manage aggressive behaviors, foster cooperation, and nurture positive conduct.

The Cheers and the Tears: Healthy Alternatives to the Dark Side of Youth Sports Today, by Shane Murphy (San Francisco: Jossey-Bass, 1999). Offers parents and coaches sensible advice and healthy alternative approaches to the competitive and stressful world of youth sports.

For Kids

Fortunately, by Remy Charlip (New York: Macmillan, 1987). This is an absolute must for young readers. It's a model on changing your unfortunates to fortunates. Ages 4 to 9.

I Made a Mistake, by Miriam Nerlove (New York: Atheneum, 1985). A young child recognizes, "It's okay to make a mistake." Ages 4 to 8.

Nobody Is Perfick, by Bernard Waber (Boston: Houghton Mifflin, 1971). A young boy finally realizes through much trial and error that nobody is "perfick," including himself. Ages 5 to 8.

Be a Perfect Person in Just Three Days! by Stephen Manes (New York: Bantam-Skylark, 1991). Milo finds a book at the library on "how to be the perfect person!" He follows the directions carefully and finally learns the message in the end: "Being perfect is boring! Besides you're already perfect just being yourself!" Ages 9 to 12.

Bad Attitude

21

Selfish
Antidote: Selflessness, Generosity, Consideration

"Me . . . me . . . me."

Dear Dr. Borba,
Okay, I admit it. Somewhere I made a huge parenting mistake. I
always tried to put my kids first and give into their every little
whim. I guess I wanted to make sure they were happy and had
great self-esteem. Well, my plan backfired big time! I now have two
selfish sons who think they rule the world. Is it too late to change
their behavior? Help!

—Judy B., a mom of two from Ann Arbor, Michigan

Bad Attitude Act Out
"But Daddy, it's my house. Why are you letting him
play with *my* stuff?"

"So what if he broke his arm? I'm going without him."

"Is it my fault they don't have food or clothes? I'm
keeping my stuff."

350

EMERGENCY ATTITUDE ℞

Change your kid's "me . . . me . . . me" attitude to "you . . . you . . . you." Teach empathy. The best cure for selfishness is to help kids feel what someone else is feeling. Choose a particularly offensive selfish act and play Pretend to Be Me. Here's how you could use it:

Suppose you fell asleep reading the paper on the couch after an exhausting day. Your little critter suddenly jumps on you, bounces up and down, and wants to play horsey. When you plead for mercy and a few more minutes of much-needed rest, she cannot understand how you could possibly not want to satisfy her desire. Tell her you have a new game called Pretend to Be Me. Have her put on your shoes, lie down on the couch, close her eyes, and pretend to be asleep after a very hard day at work. Tell her, "You're very tired and worn out." When she looks really relaxed, create an annoying loud noise and shake the couch as if you're jumping on her. Then say, "How do you feel? What would you like to say to me? Can you feel how I felt when you asked me to play horsey?" The trick is to help her think about you instead of herself.

Suppose you're waiting up late for an older kid out past his curfew. He finally comes back two hours late and can't understand why you're so upset. You get out of your chair and say, "Okay, sit in my seat. Keep watching that clock over there; now look at the door, now at the phone that should have called to tell me where you are, or ringing from the police about some accident you got into. How do you feel? Now do you understand why I'm upset?"

If you think self-centered and selfish kids are on the rise, you're right. National surveys show most parents feel they're raising selfish kids. Kids don't arrive in this world with all the symptoms of the Big Brat Factor. Research shows that our children are born with the marvelous gift to care and be concerned about others. But unless we nurture those virtues, they will lie dormant.

Sure, younger tykes are self-centered and egocentric, but most shift into the other-centered phase with experience and guidance. The problem is that unless we help stretch them into thinking about others' thoughts and feelings, many get locked into self-centeredness. One thing is for sure: selfish kids are no joy to have around. They always wants things *their* way, put *their* needs and concerns ahead of others, and rarely stop to consider other people's feelings. And that's because they want you to believe that *their* feelings are more important than the feelings and needs of others.

The obvious reason that kids are selfish is that we've spoiled them by indulging in their every whim out of guilt or the misguided perception that good parenting is all about giving. Do you have a Little Princess or Prince in your house who feels entitled to luxury and privilege? Of course, there are some other potential reasons for this bad attitude. Your child may be expressing underlying feelings of neglect, jealousy, or inadequacy. He may be trying to satisfy needs for love and attention that have been previously ignored. And remember that some kids can't think about others because they're struggling to survive the emotional pain of their everyday lives.

So let's roll up our sleeves to squelch this obnoxious bad attitude, and make sure our kids have the virtues of selflessness, generosity, and consideration.

BAD ATTITUDE ALERT

Pull out the stops. Start reversing your kid's selfish attitude now.

Diagnosis

Begin with the five questions below.

Why. Why does your kid have this attitude? Has she always been treated as if the world revolves around her? Has he learned that he is going to get his way if he keeps at you long enough? Have you been ignoring him because his selfish attitude is so obnoxious or embarrassing? What do you think is the root cause in the way your family works or doesn't work that motivates this selfishness? Are you neglecting your child or being too judgmental or demanding? Might he be craving your love and approval? Or have you put so much time and energy into just this little person that he thinks the whole world revolves only around him? What is fueling this attitude, and why do you suppose your kid continues using it?

What. Are there particular issues or things he is more selfish over? Is this about wanting stuff, wanting his way, needing more attention, feeling he "deserves" it, being jealous or resentful of siblings?

Who. Does he display the same selfish behavior to everyone or just some individuals? For instance, is he this way only with his siblings or younger kids, his friends or peers, certain relatives, or Dad or Mom? Are there some folks he does not use his selfish ways on? If so, who are they? Why are they spared?

When. Is there a particular time of day, week, or month he is more demanding? Is there a reason? Is it around the holidays? Back to school? Summer? Vacations? Birthday? Report card time? Are you seeing any pattern of when your kid is most selfish, or does he display the same attitude all the time?

Where. Are there certain places he is more likely to be selfish? How does he act when he goes shopping with you? What about at a restaurant, the movies, day care or school, or

Selfish

a certain relative's? If you notice that he is selfish in some place more than others, why? What is so different about the location that triggers the attitude?

Now take a look at your answers. Are you seeing any predictable patterns? Do you have any better understanding of your kid's selfish attitude and where it's coming from?

WHAT'S WRONG WITH YOUR CURRENT RESPONSE?

Talk to your friends. Are they seeing the same kinds of selfish behaviors in their kids? What are they doing (if anything) to halt their kids' selfishness? Are there individuals your child is *not* selfish around? What responses are they using that is causing your kid not to try his antics with them?

Try to identify the last incident when your kid was self-ish. Did you give in and buy what she wanted? Lecture her? Set a consequence? Ignore the attitude? Is this how you typically react to your kid's selfish streak? And how did your kid react to your response?

Write down the one thing you will never do again.

I will not _____

_____

FACING YOUR OWN BAD ATTITUDES

Think about when you grew up. Do you think your child-hood friends were as selfish as the generation of kids today? What might be contributing to the rise of selfishness? How are you contributing to it?

Kids are not born selfish and inconsiderate, so where is your kid learning the attitude? Could it be from your behavior? How well are you modeling selflessness to your kid? Is your example teaching her to be selfless and giving or greedy, self-centered, and inconsiderate? Are you ever accused of being selfish? Why? Which do you feel is more important: what you have or who you are? How would your kid answer that question about you?

What about your own parenting? Is there anything you might be doing to exacerbate your kid's selfishness? Here are some issues to consider: Are you compensating for a lack of material or emotional generosity you experienced in childhood? Are you lax on limits because you want your kid to like you? Do you indulge your kid's whims hoping it might improve your relationship? Do you give in to your kid's cries, whines, pouts, demands (or whatever antics used) because it's just "easier"? Do you sometimes feel guilty for not spending enough time with your kids so you buy them things to alleviate your guilt?

How important to you are the virtues of selflessness and charity? Do you share those beliefs in your walk and talk to your kids? How much emphasis is placed on philanthropy and giving in your family? Would your kids agree with your verdict?

What is the first step you need to take to fight selfishness in yourself as an example to your sons or daughters? Write down changes you need to make.

I will _____

_____

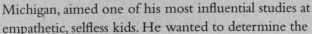

BAD ATTITUDE NEWS ALERT

Martin Hoffman, a world-renowned researcher from the University of Michigan, aimed one of his most influential studies at empathetic, selfless kids. He wanted to determine the type of discipline their parents most frequently used with their children, and the finding was clear: the most common discipline technique that parents of highly considerate children use are reasoning with them about their uncaring, selfish behavior. Their reasoning lessons helped sensitize their children to the feelings of others and realize how their actions may affect others. It's an important parenting point to keep in mind in those moments when we confront our own kids for any uncaring, selfish deed.

THE "DON'T GIVE ME THAT ATTITUDE" MAKEOVER

To eliminate your kid's selfish ways, take the following steps.

Step 1. Go Beneath the Surface

Here are some common and less apparent reasons that may be contributing to your child's selfish attitude. Check off the ones that apply to you:

☐ You're spoiling the kid for bad reasons of your own (for example, guilt, compensation, avoidance, "love").

☐ You don't treat discipline and setting limits as a high priority in your parenting.

☐ You or another adult member of your family is modeling selfishness.

☐ Your kid is feeling neglected.

☐ Your kid is jealous of a partner or sibling.

☐ Your kid resents how much you indulge yourself with luxuries and privileges.

☐ Your child has never been taught the value of selflessness.

☐ Your child has poor emotional intelligence and has difficulties identifying or understanding other people's emotions.

☐ Your child is angry, anxious, or depressed or having some other problem that makes it difficult for him to think of others.

☐ Other: _____

_____

_____

Review this list carefully, pick out the ones that most apply to your family, and start focusing on each problem with the appropriate steps below or elsewhere in this book.

Step 2. Censor Selfishness

A major step in squelching your kid's selfish attitude is simply not tolerating it. It won't be easy, especially if your kid is used to having his every whim catered to. But if you really are serious about changing this attitude, you must stand firm and be consistent. Start by clearly laying down your new attitude expectations: "In this house, you are always to be considerate of others." Then loudly state your disapproval each and every time your child acts selfishly. Be sure to state why his behavior was wrong, and if the selfish attitude continues, consider applying consequences—for example:

"That was selfish: I expect you to treat your friends the same way you'd want to be treated."

"I'm very concerned when I see you monopolizing all the video games and not sharing them with your friend. You may not treat people selfishly."

Step 3. Nurture Empathy to Decrease Selfishness

Kids who are empathic can understand where other people are coming from because they can put themselves in their shoes and feel how they feel. And because they can "feel with" someone else, they are more generous, unselfish, and caring. So nurture your child's empathy to help him see beyond himself and into the views of others. Here are three ways to do so:

- *Point out other's emotions.* Pointing out the facial expressions, posture, and mannerisms of people in different emotional states as well as their predicaments helps kids tune into other people's feelings. As occasions arise, explain your concern and what clues helped you make your feeling assessment: "Did you notice Lily's face when you were playing today? I was concerned because she seemed worried about something. Maybe you should talk to her to see if she's okay."
- *Imagine someone's feelings.* Help your kid imagine how the other person feels about a special situation: "Pretend you're a new student and you're walking into a brand-new school and don't know anyone. How will you feel?" Asking often, "How would you feel?" helps kids understand the feelings and needs of other people.
- *Ask often, "How does the other person feel?"* Look for daily situations that could nurture empathy. Then pose questions using that situation to help guide your child to consider how the person feels—for example:

Parent: Mom has had a long, hard day at the office. How do you think she feels?

Child: Kind of tired.

Parent: So what could you do to make her feel better?

Child: I guess I could turn down my TV, so it's not so loud.

Parent: That's a great idea! It would be a nice way to let Mom know you're thinking about her.

Step 4. Set Limits

One reason kids become selfish is that they are used to getting their way. Don't let them get away with that. Set clear limits, and then stick to them like glue. Don't give in to whining, pouting, tantrums, and guilt-laced admonishments of "You're the worst parent in the world!" This might be hard if you think your main role is to be your kid's best friend. Reset your thinking. See yourself as the adult, and recognize that hundreds of child development studies conclude that kids whose parents set clear behavior expectations turned out less selfish. You may have to have a serious talk with other caregivers in your kid's life who are guilty of overindulging. Let them know in no uncertain terms you are serious about curbing your kid's selfish attitude around and must have their cooperation to do so.

Step 5. Reinforce Selfless Acts

Parents who raise selfless, caring kids don't do so by accident. They intentionally make sure that their kids are aware of the rights, feelings, and needs of others. This means you need to fight the tendency to make your child feel as though the world revolves around him. You'll be much more pleased with the outcome: a more considerate, caring kid.

One of the fastest ways to increase selflessness is by "catching" your kid doing considerate and unselfish acts. Always remember to describe the deed so she clearly understands the virtue and point out the impact it had on the recipient. That will also help her be more likely to repeat the same generous deed another time:

"Did you see Charlotte's smile when you shared your toys? You made her happy."
"Thanks for taking time to ask me how my day went."
"Thanks for giving your CDs to your brother. I know you don't listen to rap anymore, but he just loves it."

The First 21 Days

Commit yourself to an FSD (Family Selfless Deeds) project to help your kids recognize what a difference their unselfish acts can make. Here are some ideas for this project:

- *Give part of your allowance to charity.* Start a new rule: a portion of weekly allowance must be set aside for charity. Even young kids can put away a portion of their allowance or gift money to give to a good cause. Some families require kids to divide their earned allowance into three categories: money to spend, save, and donate to charity.
- *Do a family sacrifice.* Give everyone in the family a big cardboard box and ask them to fill it with giveaways, including a few things they really care about, like favorite articles of clothing, toys, books, DVDs, or CDs. Then have your kids help you deliver the boxes—which can be colorfully decorated by younger kids—to your favorite charity.
- *Play the Gift of Time Game.* Everyone in the family puts their name in a hat and then blindly pulls one out. For the next twenty-one days, each family member commits to spending an age-appropriate amount of time devoted to the chosen person. For example, they can do that person's chore, help him or her complete some project, play a game, or just hang out together. It's the time spent that counts.
- *Graduate to anonymous benevolence.* The highest level of selflessness is giving away material goods or

> your precious time without anyone knowing it was you who did it. There is no recognition or rewards. You do it because it's right. This kind of attitude is the ultimate goal of parenting.

ATTITUDE MAKEOVER PLEDGE

How will you use these steps to help your kid become less selfish and achieve long-term change? On the lines below, write exactly what you agree to do within the next twenty-four hours to begin changing your kid's attitude so he is less demanding and more considerate.

_____

_____

_____

_____

_____

_____

THE NEW ATTITUDE REVIEW

All attitude makeovers take hard work, constant practice, and parental reinforcement. Each step your child takes toward change may be a small one, so be sure to acknowledge and congratulate every one of them along the way. It takes a minimum of twenty-one days to see real results, so don't give up! And if one strategy doesn't work, try another. Write your child's weekly progress on the lines that follow. Keep track of daily progress in your Attitude Makeover Journal.

WEEK 1

_____
_____
_____

WEEK 2

_____
_____
_____

WEEK 3

_____
_____
_____

ONGOING ATTITUDE TUNE-UP

Where does your child's attitude still need improvement? What
work still needs to be done?

_____
_____
_____

ATTITUDE MAKEOVER RESOURCES

For Parents
Wimpy Parents: From Toddler to Teen: How Not to Raise a Brat, by Kenneth N. Condrell (New York: Warner Brothers, 1998). Expounds on
the dangers of overly permissive parenting.

Spoiled Rotten: Today's Children and How to Change Them, by Fred G. Gosman (New York: Warner Books, 1993). A convincing statement of how spoiling kids is hurtful and specific advice on how to undo the harm.

Too Much of a Good Thing: Raising Children of Character in an Indulgent Age, by Dan Kindlon (New York: Talk Miramax, 2001). A solid testament of the dangers of overprotecting and overindulging our kids.

The Moral Intelligence of Children, by Robert Coles (New York: Random House, 1997). Thorough and research-based ideas on how to raise a moral, unselfish child.

For Kids

Me First, by Helen Lester (Boston: Houghton Mifflin, 1995). Pinkerton Pig is pushy and greedy but overcomes his selfishness when he learns that being first isn't always the best. Ages 2 to 4.

The Selfish Giant, by Oscar Wilde (New York: Putnam, 1995). A wonderful tale about a once selfish giant whose heart finally melts when he helps a small boy. Ages 5 to 8.

Number the Stars, by Lois Lowry (New York: Dell, 1989). Based on the true, compassionate story of a young Danish girl who displays the epitome of selflessness: she sacrifices her life to save her friend from the Nazis. Ages 9 to 12.

Of Mice and Men, by John Steinbeck (New York: Penguin, 1993). Explores the friendship between two stirring characters: mentally handicapped and warm-hearted Lenny and his protector, George. Heartbreaking moments depicting a world that can sometimes be cruel and selfish make for ripe moral discussions. The movie version of Steinbeck's book is also highly recommended (MGM, 1992). For teenagers.

The Kids Can Help Book, by Suzanne Logan (New York: Perigee Books, 1992). A wonderful compilation of ways kids can volunteer and make a difference in the world with their unselfishness. Ages 8 to 13.

Whipping Boy, by Sid Fleischman (New York: Harcourt, 1993). Young self-centered Prince Brat runs away with his whipping boy in this briskly told tale of high adventure that won the Newbery Medal. Ages 10 to 13.

22

Uncooperative
Antidote: Cooperation, Friendliness, Caring

"I'll do it my way."

Dear Dr. Borba,
The neighborhood kids were over yesterday, and my kid acted like the biggest jerk. I don't know a nicer way of putting it. He hoarded his CDs and video games, wanted things to go his way, never shared, and was so uncooperative that I wanted to send all the kids home right then and there. For the life of me, I don't know why they stayed. Any suggestions on how to help this kid be more cooperative would be greatly appreciated.

—Craig J., from Orange County, California

Bad Attitude Act Out
"But, Mommy, he had a turn already. Do I have to give him two turns?"

"Why should I share my laptop with him? It's my house and my stuff."

> "So what if I'm on the team? I don't want to do any work. Let them do it."

EMERGENCY ATTITUDE ℞

Enforce a sharing attitude by immediate and active intervention. The most crucial basic skill to cure an uncooperative bad attitude is sharing. If you don't know how to share, you'll never be able to take turns, work on a team, get along in a family or group of friends, or collaborate in a workplace. So you better get started early in teaching this essential good attitude. Teach cooperative play with your younger child by sitting side by side, taking turns, and sharing every toy so he experiences the give and take of everyday life. Do it in the sandbox, playing with dolls, stuffed animals, and action toys, building blocks, and working with clay. For older kids, start with board games; then graduate to playing catch, Frisbee, video games, and ultimately work projects in the home, yard, or community. In each case, you'll be teaching your kid how to work with other individuals or in a team.

Cooperation is all about working together and supporting one another, and those are tough notions for spoiled kids who are too tightly wrapped up in themselves. To really cooperate in any group—family, sports, scouting, church, club, play, or school—you must set aside your individual concerns for the needs of the group. There's no time to be self-centered, think only of yourself, and want things to only go your way.

There may be several reasons that your kid has an unco-operative attitude. He may be feeling shy and uncertain about how people feel about him, may be preoccupied with some other problem at home or school that's distracting his atten-tion, may lack social experiences that people need to learn basic friendship skills, or may have been so pampered and spoiled that he thinks he's the center of the universe and never has to share or work with others.

Cooperating is about working for the team or family or group—whatever the size. And doing so means you can't always be first, win, share, or have your own way. You have to put aside your wants and desires, and acknowledge the feel-ings and concerns of others. Learning the replacement virtues of cooperation, friendliness, and caring dramatically increases kids' chances of success in school, home, and life. It's all the more reason to curb your kid's uncooperative attitude.

BAD ATTITUDE ALERT

We're living in the age of virtual relationships where not only face-to-face but long-distance collaboration is crucial. To tune up your kid's uncooperative attitude, start now if you want to launch him toward happiness and success.

Diagnosis
Start with these five questions.

What. What exactly does your kid do or say that is uncoop-erative? Here are a few traits of kids displaying uncooperative attitudes. Mark any that your kid is displaying and add other behaviors that concern you to the list:

- [ ] Doesn't take turns
- [ ] Doesn't share
- [ ] Doesn't listen to others

- [ ] Hoards toys, tools, supplies, electronic equipment for play or work
- [ ] Tries to bully or dominate a group
- [ ] Complains about working with others
- [ ] Never compromises
- [ ] Wants things to go his own way
- [ ] Doesn't pull her own weight on a team
- [ ] Is argumentative
- [ ] Insists that demands be met immediately and his way
- [ ] Doesn't do what others ask him to
- [ ] Criticizes others
- [ ] Acts bossy; directs others to do what he wants
- [ ] Never asks others what they would like to do
- [ ] Doesn't work well with others
- [ ] Unwilling to negotiate

Who. Does he display the same attitude to everyone? Are there some individuals he is more likely to flaunt this attitude with—for instance, younger siblings, older peers, a teacher, or a coach? If so, then why does he flaunt it toward some people and not others?

Where. Are there certain places he is more likely to flaunt the attitude (at school, practice, the babysitter's, day care, scouts, play group, a certain friend's house, a certain relative's)? Why?

Why. Why is your kid so uncooperative? Does he not know how to cooperate? Does he feel slighted? Is he selfish and spoiled? Does he always wants things his way? Is he usually dominated by another kid so he feels that he can't contribute? Is he not expected to cooperate? Is he used to getting away with not complying with your requests? Is he shy, insecure, lacking friendship skills or the experience of working in a group, worried about some other problem, physically exhausted, or ill? What's fueling this attitude?

When. Are there certain times your kid displays her unco-operative attitude—for instance, during ski practice, a scout meeting, when it's time to go to day care, or during her study group? Might there be a reason? Maybe she feels excluded, doesn't have the skills to get along, feels more secure at home, or doesn't like the competition.

What is your best diagnosis of why your kid has learned this attitude? Confer with other adults who know your kid well to see if they agree.

WHAT'S WRONG WITH YOUR CURRENT RESPONSE?

How do you typically respond to your child's uncooperative actions? Do you ignore them? Lecture him? Punish? Give a stern look? Sit down next to him until he complies? Argue? What is the typical way you respond to your kid's uncooperative attitude? Does it work in curbing his bad attitude? Why or why not? How does your kid typically respond to your response?

Is there anything you've tried time and time again that has never worked in curbing your child's uncooperative attitude? Write it down to remind you not to use again it with your kid.

I will not _____

_____

FACING YOUR OWN BAD ATTITUDES

Your child learns a great deal about cooperation simply by observing your behavior. If you want your child to be more cooperative, the easiest way is to consciously demonstrate cooperative behavior in yourself so he has a model to copy. And the first step to doing so is to identify which behaviors you need to tune up. Begin by rereading the checklist above of uncooperative behaviors, and this time check off ones that might apply to *you*. Now choose one behavior to improve in yourself.

What is the first step you need to take in yourself to help your child deal with his or her uncooperative attitude? Write down changes you need to make.

I will _____

_____

BAD ATTITUDE NEWS ALERT

In the past twenty-five years, the American workplace has been transformed so that the vast majority of businesses and organizations are now team based. That means that people are now working cooperatively rather than individually. It also means that if your child is not a team player and lacks the skills of social competence, he will be handicapped from succeeding in the workplace. As Tom Peters and Robert H. Waterman, authors of the best-selling book *In Search of Excellence* point out, the impact that teamwork has on productivity is an astounding 5,000 percent! It's all the more important to break your kid of his uncooperative attitude.

THE "DON'T GIVE ME THAT" ATTITUDE MAKEOVER

To squelch your child's uncooperative attitude, take the following steps.

Step 1. Teach the Value of Cooperation

One of the most important steps to curb an uncooperative attitude is to emphasize cooperation and make sure your kid knows its value. Take time to define the meaning of cooperation, explaining the positive impact it has on others and the long-term benefits for your kid. To serve as a constant reminder, you might consider making a poster with your child listing kinds of cooperative deeds that family members can do for one another. Here are a few points to discuss:

"Being cooperative makes other kids happy" or "When you aren't cooperative and don't share or take turns, it makes the other person sad and not want to play."

"Cooperation is in your own self-interest since it is the most effective way to succeed in getting things done and achieving your own goals."

"Cooperation makes the world a nicer, more peaceful place, because it helps people get along."

"Being cooperative means you're thinking not just about yourself but also about the other person. And that's a big part of being nice."

"When you work with others as a team, you are more likely to get more accomplished because you are all cooperating and doing part of the work."

Be sure to share examples of contemporary news and history, in business, government, and your local community. For example, read books together about how the founding fathers worked as a team to solve major problems when forming this country. And don't forget the Allied Forces during World War II, the United Nations, and other examples of famous teamwork in sports and entertainment. For younger kids, point out groups in your own community that work together to help keep your child safe, like their teachers, the police, the doctors and nurses in the hospital, and firefighters.

Step 2. Expect Cooperation

Research studies find that kids who are cooperative have parents who expect them to be. Therefore, one of the easiest ways to boost cooperation is to make it a priority in your home—and the sooner you start, the better. Begin by mandating your rules and stressing that uncooperative actions are not acceptable in your family. Then call out your disapproval the moment you see any sign of an uncooperative attitude:

"That's not being cooperative. I expect you to share with your friends. Try again, please."

"In this home, we cooperate. You had a turn; now it's Sally's turn. If you can't cooperate, you can't play, and your friend will have to go home."

"How would you feel if John treated you that way and took more toys to play with? Next time, I expect you to cooperate."

Step 3. Teach Cooperative Skills; Then Find Practice Opportunities

There are many skills kids need to cooperate and you can teach them to your child. Choose one skill your kid needs to learn. Then take time to teach this skill (such as how to take turns, or share, or listen) by showing what it looks and sounds like. Just telling your kid about the skill is not enough; she needs to practice it again and again until she can use it on her own. So look for everyday practice opportunities such as during the car pool, standing in a grocery line, participating in a play group, or during chore time. Here are examples of how parents have reminded kids to practice the new skill:

- *Taking turns:* "Be sure to take turns when you play with Charlie today. Let him go first, and then it will be your turn, and then his again. Taking turns will make play time more fun because he will be happier that he has a turn."

- *Teamwork:* "Why don't you and your brother help each other finish your chores? If you both pitch in and work together, you'll both be finished more quickly so we can go to the movies."

Step 4. Set Ground Rules; Then Expect Sharing

Sharing is one of the essential skills of cooperation. Lay down family ground rules so your kids know you expect them to share and take turns. Be sure your kids clearly know your expectations. Some kids have a tough time learning to share; here are few tips to help them learn to walk the talk:

- *Use a timer.* Some kids, especially the younger set, have a tough time sharing. One way to get them started is by using an oven timer or sand timer so that they can "see" how much longer it is until it's their turn. Older kids can use the minute hands on their watches. Teach kids to agree on a set amount of time—usually only a few minutes—for using an item. When the time is up, the item is passed to the next child for his turn.
- *Put away valuables.* Tell your child to put away any personal possessions she does not want to share before her guest arrives. There are certain possessions that are very special to your child, so putting those items away before a guest arrives minimizes potential conflicts. Explain that anything your child leaves out should be shared.
- *Share only what belongs to you.* Items that do not belong to your child may not be shared unless permission is granted from the owner: "I'm sorry, we can't play with that. It belongs to my brother, so it's not something I can share."
- *Don't expect anything in return.* Emphasize that just because you share, you should not anticipate getting something back. The reason to share is that it's nice to be nice.
- *Model the value of sharing equipment.* Computers, tools, and technological expertise all have a role in working together and getting things done these days. Take a moment

to show your kids directly how in this age of technology there are so many great ways to cooperate: sharing e-mail lists, creating links on e-mail and Web site links, sharing computer files, creating cell phone networks, and making Web sites for family and friends.

The First 21 Days

Choose a Family Work-Together Project that every member can be a part of, such as putting together a picnic, planting a garden, planning a day trip or family vacation, or even spring cleaning. Then go through the cooperative steps as a group so kids experience the process of working together. Here's how to hold a family garage sale where kids must cooperate:

1. Brainstorm project possibilities and then vote. The most votes wins (in this case, let's suppose the family garage sale won the most votes). You can also share a computer to search for ideas, find resources, keep a record of each step along the way, and even create a Web site for each project.

2. Give everyone a large garbage bag or box in which to put all clothes, games, books, or whatever they want to sell.

3. Supply poster board, marking pens, and tape for everyone to make signs announcing the sale and then post them around the neighborhood. Or make the signs on your computer and print them out for posting.

4. Set out marking pens and labels for price tags; members can help each other price each item.

5. Get up early the morning of the sale, and arrange items on your front lawn or patio. Older kids can help younger kids assume responsibility for the "cash register" as items are sold.

At the end of the day, any unsold items can be donated to a charity that is chosen in a cooperative family vote. Members can also decide how to spend any earnings. Does each person keep his or her own profits, are they to be divided equally, or should they be combined into one fund and spent as a family? Not only does your family have fun and earn money, but they learn the value of cooperation by experiencing the process.

ATTITUDE MAKEOVER PLEDGE

How will you use these steps to help your kid become more cooperative and achieve long-term change? On the lines below, write exactly what you agree to do within the next twenty-four hours to begin changing your kid's attitude so he is more cooperative.

_____

_____

_____

THE NEW ATTITUDE REVIEW

All attitude makeovers take hard work, constant practice, and parental reinforcement. Each step your child takes toward change may be a small one, so be sure to acknowledge and

congratulate every one of them along the way. It takes a minimum of twenty-one days to see real results, so don't give up! And if one strategy doesn't work, try another. Write your child's weekly progress on the lines below. Keep track of daily progress in your Attitude Makeover Journal.

WEEK 1

_____

_____

_____

WEEK 2

_____

_____

_____

WEEK 3

_____

_____

_____

ONGOING ATTITUDE TUNE-UP

Where does your child's attitude still need improvement? What work still needs to be done?

_____

_____

_____

ATTITUDE MAKEOVER RESOURCES

For Parents

Good Friends Are Hard to Find, by Fred Frankel (Pasadena, Calif.: Perspective Publishing, 1996). Written by the director of the UCLA Parent Training and Social Skills Program, this parent guide is invaluable. It lays out step by step how to help kids from 5 to 12 years old make friends, cooperate, and solve relationship problems.

Learning to Play, Playing to Learn: Games and Activities to Teach Sharing, Caring, and Compromise, by Charlie Steffens and Spencer Gorin (Los Angeles: Lowell House, 1997). Over sixty unique and entertaining activities that help kids manage aggressive behavior, foster cooperation, and nurture positive conduct.

Parents Do Make a Difference: How to Raise Kids with Solid Character, Strong Minds, and Caring Hearts, by Michele Borba (San Francisco: Jossey-Bass, 1999). How to teach kids the eight indispensable skills all kids need to be successful in all arenas of their lives. See especially the "Getting Along" chapter.

For Kids

Cooperation (Values to Live By), by Janet Riehecky (Chicago: Child's World, 1990). Why cooperation is so important and is a virtue we all need to walk and talk. Ages 5 to 8.

Frog and Toad Together, by Arnold Lobel (New York: HarperCollins, 1972). Five glorious stories describe the cooperative friendship of Frog and Toad. Ages 5 to 10.

How to Lose All Your Friends, by Nancy Carlson (New York: Viking Press, 1994). A great picture book that looks at all the negative friendship consequences of uncooperative behaviors such as not sharing, never smiling, and poor sportsmanship. Ages 3 to 8.

Not Like That, Like This! by Tony Bradman and Joanna Burroughs (New York: Oxford University Press, 1988). Dad and Thomas go for a walk and find themselves in a most peculiar problem: both their heads are stuck through the iron railings of a fence. Everyone has to cooperate to get Dad unstuck.

23

Ungrateful
Antidote: Gratitude, Thankfulness, Courtesy

"This isn't at all what I wanted."

Dear Dr. Borba,
My husband and I have worked so hard to give our kids a good
life. We've always put them first and given them what we never had
when we were kids. Instead of being appreciative, they only seem to
want more. We see them turning out to be ungrateful and wanting
what everyone else has. How do we help them be more appreciative
and take joy in what they're blessed with?

—Clara B., a mom of two from Champaign, Illinois

Bad Attitude Act Out

"I know Grandma took me to Disneyland, Mommy, but
I went there before."

"I know my teacher stayed after school to help me,
but she's getting paid for it."

> "Why should I write a thank-you card? I told her 'thank you' already."

EMERGENCY ATTITUDE ℞

Volunteer your child and yourself to do some type of charitable work, such as playing with children in a homeless shelter, reading to the blind, building low-cost housing, or delivering meals to the housebound. Expose your child to those who have far less comfort, convenience, and material resources than she does. Such hands-on face-to-face experiences with poverty, deprivation, or misfortune can go a long way in helping your child appreciate everything with which she's been blessed. She may also come to realize that happiness doesn't necessarily depend on material possessions.

Studies suggest that we are producing a large population of spoiled, ungrateful kids who always seem to want more and are never quite satisfied with what they have. There are a number of factors that keep our kids from developing gratitude. For starters, we have relentless consumption-driven media that push kids to think they need more; a hectic-paced lifestyle that leaves little time to help kids count their blessings; the sometimes overwhelming impact of troubling news that focuses on the bad parts of life instead of helping kids appreciate the good. In addition, we live in a society in which busy, guilt-ridden parents bribe their kids with hoards of stuff every time they want them to do something or out of guilt for not being home much. Sometimes with the best intentions, we try to give our kids everything we always wanted and never had. Or our competitive instincts compel us to keep up with the Joneses, so we lavish our kids with the latest and best of everything. The result is a family culture that expects only the finest things in life and takes for granted a lifestyle that cannot be attained by the other 99 percent of the planet. But are our kids grateful? No. Are they jaded by a grandiose sense of entitlement? Yes. And who did this to them? We did.

This pervasive attitude of ingratitude must be reversed. Sowing the seeds of gratitude not only curtails selfishness and jealousy, but is also an integral part of raising happy, emotionally fulfilled children. Research tells us that the happiest kids are the ones who feel a sense of appreciation for life—regardless of wealth, health, or personal circumstances. One thing is clear: you must replace your child's ungrateful bad attitude with the virtues of gratitude, thankfulness, and courtesy. And the sooner you begin, the better.

BAD ATTITUDE ALERT

The war against ingratitude must start now, and the best place to begin is by analyzing the source of the problem.

Diagnosis

Here are a few questions to help you pinpoint exactly what troubles you most about your kid's ungrateful attitude so you can develop the most effective makeover to change it. Check the following items if they describe your child:

- [ ] Unappreciative or ungrateful when someone extends a thoughtful gesture toward him
- [ ] Oblivious to the luxury and privileges of his life
- [ ] Envious or jealous of other people's attributes or possessions
- [ ] Needs reminders to say "thank you" to others
- [ ] Takes for granted his safety, comfort, and good health

☐ Unsatisfied with the blessings that he has and always seems to want more
☐ Unwilling to reciprocate with gifts or kind acts to others
☐ Feels entitled to continuing privileges, luxuries, and other resources

What concerns you most about your child's lack of gratitude? Is there one thing that you might do to tame your kid's ungrateful ways? Answering these next questions will help you understand why she is resorting to this attitude.

Why. Why does your kid have this attitude? Is it just because she's spoiled? Has she been taught to value only material things? What does she gain from being ungrateful? Remember, you use an attitude because it works. Why is she continuing to use it?

What. Are there particular issues or things over which she is especially ungrateful? Are they about wanting stuff, having things to keep up with friends, using it to make the giver feel uncomfortable, being jealous of a sibling, or something else?

Who. Does she display the same ungrateful attitude to everyone? Are there some individuals she does not use her ungrateful ways on? If so, who? Why not?

When. Is there a particular time of day, week, season, or year when your kid is more ungrateful? Is there a reason? What about times when she receives gifts from others? Does she appear appreciative of what she receives?

Where. Are there certain places he is more likely to be ungrateful (at school, home, birthday parties, holidays, with friends, at a relative's home)? Why?

Now take a look at your answers. Are you seeing any predictable patterns? Do you have any better understanding of your kid's ungrateful attitude and where it's coming from? What factors might be contributing to your kid's attitude of ingratitude?

WHAT'S WRONG WITH YOUR CURRENT RESPONSE?

Now reflect on how you typically respond to your child's ungrateful attitude. Think of the last time you gave your child a special privilege or gift that you felt he was unappreciative of. What did he do that you interpreted as an ungrateful attitude? Now play back how you responded to his attitude. Was there one thing you could have done that would have changed your child's ungrateful ways or even toned them down?

What response does not curb your kid's ungrateful spirit? It might be something you are allowing, such as giving in to his every whim or never requiring him to thank others for gifts or kind deeds. It could also be allowing others to overindulge your kid. Is there one response you might never try again?

I will not _____

_____

FACING YOUR OWN BAD ATTITUDES

Did your parents instill a sense of gratefulness in you? If so, how? Did they place the same value on possessions and privileges that you do? Did they encourage you to value the spiritual things of life, such as the importance of love and relationships? Have you incorporated any of their attitudes in your parenting? If so, which ones? Which attitudes, if any, would you like to start using with your children? Write them.

Next, reflect on your current attitude. Here are a few questions to help you think about how well you are modeling gratitude to your kids. Check any that might need to change:

How well and how often do you model gratitude:

☐ To your spouse for helping you, expressing appreciation, loving, working hard, or treating you kindly

☐ To your kids for a job well done, or for everyday behaviors such as coming to the table on time, finishing chores without reminders, waiting patiently, being courteous, or conveying gratefulness

☐ To the waiter at the restaurant for providing good service

☐ To the grocery worker for bagging your groceries or helping you carry them to your car

☐ To the other driver for giving you the right of way or waiting patiently while you park

☐ To the babysitter for watching your children and keeping them safe

☐ To a stranger for holding the door open for you, holding your space in line, or helping you in some random act of kindness

☐ To yourself for your countless blessings such as your health, family, friends, home, or spirituality

The best way our kids learn gratitude is by seeing others display appreciation and gratitude in those everyday, unplanned moments. Those examples are ones they are most likely to copy. For instance, how often do your kids see you convey your appreciation with hugs, words, or small notes to others for their kindnesses bestowed on you or your loved ones? Even more important, how often do you tell your kids how much you appreciate them? Think of one simple way you could be a better example of gratitude to your children. Write how you will use it within the next twenty-four hours to tune up the attitude.

I will _____

_____

BAD ATTITUDE NEWS ALERT

We're dealing with a fresh rash of hyper-consumer kids who buy, buy, buy, and won't take no, no, no for an answer. A national survey of youth commissioned by the Center for a New American Dream found that the average American kid aged twelve to seventeen who asks his or her parents for products that have been advertised *will ask nine times until their parents finally give in*. For parents of "tweens," the problem is particularly severe: more than 10 percent of twelve to thirteen year olds admit to asking their parents *more than fifty times* for products they've seen advertised. The key trend here is clear: *our kids don't give up until we give in*. So don't give in: saying no and meaning it is one of the best ways to ensure that your kid kicks his ungrateful attitude.

THE "DON'T GIVE ME THAT ATTITUDE" MAKEOVER

To eliminate your child's ungrateful attitude, take the following seven steps.

Step 1. Set Limits
Fight the tendency to overindulge your child with too many things. After all, having too much is one way to squelch

gratefulness. So add the word *no* to your vocabulary. Then don't feel guilty about using it with your kids. Always giving kids what they want does not help them learn to be grateful and appreciative of what they have.

Step 2. Verbalize Gratitude

Our kids do many thoughtful deeds throughout the day, but we often overlook them. Well, don't! Hearing you verbalize gratitude is one of the easiest ways to boost kids' grateful hearts as well as walk *and* talk gratitude. Just be sure to tell your kids *what* they did that you appreciate. Not only will they be more likely to repeat their kind action, but they will copy your example and send "appreciation messages" to others deserving *their* thanks.

"Kevin, thanks for remembering to take out the trash. I appreciate your helpfulness."

"Thanks for giving me a moment by myself, Yulrika. I had a really hard day at work, and I appreciate your thoughtfulness."

Step 3. Help Your Child Tune into What Makes Others Happy

Grateful hearts are created not from centering on personal needs but centering on others. Help your child focus on what others appreciate. It's an easy but powerful way of boosting his understanding of gratitude, as well as helping him recognize simple ways to make others happy. Here's an example:

Parent: Uncle Ken has been with us for two days. What have you noticed that he appreciates?

Child: He was really happy when I talked with him yesterday.

Parent: You're right! I bet he'd really be grateful if you did that again today. Why not do it again to make him happy?

Step 4. Help Your Kid Imagine the Recipient's Feelings

One way to help your child understand the impact of gratitude is by having him imagine how the recipient of his kind actions feels. Suppose your child just sent a thank-you card to his aunt for the birthday present he received. Use it as an opportunity to help your child recognize his aunt's feelings when she receives the card by having him pretend to be the recipient: "Pretend you're Aunt Helen right now. You open up your mailbox and find this card. How will you feel when you read the card?"

Step 5. Require Thank Yous

Writing thank-you cards to others is a habit of gratitude we should encourage in our children. This is another way kids learn to consider other people's feelings rather than just their own. The problem for most parents is getting kids to write these notes without a struggle. One way is to allow kids to create their own way of thanking the person. A few creative thank-you ideas for kids might include:

- *Video.* Make a tape of a video just for that person that expresses appreciation.
- *Photo.* Take a photo of the child wearing or using the gift. The developed print makes an instant postcard; the child just writes a brief note on the back and addresses and mails it.
- *Puzzle.* Write the thank-you on a piece of card stock, and then cut it into a few pieces like a jigsaw puzzle.
- *Cereal spell out.* Spell out the thank-you use M&M's or alphabet cereal glued on a piece of cardboard.

Step 6. Create Family Gratitude Rituals

One of the best ways kids incorporate gratitude is by establishing family rituals in which everyday blessings are acknowledged and not overlooked. Here are examples for gratitude some families have adopted:

- For young kids, make a game of saying "Thank You ABCs" anytime and anyplace. You and your kids say the alphabet together, but for each letter, also try to include something you are grateful for. It goes something like this: *A, Aunt Helen; B, my brother; C, my cat;* and so on. Families with small kids rarely get beyond *H,* but the point is that you're having fun together, and your kids are also learning to be appreciative.
- Say a prayer of thanks as a family before meals.
- With an after-meal "gratitude share," each person reveals one thing he or she is grateful for that happened during the day and why.
- As a bedtime ritual, you and your child exchange messages of appreciation for one another followed by a goodnight hug and kiss.

Step 7. Require Giving

Research shows that kids' grateful spirits are developed through experience, so find opportunities for your child to give to others. Those moments will help him see how grateful others are for his kind gestures. In turn, he will be more likely to incorporate the virtue of gratitude into his daily behaviors. You might take homemade cookies to a nursing home, rake leaves for an elderly neighbor, deliver children's books your family no longer reads to a homeless shelter, or visit a lonely relative or friend. Hands-on giving is really the best way for kids to appreciate the power of gratitude. It's also a wonderful way for them to recognize that often the most appreciated gifts are ones that come straight from the heart.

The First 21 Days

Start a Count Your Blessings Campaign in your family. For younger kids, start a nighttime tradition in which each family member is encouraged to give thanks for at least one thing that happened during the day. Watch your kids' gratitude multiply for even the simplest kind acts because your family is more intentional at noticing and then acknowledging them. For older kids, have them keep a Gratitude Journal with an entry each day that documents something they've done or seen that expresses an attitude of gratitude and appreciation for the blessings of life. Another idea is to encourage your children to do one random act of kindness each day for someone in the family, at school, among their friends, but even a perfect stranger. This can be planned or spontaneous or must be shared before the day is over. *Hint:* Suggest they see the film or read the book titled *Pay It Forward.*

ATTITUDE MAKEOVER PLEDGE

How will you use these steps to help your kid become less ungrateful and achieve long-term change? On the lines below, write exactly what you agree to do within the next twenty-four hours to begin changing your kid's attitude so he is less ungrateful and more appreciative.

_____

_____

_____

THE NEW ATTITUDE REVIEW

All attitude makeovers take hard work, constant practice, and parental reinforcement. Each step your child takes toward change may be a small one, so be sure to acknowledge and

congratulate every one of them along the way. It takes a minimum of twenty-one days to see real results, so don't give up! And if one strategy doesn't work, try another. Write your child's weekly progress on the lines below. Keep track of daily progress in your Attitude Makeover Journal.

WEEK 1

_____
_____
_____

WEEK 2

_____
_____
_____

WEEK 3

_____
_____
_____

ONGOING ATTITUDE TUNE-UP

Where does your child's attitude still need improvement? What work still needs to be done?

_____
_____
_____

ATTITUDE MAKEOVER RESOURCES

For Parents

Don't Sweat the Small Stuff with Your Family: Simple Ways to Keep Daily Responsibilities and Chaos from Taking Over Your Life, by Richard Carlson (New York: Hyperion, 1998). Ninety-eight brief essays that address small, meaningful ways to avoid being overwhelmed with life and instead be grateful for what we have.

Simple Abundance Journal of Gratitude, by Sarah Ban Breathnach (New York: Warner Books, 1996). A day-to-day journal interlaced with inspirational quotes to remind you to count your blessings.

For Kids

Fox and Heggis, by Sandra E. Guzzo (Morton Grove, Ill.: Albert Whitman & Co., 1983). Fox is eager to buy a special hat, but his generosity to his friends prevents him from getting it. His friends find the perfect way to thank him for his kindness. Ages 3 to 6.

Gratefully Yours, by Jane Buchanan (New York: Farrar, Straus & Giroux). A young girl rides the Orphan Train from New York to Nebraska, where she must face a strange new life with a farmer and his wife, who is grief-stricken over the loss of her children. Ages 9 to 12.

Lady in the Box, by Ann McGovern (Hollidaysburg, Pa.: Turtle Books). A young brother and sister bring food and a warm scarf to a homeless woman despite their mother's warning to never talk to strangers. Ages 4 to 8.

The Giving Tree, by Shel Silverstein (New York: HarperCollins, 1964). The story that has become a classic of a boy who grows into manhood and of a tree that gives him special gifts through the years. A wonderful parable about giving for all ages.

The Giver, by Lois Lowry (New York: Laure Leaf, 2002). This thought-provoking novel deals with a twelve year old's struggle to discover the disturbing truth about the hypocrisy in his world. What would it really be like to live in a pain-free world? To do so, one would have to give up humanity. Ages 10 and up.

Bad Attitude

24

Unhelpful
Antidote: Helpfulness, Diligence, Generosity

"You do it."

Dear Dr. Borba,
We're noticing a most unbecoming attitude in our seven year old.
Whenever he's asked to help, we get one of those "you've got to be
kidding" looks. Today I politely asked him to help clear the dinner
table, and he had the nerve to ask how much I'd pay. Is it too much
to expect your child to lend a hand? Lately, I feel more like a
banker than a mom.

—Barbara K., a mom from Madison, Wisconsin

Bad Attitude Act Out

"I'm too busy, Daddy. Would you please do it for me?"

"Taking out the trash is yucky."

"I'll rake our leaves, but how much are you going to
pay me?"

EMERGENCY ATTITUDE ℞

Make a clear and specific list of chores. Sit down with the whole family, invite an open discussion, and get everyone to agree on a day-by-day schedule that spells out household responsibilities. Include putting away dishes, sweeping the kitchen, dusting the furniture, sponging the counters, feeding the pets, and other basic jobs. Choose appropriate chores for younger and older kids. Then from this moment forth, expect your kids to be helpful and take an active role helping around the house. Remember that you're creating a home and not running a bed-and-breakfast establishment, so unless they're paying you rent and a salary, get your kids to start helping out.

Heard these sweet words from your darling offspring lately: "How much do I get if I help? That's not my job." If so, your kid may be suffering from the Big Brat Factor epidemic with a subdiagnosis: *Unhelpfulitis*. And watch out: this ailment is especially lethal to character development and can be damaging to family harmony.

Many factors play a role in producing unhelpful kids, but two stand out. First, we're expecting kids to be less helpful these days. For whatever reason—such as our hectic pace or their overscheduled lives—parents tend to excuse kids from helping: "His schedule is so tight: he needs time to relax. It's easier to do it myself" or "She works so hard in school, and needs a break."

Many kids go through a developmental period at two to four years old when they really want to be helpful to show off their new skills and please you. Unfortunately, we don't always take advantage of their innocent desires to help out, and so that temporary window of opportunity is closed. And is it really tough to open up again! Too often when older kids are asked to help us out, they expect to be paid, and all too often we open up our wallets and comply. The result is a gradual extinguishing of helping, supporting, caring attitudes fueling selfish, me-me-me attitudes instead. The first step to helping kids learn this new attitude is to get them off the couch and expect them to lend a hand. It's a good way to begin teaching them the virtues of helpfulness, diligence, and generosity that they will need for developing good moral character and becoming selfless, contributing members of society. And the sooner we start the better.

BAD ATTITUDE ALERT

As parents, we all need more help, so teaching and expecting our kids to do their share not only helps the family but prepares them to be productive and successful individuals who contribute to their home, school, community, and society at large.

Diagnosis
Being unhelpful doesn't happen all by itself. Here are some questions to ask to find out where this bad attitude is coming from.

Why. Why does your kid have this attitude? Is he not expected to help out? Has someone always rescued or excused her from household duties? Have good grades or violin or swimming or something else been prioritized over helpfulness? Has no one ever taught him how to do basic household chores? Where did she get this notion that she's a prima donna and does not have to lift a hand?

What. Are there particular issues he is more unhelpful about? For instance: Laundry? Her bedroom? Pets? Siblings? Are there any jobs your kid does willingly?

Who. Does he display the same unhelpful behavior to every-one? Are there some individuals he does not use this attitude on and is more helpful with? If so, who?

When. Is there a particular time of day, week, or month when he is less helpful? Is there a reason? For instance, might his schedule be too crammed? Is he tired? Is there friction with another person?

Where. Are there certain places he is more likely to be unhelpful (at school or day care, in your yard, inside the home, at Grandma's)? Why?

Now take a look at your answers. Are you seeing any predictable patterns? Do you have any better understanding of your kid's unhelpful attitude and where it's coming from?

WHAT'S WRONG
WITH YOUR CURRENT RESPONSE?

Studies have shown that kids a few decades ago were much more helpful than kids today. What's changed in today's lifestyle that's causing helpfulness to decline? What's changed in your lifestyle that might be triggering your kid's unhelpful attitude? Do you leave everything to hired help? Do you eat out so often that your kids don't know what a dishwasher looks like? Is your kid so overscheduled with tutoring, sports, music lessons, dance, and social activities that there's no time for household chores? Are you so concerned about getting your kids into the best schools starting from age three on that the virtue of helpfulness isn't even on your radar screen? Are you so exhausted with your own busy schedule that you just don't have the energy to insist that your child help out at home? How does all this affect how you are responding to your kid's unhelpful attitude?

Now reflect on how you typically respond to your child's unhelpful attitude. Did you ignore him? Excuse him?

Do the task for him? What did your kid learn from your response? Write down one thing you will never do again to curb your kid's unhelpful attitude.

I will not _____

_____

FACING YOUR OWN BAD ATTITUDES

Take a serious look in the mirror to see if your kid's unhelpful attitude may be mirrored from your attitude. Here are a few questions to help you assess just how well you are boosting your kids' attitude or if your own attitude just may be derailing it:

☐ Do you expect your kids to lend a hand around the house? For instance, do your kids have set chores, responsibilities, or duties? Is your kid clear on those chores? Do you consistently expect those duties to be completed? Or do you feel you are doing your kids a favor by not requiring them to help at home because they are so busy?

☐ Do you reward your kids for helping? Do they expect to be compensated for any help they provide? Always providing monetary compensations or material treats for helpful gestures makes kids learn to expect payment. Is that the attitude you want in your child?

☐ Do you come to your child's rescue and complete her assigned tasks or make an excuse for her lack of helpfulness? Have you noticed other members of your family—siblings, relatives, partner—finishing her chores and letting her off the hook? What message is that sending to her?

☐ Are your standards of perfectionism so high that you don't want your kid to help because the end product

won't be good enough or you just find yourself redo-
ing the task so it meets your standards?

☐ Do your kids know that you value helpfulness? Have
you stressed your beliefs to your kids? How often do
you talk to your kids about helpfulness and why it is
important?

☐ Do you consistently thank those who help you, or do
you take them for granted or forget to voice your
appreciation?

To learn new behaviors, you need good models to copy,
so think how often your kids see you acknowledging helpful
behaviors. Before you begin tuning up the attitude in your
kid, think how you can tune up helpfulness in your behavior.
What is the first step you need to take to tune up helpfulness
in yourself as an example to your sons or daughters? Write
down changes you need to make.

I will _____

_____

BAD ATTITUDE NEWS ALERT

Research by Dan Kindlon, Harvard
psychologist and author of *Too Much of
a Good Thing: Raising Children of Character
in an Indulgent Age,* found that kids who get an
allowance but do not have to do chores to earn it are
at a greater risk for depression and tend to be self-
centered. His studies also found that teens who are not
required to regularly help out around the house are
more likely to see themselves as spoiled: they know
they're getting something for nothing.

THE "DON'T GIVE ME THAT ATTITUDE" MAKEOVER

To eliminate your child's unhelpful attitude, take the following steps.

Step 1. Expect Helpfulness

One of the biggest mistakes parents make is assuming their kids will help out without being asked—or paid. Don't make that mistake. If you want your kid to be helpful and a contributing family member, then model, reinforce, and nurture those behaviors. Expect your kid to help out at home and willingly lend a hand whenever asked and to do so without being paid.

Make sure your kid knows your expectations. Don't be vague, indirect, or make the mistake of assuming that kids know how to lend a helping hand. Instead, specify exactly what they can do to be supportive on any given day, and then expect the behavior. Here are some ideas about how to do this:

"We're going to Aunt Carol's today. You know how much she appreciates your helping her set the table, so be sure you do."

"Mom is coming home soon and has had a really hard day. Why don't you tell her you'll help fix dinner? I know she'll be thankful."

When they get the idea of how to lend a hand, encourage the behavior:

"I'm having the Kanes for dinner tonight. What could you do to help me out at dinnertime?"

"We're leaving on our vacation tomorrow, and there's lot to do. How will you help?"

Step 2. Delegate Exact and Specific Home Duties

The earlier you expect your kids to take an active role in helping around the house, the easier you'll find it is to get them to lend a hand. Even kids as young as three years old can help around the house by picking up toys, feeding the dog, and taking out small trash cans. So gather all the troops and brainstorm ways they can help out at home. Then ask each member to volunteer to do a few tasks each week. If your kids don't volunteer, you assign each one the jobs and specify when they are to be completed. Here are a few job possibilities:

- *Set and clear the table:* rinse off dirty dishes, put dishes in dishwasher, put clean dishes back in cupboards
- *Gardening:* weed, water plants, rake leaves, mow lawn, sweep patios
- *Bathroom:* wash counters and sinks; clean showers, toilets, tub; fold towels
- *Pets:* feed, take on walks, brush, bathe, clean out the cage, change the litter, play with them
- *Laundry:* put dirty clothes in hamper, empty the hamper, sort lights and darks, fold clean laundry
- *Recycling:* stack magazines and papers
- *Dust furniture, vacuum*
- *Clean the car:* wash exterior, clean out trash, vacuum, clean windows
- *Windows and mirrors:* clean using spray bottle
- *Take out the garbage:* empty wastebaskets

Step 3. Teach How to Be Helpful

Once you delegate specific duties, go through each job step-by-step at least once with your kids so that they clearly know how to do it. When you're sure they are capable of the task, post a chart on the refrigerator listing each kid's home duties, and then expect them to do it on their own. *Whatever you do, don't do any task your kid can do for herself.* She'll never learn to be helpful or responsible if she knows you'll finish the job for her. And don't overlook one of the best ways to boost helpfulness: everyone—you included—pitches in on a specified day and time (such as Wednesday night or Saturday morning) and does family chores together. When they are completed, many families celebrate by having breakfast together, a lunch out, or watching a fun family video.

Step 4. Acknowledge Helpful Behaviors

Show your kids how you value helpfulness by acknowledging the behavior in your kids and others. Be sure to describe the deed so your kids know what was helpful and why you appreciate it:

"Did you notice how helpful Jason was today at the party? He asked if I could use a hand in setting up the games. I admire his thoughtfulness."

"Priya, thanks for helping me pick up the dirty clothes. You did so without being asked! I really appreciate your helpfulness."

Step 5. Set a Consequence
If the Unhelpful Attitude Continues

Anytime you see your kids slack off, let others do the work, and if they do not help out, call them on it. Explain why their behavior is unacceptable, firmly restate your expectations, and then insist on helpful behaviors: "You're a member of this family, so you're expected to help out. Turn off the TV, and go help Dad sweep the patio." If your kid doesn't comply, set a consequence: "In this house you help first, then you play. If you don't, you will lose the privilege of using the family room for the day" (or another appropriate option). The consequence should be anything you can maintain control over, such as the TV, phone, or computer. It should also fit the crime and be appropriate to your child's age. Once stated, *don't give in until your kid starts helping.*

Step 6. Find Ways to Serve Others as a Family

One of the best ways for your kids to learn helpfulness is through doing helpful deeds, and what better way than doing so as a family? Look for a way your family can lend a hand to others: reading to the blind, coaching underprivileged kids, serving soup to the needy, making quilts for the homeless. Then commit to doing the service regularly together so your kids learn a sense of social responsibility and how helping others can make a difference in the world.

The First 21 Days

Find an age-appropriate Pitch Right In Project to teach your child a more helpful attitude. Be sure it is an activity where the emphasis is on his contribution to someone or something else rather than any kind of a personal gain. Whenever possible, capitalize on your kid's individual skills and interests. For example, if your younger child loves to draw, she might make cards to bring to a nursing home for the elderly to enjoy or send to their loved ones. Or if your toddler loves flowers and the out-of-doors, set her loose in the park with a large garbage bag and a pair of latex gloves and have her pick up trash. For an older kid, there are many possible projects that emphasize helpfulness, including collecting clothing and blankets from neighbors to distribute to the homeless; collecting or repairing toys to donate to local charities; helping coach younger kids in a favorite sport, dancing, or gymnastics; or tutoring kids in a subject of special interest or achievement like math, computers, science, or English as a second language.

ATTITUDE MAKEOVER PLEDGE

How will you use these steps to help your kid become less unhelpful and achieve long-term change? On the lines below, write exactly what you agree to do within the next twenty-four hours to begin changing your kid's attitude so he is more helpful and considerate.

_____

_____

_____

THE NEW ATTITUDE REVIEW

All attitude makeovers take hard work, constant practice, and parental reinforcement. Each step your child takes toward change may be a small one, so be sure to acknowledge and congratulate every one of them along the way. It takes a minimum of twenty-one days to see real results, so don't give up! And if one strategy doesn't work, try another. Write your child's weekly progress on the lines below. Keep track of daily progress in your Attitude Makeover Journal.

WEEK 1

_____

_____

_____

WEEK 2

_____

_____

_____

WEEK 3

_____

_____

_____

ONGOING ATTITUDE TUNE-UP

Where does your child's attitude still need improvement? What work still needs to be done?

_____

_____

_____

ATTITUDE MAKEOVER RESOURCES

For Parents

Didn't I Tell You to Take Out the Trash: Techniques for Getting Kids to Do Chores Without Hassles, by Foster W. Cline and Jim Fay (Golden, Colo.: Love and Logic Press, 1996). Focuses on the importance of chores and offers tools for getting kids to do them without hassles.

Chore Wars: How Households Can Share the Work and Keep the Peace, by James Thornton (Berkeley, Calif.: Conari Press, 1997). Strategies to ease chore battles and boost cooperation.

Home Allowance and Chore Kit: Larry Burkett's Money Matters for Kids: Ages 6–16, by Larry Burkett (Colorado Springs: Chariot Victor Publishers, 2000). Written from a Christian perspective, it addresses how to teach kids to contribute to the family without expecting to be paid. Ages 6 to 16.

For Kids

Alfie Gives a Hand, by Shirley Hughes (New York: Lothrop, Lee & Shepard, 1983). When Alfie is invited to a birthday party without his mother or sister, he finds that he must put down his security blanket to be able to be helpful. Ages 3 to 7.

Au Revoir, Les Enfants (Orion, 1987). This video tells the true story of an eleven-year-old boy attending a Catholic boarding school in Nazi-occupied France who discovers that three classmates are Jews in hiding from the Nazis. Moving scenes describe the helpful compassion of those who risked their lives to shelter them. Ages 10 and older.

Helping Out, by George Acona (Boston: Houghton Mifflin, 1985). Eloquent black-and-white photographs depict the special relationship between adults and children working together in many different settings. Ages 4 to 8.

The Kids Can Help Book, by Suzanne Logan (New York: Perigee Books, 1992). A wonderful compilation of ways kids can lend a hand to make a difference in the world. Ages 8 to 12.

PART 3

Beyond the Crisis

The greatest discovery of my generation is that human beings can alter their lives by altering their attitudes of mind.
—William James

Okay, you've targeted your kid's worst attitudes to work on, you've read the right chapters, you've designed a specific makeover plan, and you've even identified some of those same attitudes in yourself. You've realized change isn't going to be quick or easy, so you've committed yourself to be consistent, relentless, tenacious, and perseverant.

Many of you have kept up your Attitude Makeover Journal, and some of you may have met regularly with your parent support group. You may have even read a few of the extra resources. In fact, you're well on your way to making significant changes in your children's bad attitudes and can see that not too far down the road, there's a real possibility that you'll succeed in putting out the fire and moving out of crisis mode.

Congratulations! I knew you could do it. What you've achieved so far is commendable and no small piece of cake. You've made some crucial repairs, you've done a lot of important remodeling, and you may have even added a room or two. But now you need to take an even longer view to imagine the future shape and foundation of your entire family structure—the place where you dwell both literally and spiritually. You need to create a permanent new way of being together, of relating to one another in your personal, domestic, and community life.

Real change takes more than just reading a book and starting to walk the talk. Our ultimate goal is not only eliminating our kids' bad attitudes, but also giving them an entirely new worldview based on a solid foundation of strong values and good moral examples. And if we don't, there's a good chance that they will slip back to their old bad attitudes and aimless view of the world.

It's going to be just great when your kid turns the corner and gets rid of these bad attitudes you've been working on. But he won't know where to go from there unless you can provide him with a new view based on your own solid knowledge, experience, and moral beliefs. So let's move on. Let's get out of the reactive, emergency, crisis mode. Let's go forward to the place where we can prevent this epidemic from ever happening again. Let's begin to convey a positive, proactive view of how to live that our kids can adopt and enjoy for the rest of their lives. And the good news is that not only will this help our children, but it's the best hope we have for a world that is decent, sane, and humane.

So let us begin. There are a few basic tenets and solid life principles that have lasted through the ages. In some shape or form, these principles appear in all cultures, religions, and civilizations. And the main thing they all have in common is not just preventing bad attitudes from happening and that brat factor from taking hold, but they cultivate a society whose children are not spoiled, selfish, defiant, and insensitive but rather selfless, compassionate, respectful, and empathic. In the end, they are the kinds of kids that we all hope and dream for.

Different religions, cultures, and spiritual disciplines have their own unique language in expressing these life principles. But here is my version of the basic list. It's what we can do as parents and also convey into all the relationships and activities in our lives.

The Ultimate Principles for Inspiring Human Attitudes
1. *Be loving.* It's the greatest gift and greatest blessing. It's the basis of all relationships and morality. The more love and kindness you give, the more you receive. Remember that the best gift you can give your child is of yourself.
2. *Be consistent.* Regularity, structure, and clear boundaries create trust. It's what your child needs to feel safe and secure, so provide it.
3. *Be a good example.* Provide the kind of moral model you want your children to copy. Your child needs someone to look up to.
4. *Be authentic.* Never fake a feeling or act out a phony behavior. Your children need you to be sincere, genuine, and your real self at all times.

5. **Be present.** Be here now. Don't let work and other distractions interfere with remaining in the moment in direct contact and communication with your child and other loved ones.

6. **Be positive.** Things often turn out on the basis of your way of looking at it. If you're optimistic and hopeful about the future, it may turn out to be self-fulfilling.

7. **Be patient.** Slow down and get in sync with your kids. Life goes by all too quickly, so why speed things up? And don't forget, change takes time.

8. **Be persistent.** Life is a long-distance run. Perseverance pays off, so never give up, especially when it comes to helping your kids.

9. **Be selfless.** Get out of your shoes, put your energy into others, and take your kid along with you on the journey.

10. **Be active.** Don't just sit there. When you have a good idea or realize something is wrong, be proactive. Your actions will show your child that the only way to accomplish deeds large or small is by plunging full speed ahead.

11. **Be simple.** Your child doesn't need a whole lot to be happy; in fact, less really is better. It will help him develop appreciation and gratitude for the essential things in life.

12. **Be believing.** Every human being needs something to live by: a set of guiding principles, a sense of right and wrong. You need to be clear, conscious, and consistent with it, so your child knows where you stand and has the opportunity to follow.

13. **Be open.** Flexibility is strength. Learning new things, having new ideas, and allowing exposure to other points of views and ways of being are lessons you need to experience and pass on to your kids.

14. **Be empathic.** Above all else, the most important virtue humans can aspire to is the ability to understand and get inside another person's feelings. Empathy is the effective antidote to attitudes that are selfish, insensitive, and cruel.

And the best way our children can learn it is by experiencing our empathy for them.

This isn't such an easy world for parents and children alike. We're living in uncertain and dangerous times. The attitudes we see in our children to some extent not reflect only our family dynamics but also the influence of the world at large. The problem is acute, and the stakes are high. There are some things way out of our control, but the one thing we can do is be parents.

Everything we do now is going to have an impact on our children and their world to come. So stop the blaming, the excusing, the rescuing and compromising, and start putting all your energy into what really matters: helping your children make the journey from bad attitudes to solid character. Ultimately, when all is said and done, it's not how many goals they score, what academic degree they achieve, or how much money they'll make that matters. It's the kind of life they live and the world in which they live it.

References

PART ONE:
CONFRONTING THE CRISIS

Studies suggest this generation is volunteering more than ever, stated by S. Culbertson, head of Youth Service America, a Washington resource center for volunteering: N. Gibbs, "Who's in Charge Here?" *Time,* Aug. 6, 2001, p. 48.

Two-thirds of school police officers say younger children act more aggressively: R. Carroll, "School Police: Youths Getting More Aggressive," *Desert Sun,* Aug. 20, 2003, p. A5.

Three-quarters of Minnesota kids say kids materially spoiled and generally irresponsible: M. E. Baca, "Mindworks: Kids Admit They're Spoiled but Not Solely at Fault," *Star Tribune,* Dec. 3, 2001.

Kid nags nine times to get parents to buy product, cited by J. S. Chatsky, "Parties Without the Presents," *USA Weekend,* Apr. 6, 2003, p. 22.

Two out of three parents say kids measure self-worth by possessions, cited by M. Elias, "Ads Targeting Kids," *USA Today,* Mar. 22, 2000, p. D5.

Poll of 1,005 adults conducted by KRC Research and Consulting with assistance from U.S. News pollsters, cited in J. Marks, "The American Uncivil Wars," U.S. News Online [http://www.usnews/issue/civil.htm]. Apr. 22, 1996.

Survey (12 percent of adults perceive kids are raised to be respectful) reported by A. Siegler, "What a Nice Kid," *Child Magazine,* 1997, cited in R. Taffel, *Nurturing Good Children Now* (New York: Golden Books, 1999), p. 58.

Survey conducted by Time/CNN parental perception of children as spoiled cited in Gibbs, "Who's in Charge Here?" p. 46.

AOL Time Warner poll finding 85 percent of respondents say American kids spoiled, cited in D. Kindlon, *Too Much of a Good Thing: Raising Children in an Indulgent Age* (New York: Hyperion, 2001), p. 197.

Research stating overindulged kids from affluent families are less likely to be happy, cited in D. G. Myers, "The Funds, Friends and Faith of Happy People," *American Psychologist,* 2000, *55,* 56–57.

Data on materialism: Average American kid sees 50 to 100 TV commercials a day, from M. Elias, "Ads Targeting Kids," *USA Today,* Mar. 22, 2000, D5.

Three billion dollars spent on advertising directed at kids, from a Time/CNN poll cited on CNN News July 30, 2001 [http://money.cnn.com/2001/07/30/living/v_smart_assets].

Kids spending $36 billion annually, study conducted by Penn State Smeal College of Business: M. Goldberg, "Understanding Materialism Among Youth," *Journal of Consumer Psychology,* Aug. 24, 2001.

PART TWO:
TWENTY-FOUR ATTITUDE MAKEOVERS

1 Arrogant
Adults stating need to display skills to gain parental love: R. Baumeister (ed.), *The Self in Social Psychology* (Philadelphia: Taylor and Francis, 2000).

2 Bad-Mannered
Poll of 1,005 adults conducted by KRC Research and Consulting with assistance from U.S. News pollsters, cited in J. Marks, "The American Uncivil Wars," U.S. News Online [www.usnews/issue/civil.htm]. Apr. 22, 1996.

3 Bad-Tempered

Students hitting out of anger: Josephson Institute and CHARACTER COUNTS! Coalition, "1998 Report Card on the Ethics of American Youth." [www.josephsoninstsitute.org/98-Survey/violence/98survey.htm]. Oct. 19, 1998.

American Medical Association, *Physician's Guide to Media Violence* (Chicago: American Medical Association, 1997).

D. Shrifrin, "Three-Year Study Documents Nature of Television Violence." *AAP News,* Aug. 1998. [http://www.aap.org/advocacy/shifrin898.htm].

Number of violent acts on television viewed by age eighteen quoted in R. Taffel, *Nurturing Good Children Now* (New York: Golden Books, 1999), p. 18.

Conclusion that viewing entertainment violence leads to increases in children's aggressive behavior, cited by American Academy of Pediatrics, "Joint Statement on the Impact on Entertainment Violence on Children, Congressional Public Health Summit," July 26, 2000. [http://www.aap.org/advocacy/releases/jstmtevc.htm].

Televised violence contributes as much as 15 percent of kids' aggressive behaviors, cited by the American Psychological Association, "Summary Report of the American Psychological Association Commission on Violence and Youth," in *Violence and Youth: Psychology's Response,* Vol. 1 (Washington, D.C.: American Psychological Association, 1993), quoted in J. Garbarino, *Lost Boys* (New York: Free Press, 1999), p. 198.

4 Cheats

Rates of student cheating as cited in K. Kelly, "Parents in a Haze?" *U. S. News and World Report,* May 26, 2003, p. 44.

Who's Who Among American High School Students survey of cheating as cited in C. Kleiner and M. Lord, "The Cheating Game," *U.S. News and World Report,* Nov. 22, 1999, pp. 55–61.

Eighty-four percent of college students cheating, cited in *U.S. News and World Report,* Nov. 22, 1999, pp. 55–61.

5 Cruel

National School Safety Center, cited in A. Mulrine, "Once Bullied, Now Bullies—with Guns," *U.S. News and World Report,* May 3, 1999, p. 24.

N. Eisenberg, *The Caring Child* (Cambridge, Mass.: Harvard University Press, 1992).

Survey (43 percent of children afraid to use school bathrooms), cited by A. Mulrine, "Once Bullied, Now Bullies—with Guns," p. 24.

Research (1 to 7 ratio of school children as bully or victim), cited by C. Goodnow, "Bullying Is a Complex, Dangerous Game in Which Everyone's a Player," *Seattle Post-Intelligencer,* Sept. 1, 1999. [http://www.seattle-pi.com/lifestyle/bull1at.shtml].

Research by the National Education Association quoted by S. Fried and P. Fried, *Bullies and Victims* (New York: M. Evans, 1996), p. xii.

E. Midlarksy and J. H. Bryan, "Affect Expressions and Children's Imitative Altruism," *Journal of Experimental Research in Personality,* 1972, *6,* 195–203.

Research (repeated viewing of violence reduces kindness) by R. S. Drabman and M. H. Thomas, "Does Media Violence Increase Children's Toleration of Real-Life Aggression?" *Developmental Psychology,* 1974, *10,* 418–421.

M. Levine, *See No Evil* (San Francisco: Jossey-Bass, 1998), p. 43. Levine quotes R. E. Goranson, "Media Violence and Aggressive Behavior: A Review of Experimental Research," in L. Berkowitz (ed.), *Advances in Experimental Social Psychology* (Orlando, Fla.: Academic Press, 1970).

M. Hoffman, "Parent Discipline and the Child's Consideration for Others," *Child Development,* 1963, *34,* 573–588.

6 Demanding

A. P. Goldstein, *Violence in America: Lessons on Understanding the Aggression in Our Lives* (Palo Alto, Calif.: Davies-Black Publishing, 1996), p. 15.

7 Domineering

Findings from the National Center for Clinical Infant Programs, cited in D. Goleman, *Emotional Intelligence* (New York: Bantam Books, 1995).

8 Fresh

Survey of adults on whether kids are raised to be respectful reported by A. Siegler, "What a Nice Kid," *Child Magazine,* 1997, cited in R. Taffel, *Nurturing Good Children Now* (New York: Golden Books, 1999).

9 Greedy

Limiting TV viewing reduces materialism, cited in T. Robinson and others, "Effects of Reducing Television Viewing on Children's Requests for Toys," *Journal of Developmental and Behavioral Pediatrics,* 2001, *22,* 179–184.

J. E. Grusec, "Socializing Concern for Others in the Home," *Developmental Psychology,* 1991, *27,* 338–342.

Study that kids don't have the control to save money, cited by M. Elias, "Ads Targeting Kids," *USA Today,* Mar. 21, 2000, p. D5.

10 Impatient

Impulsivity has risen more than 700 percent: L. Tanner, "Study Suggests More U.S. Kids Have Problems with Behavior," *Desert Sun,* June 6, 2000, p. A5.

Research on the benefits of patience: Y. Shoda, W. Mischel, and P. K. Peake, "Predicting Adolescent Cognitive and Self-Regulating Competencies from Preschool Delay of Gratification," *Developmental Psychology,* 1999, *26,* 978–986.

11 Insensitive

Longitudinal study on children's empathy: R. Koestner, C. Franz, and J. Weinberger, "The Family Origins of Empathy Concern: A 26-Year Longitudinal Study," *Journal of Personality and Social Psychology,* 1990, *58,* 709–717.

Study on boys' empathy levels: S. Bernadette-Shapiro, D. Enrensaft, and J. L. Shapiro, "Father Participation in Childcare and the Development of Empathy in Sons: An Empirical Study," *Family Therapy,* 1996, *23*(2), 77–93, cited in K. Pruett, *Fatherneed: Why Father Care Is as Essential as Mother Care for Your Child* (New York: Free Press, 2000), p. 48.

12 Irresponsible

Time/CNN poll on kids doing fewer chores: N. Gibbs, "Who's in Charge Here?" *Time,* Aug. 6, 2001.

13 Jealous

W. Sears and M. Sears, *The Discipline Book* (New York: Little, Brown, 1995), p. 216.

14 Judgmental

National Parent-Teacher Organization findings on ratio of parent put-ups to parent put-downs, cited in S. Marston, *The Magic of Encouragement* (New York: Morrow, 1990).

15 Lazy

Increase in self-satisfaction for those who maintain goals from M. Elliott, "Time, Work, and Meaning" (unpublished doctoral dissertation, Pacifica Graduate Institute, 1999) and cited by D. Niven, *The 100 Simple Secrets of Successful People: What Scientists Have Learned and How You Can Use It* (San Francisco: HarperSanFrancisco, 2002), p. 197.

Increase in teen suicide: J. Cloud, "What Can the Schools Do?" *Time,* May 3, 1999, pp. 38–40.

16 Manipulative

E. W. Swihart Jr. and P. Cotter, *The Manipulative Child: How to Regain Control and Raise Resilient, Resourceful, and Independent Kids* (New York: Bantam Books, 1998), p. xiii.

17 Narrow-Minded

American youth are displaying intolerant actions at younger ages, cited in M. Borba, *Building Moral Intelligence: The Seven Essential Virtues That Teach Kids to Do the Right Thing* (San Francisco: Jossey-Bass, 2001), p. 192.

Survey of hate crimes of Massachusetts high schools: L. M. Everett-Haynes, "Hate Crimes Prompt Campus Campaign," *Arizona Daily Wildcat,* Jan. 13, 2000.

Review of Higher Education, cited by J. Levin and J. McDebitt, *Hate Crimes Revisited: America's War on Those Who Are Different* (Boulder, Colo.: Westview Press, 2002), p. 116.

18 Noncompliant

Rise in defiant, disrespectful kids, cited in T. Lickona, *Educating for Character* (New York: Bantam Books, 1991), p. 15.

New York Times, June 26, 1997, p. A17, quoted in M. Medved and D. Medved, *Saving Childhood* (New York: HarperCollins, 1998), p. 171.

Louisiana lawmakers: R. Tanner, "States Debate Proposals for Courtesy in Schools," *Desert Sun,* May 29, 2000, p. A5.

19 Pessimistic

Research concluding that parents can teach optimism: M. Seligman, *The Optimistic Child: A Revolutionary Program That Safeguards Children Against Depression and Builds Lifelong Resilience* (Boston: Houghton Mifflin, 1995), p. 8.

Kids ten times more likely to be seriously depressed: M. Seligman, *The Optimistic Child,* pp. 37–45.

20 Poor Loser

National Association of Sports Officials concerns reported by S. Smith, "Is the Choice Sportsmanship or Death?" Knight Ridder/Tribune Information Services [www.youthdevelopment.org]. July 23, 2000.

21 Selfish

Discipline technique to produce unselfish kids: M. Hoffman, "Development of Prosocial Motivation: Empathy and Guilt," in N. Eisenberg (ed.), *The Development of Prosocial Behavior* (Orlando, Fla.: Academic Press, 1983).

22 Uncooperative

T. Peters and R. Waterman, *In Search of Excellence* (New York: Warner Books, 1988).

23 Ungrateful

Kids and commercialism: survey conducted by Center for a New American Dream, Takoma Park, Md.: Aug. 21, 2002. [http://www.newdream.org/campaign/kids/].

24 Unhelpful

Kindlon's research on helpfulness and spoiled teens, cited in D. Kindlon, *Too Much of a Good Thing: Raising Children of Character in an Indulgent Age* (New York: Talk Miramax Books, 2001), p. 206.

PART THREE:
BEYOND THE CRISIS

G. Van Ekeren, *The Speaker's Sourcebook: Quotes, Stories and Anecdotes for Every Occasion* (Upper Saddle River, N.J.: Prentice Hall, 1988), p. 57.

About the Author

Michele Borba, Ed.D., is an internationally renowned educator who is recognized for her practical, solution-based parenting strategies to strengthen children's behavior, self-esteem, and moral development and to build strong families. A sought-after motivational speaker, she has presented workshops to more than 750,000 participants worldwide and has been an educational consultant to hundreds of schools.

Dr. Borba frequently appears as a guest expert on television and radio, including NPR talk shows, *Today, The View, Fox & Friends, CTV's Vicki Gabereau,* and *Canada AM.* She has been interviewed by numerous publications, including *Newsweek, U.S. News & World Report, Redbook, Better Homes & Gardens, Chicago Tribune,* the *Los Angeles Times,* and the *New York Daily News.* She serves as an advisory board member for *Parents* magazine.

Dr. Borba's numerous awards include the National Educator Award, presented by the National Council of Self-Esteem. She is the award-winning author of eighteen books, including *No More Misbehavin': 38 Difficult Behaviors and How to Stop Them; Building Moral Intelligence,* cited by *Publisher's Weekly* as "among the most noteworthy of 2001"; *Parents Do Make a Difference,* selected by *Child Magazine* as an "Outstanding Parenting Book of 1999"; and *Esteem Builders,* used by over 1.5 million students worldwide. Her proposal to end school violence (SB1667) was signed into California law in 2002. She lives in Palm Springs, California, with her husband and three sons.

To contact Dr. Borba regarding her work or media availability, go to www.MicheleBorba.com or www.moral intelligence.com.